Praise for George Osborne: The Austerity Chancellor

'Janan Ganesh's *George Osborne: The Austerity Chancellor* treads with skill and flair the awkward line between authorised and unauthorised biography. Ganesh … has an intuitive grasp of the Tory psyche … Revealing, penetrating, stylish and superbly written. Honestly, it's a page-turner.'
– Matthew Parris

'This timely book will be widely read by those wishing to understand one of the most powerful politicians of recent times. A lively account of the Chancellor's career … it contains a great deal of fascinating new information.'
– Peter Oborne, *Daily Telegraph*

'Ganesh's dissection of what has driven the intellectual and political revival of the Tories is forensic and incisive.'
– Anne McElvoy, *Mail on Sunday*

'Detailed and illuminating … an important biography.'
– *The Guardian*

'Well researched, thoughtful and full of nuggets buried into the smoothest of prose … Ganesh treads deftly.'
– *Independent on Sunday*

'This excellent biography … an insight into one of today's most important politicians is extremely valuable.'
– *Sunday Express*

'Janan Ganesh has produced a book that readers of all sorts will enjoy and dip into in the future. The author really knows his stuff.'
– *Financial Times*

'Excellent biography.'
– John Rentoul

'A pacy, well-researched book.'
– *The Spectator*

'Fascinating biography.'
– Ted Jeory

'Ganesh spills the beans as politely as possible.'
– *Belfast Telegraph*

'Janan Ganesh produces a meticulously researched biography.'
– *Oxford Today*

GEORGE OSBORNE
The Austerity Chancellor
JANAN GANESH

Biteback Publishing

First published in Great Britain in 2012
This edition published in 2014 by
Biteback Publishing Ltd
Westminster Tower
3 Albert Embankment
London SE1 7SP
Copyright © Janan Ganesh 2012, 2014

ISBN 978-1-84954-754-3

10 9 8 7 6 5 4 3 2 1

A CIP catalogue record for this book is available from the British Library.

Set in Baskerville and Grotesque

Printed and bound in Great Britain by
CPI Group (UK) Ltd, Croydon CR0 4YY

MIX
Paper from
responsible sources
FSC® C020471

To my parent

Contents

Acknowledgements

'Isn't he a bit young for a biography?' was the inescapable reaction whenever I spoke of my interest in chronicling the life of George Osborne. If you're good enough, you're old enough, say football managers. If you're interesting enough, you're old enough, say I. Not only is he the author of an austerity programme that must count as the most important and contentious thing happening in modern Britain, but his path to power takes in most of the past two decades of politics. This is the story of an epoch – the ordeal of Conservatism, or the New Labour imperium – as well as a man.

It is also very much a book by a *Financial Times* and former *Economist* journalist about the Chancellor of the Exchequer. It charts the arc of his political ascent, and of his economic thinking. His personal life as an adult is addressed in parts, but not dwelt on.

The first, faint intimations of the idea came to me in the summer of 2010, when this previously elusive and inscrutable politician was imposing himself as Chancellor.

Having previously spent two years at Policy Exchange, a peerless immersion course in the ideas and personalities of the British centre-right, I was in a better position than many journalists to study his story. However, it was not until the turn of 2011 that my interest hardened into intent. I began researching his life that summer.

I have interviewed more than a hundred people who have known Osborne, including friends, schoolmates, student peers, colleagues, Cabinet members, journalists, businessmen, underlings, backbench MPs, peers and political opponents. I am grateful to all of them for the time they took to speak to me. Many did so on condition of anonymity; any quote that does not have a reference was taken from a private interview. I have employed no assistance at all in the research or writing, so any mistakes or misjudgements are mine.

This is not an authorised biography. I approached Osborne with the idea via his chief of staff, Rupert Harrison, not the other way around. Neither the Chancellor nor anybody in his office has seen any of the manuscript in advance of its publication, or sought any veto over anything. However, he has provided cooperation, including three interviews, and shown fairness and forbearance throughout.

This book would not exist were it not for Iain Dale, Sam Carter and others at Biteback, who took a chance on a first-time author. I am also indebted to John Micklethwait, the editor of *The Economist*, for giving me my break in journalism, and to Lionel Barber, the editor of the *Financial Times*, for trusting me with a column in his extraordinary newspaper. If only those who have lost confidence in journalism could meet either of these men.

Much of this book was written during weekends in a deserted office, my favourite place to work. But as I write these final words, I look out across Hampstead Heath, my favourite place in the world.

Janan Ganesh
London, June 2012

Prologue

'This is the unavoidable Budget.' Summoned to speak at 12.34 p.m. on Tuesday 22 June 2010, the new Chancellor of the Exchequer itemised the monstrosities of his economic inheritance. In all of Europe only neighbouring, unravelling Ireland was running a deeper fiscal deficit, he told the House of Commons. A quarter of all the expenditure cascading out of the Treasury was borrowed from financial markets. Those self-same creditors were questioning the liquidity, and sometimes the very solvency, of governments in finer fiscal fettle than his. The world's first industrial nation was flirting with ruin.

After only six weeks in office, he had not called this 'emergency' Budget to merely report on the demons menacing his country. He was also here to slay them, or at least keep them at bay. Britain was to pay its way out of looming devastation with the greatest fiscal retrenchment since the war. Taxes, including the Value Added Tax levied on ordinary purchases, would go up, while government departments girded themselves for cuts amounting to around a quarter of their budgets over five years. The previous decade – all prosperity and profligacy – suddenly seemed a thousand centuries ago.

This was austerity, and here was its author. His rhetoric of rectitude – all 'prudence' and 'virtue' and 'responsibility' – came in a squeaky pitch emanating incongruously from a brawny frame of around six feet, two inches. Attractive in an ethereal way, he wore the same combination of pale skin and dark hair favoured by vampires and members of The Cure, but, on closer study, he actually resembled nobody so much as the Beatles's Svengali, Brian Epstein. Two centuries earlier – powdered, wigged and pompadoured – he might have frolicked as a Regency fop. Even his name, George Osborne, is shared with the louchest character in Thackeray's *Vanity Fair*.

However, nothing in the Chancellor's words, and little in his cool, ambitious character, suggested frivolity. All the world's a stage, but Osborne had only ever wanted to perform in the Mother of Parliaments. As a prematurely political schoolboy, he had studied its legends and sacraments. He did not need to be told that he was the youngest Chancellor since Randolph Churchill, or that his ministerial red box was once carried by Gladstone, or that he was separated from his Labour opponents by two swords' length. Some journeys to power only make sense in retrospect, but his, for the most part, had been planned and deliberate. As he gripped the despatch box, he was touching the tangible realisation of a youthful dream.

The Budget was the culmination of another great story of Osborne's life: his mission to get his riven, radioactively unpopular Conservative Party back into government. He had recognised before almost anyone else – before even David Cameron, now the only politician in the land who outranked him – that the Tories had to remake themselves for the modern world. This stranger to personal adversity had endured the long ordeal of Conservatism: three election defeats, four fallen leaders, uncountable slights, humiliations and ignominies. Now, after fourteen Labour Budgets impotently cursed by the erstwhile natural party of government, here was a Tory Chancellor with the power to decide, to act, to rule. But it was an imperfect comeback. Sitting on either side of him as he spoke were Nick Clegg and Danny Alexander, chieftains of another party. Osborne was a coalition Chancellor, a politically bound Chancellor.

For the country, and a watching world, the Budget was more of a beginning than an end. Osborne was laying a colossal bet on the future – that the private sector would rebound as the state pulled back. At stake were not only his own prospects of leading the country one day, and his party's chances of winning an election for the first time since he was a student, but the livelihoods of millions. He was always a gambling soul, a backgammon wizard at school whose extended family included a couple of casino moguls. He had gambled by fastening himself to a leadership hopeful called William Hague in 1997, by standing for the fraught constituency of Tatton four years later, by accepting the job of shadow Chancellor at the absurd age of thirty-three, and by unveiling a sensational overhaul of inheritance tax as his party toyed with doom in 2007. His latest punt was an economic necessity, he said. A reckless experiment in dogma, countered his opponents. In the background, a small country called Greece, and a big currency called the euro, rumbled portentously.

For all that he looked like a vestige of another century, Osborne was a creature of his time. In an age of professional politicians, he was the most professional and the most political. For eighteen years, he had advised, plotted, networked, schemed, spun, strategised, campaigned, conspired and above all climbed, all within earshot of Big Ben. The world of Westminster insiders, or the 'guild' as he called it, was all he had ever known. In an age of secular liberalism, he was as free-wheeling as any politician, a son of post-modern, post-national London, for whom hang-ups about race, sexuality or personal morality were marks of troglodyte backwardness. In an age of pragmatism, he was almost physically allergic to ideology. In an age characterised by a cult of youth – where politicians, businessmen and newspaper editors were getting younger as the wider population aged – he was a Chancellor who was not yet forty. And in an age of austerity, he was a flinty pioneer, perhaps the boldest finance minister in the West in getting to grips with his country's devastated accounts.

'Today, we have paid the debts of a failed past,' he said, returning to his seat, the shoulder pats of his colleagues and the voluble scorn of his Labour opponents. But he had his own past: a story of debts owed and credit earned, of ideals and interests, of personal success in a failing party – and of an upbringing that was anything but austere.

Youth

1971–1993

'Whenever you feel like criticizing anyone, just remember
that all the people in this world haven't had the
advantages that you've had.'
The Great Gatsby

I.

It's a London Thing

'It's not as if I grew up in a stately home with a deer park.'

Ireland gave the Conservative Party its guiding philosopher, Edmund Burke, its most distinguished Foreign Secretary, Viscount Castlereagh, and its greatest warrior, the Duke of Wellington. In a roundabout way, it also provided the Tories with the current Chancellor of the Exchequer. Incongruously for such a metropolitan man, George Osborne's roots lie in the clammy sod of Wexford and Tipperary. The baronetcy he stands to inherit was established in these counties.

The family title originated in 1629, when Richard Osborne was made a baronet after thirteen years of service as a joint clerk in the King's Court of Ireland. The Osbornes joined the Protestant elite, known bitterly as the Ascendancy, that began to dominate the largely Catholic island from the late seventeenth century. Politics and the professions were cut off to Catholics and even non-conformist Protestants such as the Presbyterians. Titled, and denominated in the established Church, the Osbornes faced no such bar. Sir Richard became a Member of Parliament in the Irish House of Commons. Throughout the following two centuries, Osborne baronets were parliamentarians, barristers, sheriffs and justices of the peace. They were a public, if not political, family.

It is George Osborne's grandfather, a soldier, who stands out among the seventeen Osborne baronets. Sir George Francis Osborne was born on 27 July 1894. After his military education at Sandhurst, he was wounded twice in the First World War while serving on the Western Front. His reward was the Military Cross, introduced in 1914 as the third-highest decoration in the British armed forces. He loomed large enough over succeeding generations of Osbornes that his grandson, the future Chancellor, would decorate a wall of his childhood bedroom with war memorabilia. Less exaltedly, and inadvertently, Sir George also sparked the family's relationship with upmarket gambling. His second wife, Mary Grace Horn, was the mother of John Aspinall, who would establish the private casino in Mayfair that still carries his name. Sir George died in 1960. A quarter of a century later, his grandson would take his name in favour of the one he had been given at birth.

The third child, and first son, of Sir George and Mary would show a different kind of derring-do to the old war hero. Peter Osborne, George Osborne's father, plunged a family name synonymous with civic life into the unruly swirl of private enterprise. He was born on 29 June 1943 in Barnham, Sussex, and his education was conventional enough for a privileged Englishman: Wellington College in Berkshire and then Christ Church College, Oxford. When the young graduate stepped out into mid-1960s London, the pulsating city drew out his inner rebel. Chelsea folklore tells of a left-leaning, velvet-suited *bon viveur*. A plucky attempt at a conventional career with Singer & Friedlander, a merchant bank, fizzled out. Two decades before the Big Bang, London's financial district was a sleepy and cloyingly old-fashioned place. Peter served exactly a year in the job before concluding that 'the City wasn't for me'.[1]

Even the woman that Peter fell in love with was at the

adventurous end of what might have been expected of a man of his background. A former debutante, Felicity Loxton-Peacock, George Osborne's mother, was of similar social standing. But she was cosmopolitan, even exotic. Her mother was a Hungarian-born artist, her home was Belgravia rather than the Home Counties, and her politics were even more liberal than Peter's: a blend of pacifism, civil-libertarianism and social democracy that, in the 1960s, was nothing like as ubiquitous among the metropolitan rich as it is now. The attraction between the two dissenting souls was not hard to explain. Peter would marry Felicity on 16 October 1968.

In the meantime, he needed an income. He spent a while buying and selling old books (a passion, along with opera) but his prospects only really lifted when he met a hippy and former art student who was dating, and would soon marry, his older sister Jennifer. His name was Antony Little, and he was already conversant with design and retail, having produced an iconic black and gold logo for Biba, a fashion outlet that opened in Kensington in 1964. Peter and Antony became friends and, when the latter married Jennifer in 1966, brothers-in-law too. In retrospect, it seems inevitable that their complementary gifts would also nudge them into working together. Peter was of an enterprising bent while Little, who was six months older, sparkled creatively. They leased a shop together but aborted their planned venture, which envisaged Peter selling antiquarian books while Little used the basement as a design studio.

Instead, they elected to collaborate directly. The great loosening-up of tastes and mores in the 1960s was transforming the way people dressed, loved, socialised – and decorated their homes. There was demand, especially among the well-to-do, for bolder wallpaper designs. It passed unnoticed by stodgy mass-market producers but not by one restless entrepreneur and his artistic friend. They regarded the wallpaper on offer in mainstream outlets as 'porridge' and sought to displace it with tastefully vivid, expensively manufactured alternatives of their own.[2] On 27 November 1967, Osborne and Little Ltd, an interior fabrics concern, was incorporated.

The pair set up shop in the Old Brompton Road, a commercial thoroughfare that runs west from South Kensington tube station. Peter made the short journey there every morning from the home he shared with Felicity, who helped to drum up business, in Bridstow Place in Westbourne Grove. Rapid success allowed the firm to upgrade to a glamorous perch on the King's Road in Chelsea, which is still the home of its flagship store. Osborne and Little became one of a handful of brand names regarded as indispensable to a certain kind of upmarket lifestyle, as Little recollected in 1995. 'If people wanted frocks they went to Mary Quant. If they needed a casserole dish they went to Terence Conran. If they wanted wallpaper, they came to us.'[3]

So it was a prosperous, well-connected and cosmopolitan home that Gideon Oliver Osborne was born into on Sunday 23 May 1971, at St Mary's Hospital in Paddington. But it was a grey and struggling country that he entered too. Ted Heath, confronted by an economic malaise that would not truly lift until the mid '80s, was beginning to flail and flounder as Prime Minister. London had stopped swinging. A dour Arsenal side dominated English football, and the charts were mired in a no man's land between the fall of the Beatles and the explosion of punk.

The new arrival was Peter and Felicity's first child. By then, the family had moved from Bridstow Place to Kildare Gardens, an attractive crescent of balconied properties a few streets away. They lived at No. 15. Osborne's earliest memory is of riding around the communal green on a red tricycle with Imelda Trafford, a girl of the same age who lived next door.

Before London emerged as the home-from-home for the global rich, few of its neighbourhoods were forbiddingly expensive. Areas now colonised by the very wealthy were, in the 1970s, defiantly bohemian. The narrow sliver of west London where Osborne grew up was among them. Even now, Westbourne Grove is bordered to the north by some of the city's most troubled housing estates, while nearby Bayswater, where the Osbornes moved in 1976, has more three-star hotels than any neighbourhood could want. Back then, these areas were even rougher around the edges, and Felicity would grumble about prostitutes walking the streets near her home.

Whatever the nuances of his privilege, Osborne enjoyed a gilded start to life. He was sent to the private Chelsea Open Air Nursery, where he passed the day riding scooters and building bunkers out of wood and tarpaulin. Home improvement was a theme of Osborne family life in these years. When he was five, they moved to 36 Porchester Terrace in Bayswater, a large but derelict house that his father set about renovating. It took a year, and copious supplies from Osborne and Little, to remake a fraying property with only two usable rooms into a plush family home. Osborne was given the top room, a front-facing loft conversion. The burgeoning success of his father's business had made the renovation affordable.

The Osbornes grew wealthier over the course of their eldest son's youth but there was turbulence along the way. He was always aware of when business was good, and when it was not. By the turn of the '80s, Osborne and Little went public and his father was able to take money out of the company for the family. Their budget tightened as the recession struck soon after but the mid '80s boom allowed them to buy a country home, the Vinnicks, near Newbury, and just a few miles from Peasemore, the Berkshire village idyll where David Cameron, whom Osborne would not meet for another decade, had grown up. The next recession, in the early 1990s, by which time Osborne was at university, saw the family trade their main residence for a smaller house in St Petersburg Place, a few streets along in Bayswater.

For most of Osborne's youth, though, 36 Porchester Terrace was home. The place eventually bustled with three more boys: Benedict George was born on 25 July 1973, Adam Peter on 25 March 1976 and Theo Grantley on 28 March 1985. Despite its spaciousness – there was a bedroom for each son and a separate playroom they all shared – the house bore the scars of the rampaging quad. Again, supplies from Osborne and Little were called upon. Felicity was 'a lovely mother', remembers one of Osborne's childhood friends. Peter was also popular with visiting children, 'a funny mix of bohemian and old-school aristocrat' who would sometimes do the school run.

Much is made of Osborne's material privilege but his advantages in life went beyond money: loving parents, close siblings, a hovering crowd of grandparents and extended family, and an absence of divorce, bereavement and serious illness. If Osborne sometimes seems like a man unmarked by life, it is because he is. The thirst for status and power that astonishes those who have known him as an adult cannot be traced back to any transformative trauma or hard luck story. There is no equivalent of the debilitating stroke suffered by Tony Blair's father when the future Prime Minister was eleven, or the hardship known by the young John Major. Being the eldest son of a successful father invited pressure, of course, and Osborne's teenage years brought more academic achievement than social success, but these footling grievances scarcely explain the magnitude of his ambition and the intensity with which he pursues it.

The Osbornes' friends were art dealers, designers and writers. When guests were entertained at Porchester Terrace, the boys mingled easily with them. It was a stimulating environment – a less political and more cultural version of the atmosphere the Miliband brothers were growing up in across town in Primrose Hill, an exquisite enclave of north London *cognoscenti*. Eager to shift his image as a typical Tory, Osborne often plays up this background in liberal, eclectic London. 'It's not as if I grew up in a stately home with a deer park,' he protested in 2008.[4]

But it may be less of an advantage than he assumes. No other major Western city is quite so dominant over, and quite so different from, its host nation. Londoners can incur suspicion and bafflement from other Britons. Sure enough, few have made it to the apex of politics in the post-war era. The only Prime Minister in Osborne's lifetime who grew up in the capital was Major, and the modesty of his Brixton boyhood made him a very different political proposition to a baronet's son. Osborne, a diligent student of political history (nicknamed 'knowledge' by his brothers, more teasingly than admiringly), will know that Hampstead's own Nigel Lawson is the last occupant of either of the two great offices of state whose upbringing was both wealthy and metropolitan.

If growing up in London failed to give Osborne an electoral advantage, it certainly left him with a way of looking at the world. Indeed, it is geography, far more than class, that explains the kind of politician he has become. On issues of race, sexuality and personal morality, he is as liberal as any senior figure in any major party. His parliamentary voting record includes support for gay adoption and opposition to lowering the 24-week time limit for abortion. It is hard to think of a front-rank politician who has employed as many advisers from ethnic minority back-grounds – the likes of Rohan Silva, Ramesh Chhabra and Sajid Javid have all flown under his wing – or one who is so utterly undemonstrative about having done so. For Osborne, and for

Londoners generally, modernity and cosmopolitanism are assumed and not evangelised. Indeed, it is sometimes possible to fault him for an unreflective liberalism, an *a priori* rejection of culturally conservative positions.

The intellectual legacy of Osborne's metropolitan youth goes beyond this cultural liberalism. A Shire Tory Chancellor would not show quite the same zeal for scything planning restrictions on greenfield development, or extending Sunday trading. Awkwardly for Conservative authors of the Big Society, including David Cameron and his former adviser Steve Hilton, Osborne is also wary of using government policy to foster a more communal culture. For him, the state exists to provide a framework of laws and services. It does not take a qualitative view of what society 'should' look like, or offer any conception of the good. If this reads like a dry, atomised view of society, then it is nevertheless rigorously liberal and unmistakably metropolitan. London fosters tolerance, but it also breeds a kind of post-modern rootlessness. Bayswater and tight-knit Peasemore are separated by fifty miles geographically and light years culturally.

All of Osborne's schooling took place in the capital. He moved from Chelsea Open Air to Fox Primary School, in the state sector, before arriving at Norland Place, an exclusive primary in Holland Park, at the age of seven. There he was reunited with Ben Slotover, a boy from Knightsbridge whom he had first befriended at nursery. Their parents knew each other and would often holiday together, but the boys were closer. Slotover recalls the young Gideon Osborne, or 'Giddy' as his friends knew him, as a 'rambunctious boy' who was 'up for everything'.[5]

Norland Place was 'extremely conservative', recalls a classmate. While boys did their sums, girls would play dress-up. Maths was not something for the fairer sex but Osborne relished it. Pupils were ranked according to how many of their multiplication tables they could recite. He and Slotover, both of whom had received extra tuition at home, were joint first in completing the twelve times tables. In a boyish trial of his competitive zeal, Osborne volunteered to learn number thirteen. His teacher had to mark him using a calculator but victory was his. Another teacher, Miss Hutchings, sought to foster competition by dividing Osborne's class into 'concords' and 'harriers', but this proved more effective than she had bargained for. Things got out of hand and culminated in a playground melee in which the two tribes rolled heavy rubber tyres at each other. Osborne, a concord, 'got stuck in', according to one of his bruised victims.

In 1980, Osborne began preparatory school, where the education of privileged children really takes shape. His parents chose Colet Court in Barnes, the feeder school for adjacent St Paul's, where Osborne would migrate at the start of his teenage years. (John Colet, a fifteenth-century churchman, founded St Paul's School and scholarships there still bear his name.) Colet Court, which was for boys only, was 'a hideous prefab building that looked as though it would have had asbestos all over it', remembers one of Osborne's contemporaries there.

Slotover followed Osborne to prep school, where they befriended a South African boy named Mungo Soggot whose family had left their troubled country just three years earlier. Soggot's mother Greta would often drive Osborne and her son to school; when he was old enough, the future Chancellor would take the number 9 bus from Kensington High Street. Their gang of friends also included Ken Harris, Nathaniel Billington and Alexander Ramm. There was another Nathaniel at the school. His surname was Rothschild. But, remembers one of Osborne's crowd, 'we didn't really hang out with him'.

Fairer of hair and frecklier of cheek than the adult version, the young Osborne was 'a mixture of maturity and mischief', says Soggot, a characterisation that gets anyone who knew him as a boy nodding.[6] He had the seriousness of an older sibling and the playfulness of a child to whom life had been exceptionally kind. He was not yet an academic high-performer, though. Osborne would go on to shine, even sparkle, at St Paul's but he struggled at prep school. Colet Court was intensely competitive and aggressively streamed. There were four classes of roughly twenty in each year, and every test and half-term report helped to determine the set in which a boy was placed.

The staff, too, were a fearsome bunch. Glen Mowbray, who taught Latin, imposed exacting standards. One of the history teachers, a former army man who went by the improbably apposite name of Major Payne, watched over boys as they copied out page after page from textbooks by longhand. Some of Osborne's peers now complain that teachers were hired on the basis of their expertise in their subject, rather than their actual gift for teaching. The result was a pitiless environment for children who were not innately gifted. Osborne was below average at every subject and, at the start of his second year in 1981, he was relegated to the lowest stream. A classmate recalls Osborne finding out the news by seeing his name on a list pinned to a wall. He was visibly crestfallen but stirred to redeem himself. 'I remember his absolute determination to get out of that stream.' He did it in one term.

One shortcoming Osborne would never fix was his athletic incompetence. Tellingly, he avoided Colet Court's sports field in favour of its computer room. Osborne has a fervour for technology – as shadow Chancellor, he cycled to work in a Mozilla t-shirt – and it started early. The home computer market at the turn of the '80s pitted the BBC Micro, which was favoured by aspiring programmers, against the ZX Spectrum, which boasted better games. Osborne and Slotover each had a BBC Micro and regarded Spectrum fans as irredeemable dilettantes. Weekends were whiled away programming new games using pages of code provided in the computer's official magazine, *BBC Micro User*. To accelerate the process, one of them would read out the code while the other typed. Their parents revered the machine as a little miracle for keeping the boys quiet for entire weekends. Whenever Osborne and Slotover telephoned each other, the conversation would start with the same enquiry: 'Anything new with the computer?'

Osborne's parents did not ration his access to the television either, and he took advantage. *The A-Team* was his favourite show, but he was similarly captivated by the avuncular doodling of Tony Hart. When the family went on holiday – usually to southern Europe, sometimes more daringly to Russia and Sri Lanka – he would leave a list of programmes for the house sitter to record. At the cinema, he and Slotover devoured *The Empire Strikes Back*, *Superman 2*, *Beverly Hills Cop* and *Octopussy*. They watched *E.T.* and *Ghostbusters* on video. They tried *Apocalypse Now* but, like more seasoned audiences, found it too meanderingly pompous to stick with. He was not old enough to watch Ridley Scott's *Alien* but, having discerned its gruesome contents from the snatched testimonies of adults he overheard, he told awed friends of the scene in which a hideous extra-terrestrial explodes out of a man's chest. Felicity would occasionally challenge her son and his friends with obscure British independent films, taking them to see *Blackjack* and *The Riddle of the Sands*, but, confesses Slotover, 'We liked the Hollywood stuff better.'[7]

In his tastes and temperament, then, Osborne was typical of a boy approaching adolescence. However, these years also saw the first intimations of something less common: an interest in politics, or at least public life. His fascination with history, the subject in which he would immerse himself academically for the next decade, was obvious to any visitor to his bedroom. The spacious perch at the top of 36 Porchester Terrace included the usual accoutrements of formulaic boyhood: a computer, a Rubik's cube, a stamp collection ('Of course he had to have a penny black,' says a friend). But there was also a poster of Winston Churchill (Slotover had one of David Bowie) and a display case of war memorabilia.

Osborne never missed an episode of satires such as *Not the Nine O'Clock News* and *Yes, Minister*. While his family were not especially political, international events were the subject of dinner-table chatter. At the age of just seven, he was gripped by the murky murder of the Bulgarian dissident Georgi Markov, assassinated with a ricin-tipped umbrella on Waterloo Bridge, and scrawled pictures of the incident at school.

Osborne would help his mother run an Amnesty International stall at local church fêtes. Friends at Colet Court recall him as wholly unique at their school in bringing up politics as a subject of conversation. As part of a school trip, he was given a tour of Parliament by James Callaghan, who had only left Downing Street a few years earlier. He was captivated.

Then, on the eve of moving up to St Paul's School in 1984, Osborne made what some cynics suspect was his first political decision. For almost as long as he could remember, he had grumbled to his parents about his name. Tired of fielding the grievance, Felicity finally suggested doing something about it. With a trip to a deed poll office, her first-born became George Gideon Oliver Osborne. He chose his new name in honour of his war-hero grandfather; that it required no change of initial was a bonus. (It did not seem to occur, or matter, that George Osborne was also the name of a pretty scoundrel who perishes in the Battle of Waterloo in Thackeray's *Vanity Fair*.) His friends were discombobulated by the news: Slotover assumed that only adults could change their names, and Soggot had never heard of a deed poll before. Surprisingly quickly, though, they adjusted to it, and so did everyone else in Osborne's life.

Although Osborne has always said simply that he disliked the name Gideon, some doubt that he was moved by aesthetic revulsion alone. Theories abound as to what an alternative motive might have been. One is easy to discount. Despite speculation to the contrary, he was never bullied over his name. In a cosmopolitan school of Mungos and Nathaniels, a boy called Gideon did not stand out. His brothers ribbed him, as they do to this day, but only after he foolishly let them know that he found his name embarrassing.

Neither is there much to verify the whispers that he wanted to avoid the name's ethnic and religious connotations. Certainly, a boy named Gideon from a business family who attended a school like St Paul's would be assumed to be Jewish. Anti-Semitism was not unknown in England's posher playgrounds as recently as the '80s; 'Gid the Yid' is the kind of ugly taunt that did the rounds, and some suspect that Osborne received it. There is nothing to suggest that he actually did, however. In any case, it seems improbable that someone whose closest friends throughout his school years were Jewish would be much bothered about being mistaken for a Jew himself.

The most cynical theory about Osborne's name change is also the most popular. It is plausible that he was already set on a career in public life and feared that a name as baroque and rarefied as Gideon would hold him back. Friends and adults certainly teased him with this suggestion at the time. When a friend's mother heard that Osborne had changed his name, she exclaimed 'Watch out, that boy will be Prime Minister!' Osborne's confession to a newspaper in 2005 that, as a child,

he could not think of 'anyone who I liked or who was successful who was called Gideon' certainly seems to betray precocious
ambition.[8] Most of his school friends doubt that his decision was
quite as calculated as that, including Soggot, but all attest to his
early and avowed interest in a political career. Whenever anyone
pressed him to explain his name change, he stuck, like a disciplined politician uttering his party's line-to-take, to the laconic
form of words he uses to this day: 'I just didn't like it.'

Ultimately, the question of why Osborne changed his name
is less compelling than the fact that he did. Put aside the myth
and the mockery, and it is an extraordinary thing for a boy to
do. 'It is of a piece with his character,' says one of his old school
friends, who remains close to him. 'He ploughs his own furrow.'
Any attempt to mock him fell flat, as it became obvious that he
simply did not care about what others thought. He was magis-
terially impervious to social pressure. Osborne is comfortable
with being a man apart, and loath to accept life as something
that simply happens to a person. He would evince this unshake-
able self-direction at St Paul's, during his gap year, in his time at
university and throughout his vertiginous rise to power. And he
would do so as George.

2.

History Boy

'When he walked into a room, you'd know
something fun was going to happen.'

Follow the Thames west from St Paul's Cathedral and it will eventually skirt by the school that takes its name from Wren's baroque masterwork. St Paul's School occupies forty-five acres in Barnes, an inner suburb on a peninsula that juts into the river next to Hammersmith Bridge. There is an esoteric debate to be had about the school's precise grade of poshness. Ed Vaizey, a Conservative minister and Old Pauline, remembers it as 'very Jewish and very down to earth'.[9] It is academically peerless but lacks the aloof mystique of a boarding school. It has existed in one form or another for half a millennium, but many of its buildings are new and unprepossessingly utilitarian. Paulines tend to be the offspring of upper middle-class lawyers and bankers rather than the scions of international aristocracy who favour Eton, Harrow and Westminster.

Still, these are hairline distinctions between a few gilded institutions at the very summit of Britain's vertiginously stratified schools system. A boy who goes to St Paul's is getting a chance at life that most will never receive, and many would struggle to even fathom. In the autumn of 1984, that chance fell to George Osborne. St Paul's could have been an ordeal for him. After all, he arrived at the ferociously academic school as a middling performer. Having failed to make the scholarship set from Colet Court, he got in through the common entrance exam. Neither was he much good at sport, which vied with study for primacy in the school's life. 'I get my exercise from typing and writing,' he would tell friends.

As it turned out, Osborne became a minor legend at St Paul's – a star pupil and a provocative presence. His breakthrough came quickly. In his first year, there was a chance at a scholarship for boys who had missed out on one initially. Osborne was entered for this exam by his teachers because they thought he needed practice in pressured situations, not because they expected he would pass. Yet when the roster of successful applicants was announced in a school assembly, Osborne was among them. 'I remember my complete astonishment when they read out my name,' he says, more than a quarter of a century later.[10] His appointment as a John Colet Scholar gave him a miniature silver fish to wear on his lapel, symbolising Christ's miraculous catch in the Sea of Galilee. It also left him with a trust in his own intellect that has never faded.

Osborne fell in love at St Paul's. The object of his ardour was history. He first took to it at Colet Court, where Major Payne would tell stories of his time as a soldier in Palestine during the Second World War. At St Paul's, this embryonic interest in the past was cultivated by some exceptional teachers. One of them, Keith Perry, held discursive tutorials that encouraged his charges to take a view on events. 'He operated as a kind of university professor,' remembers Osborne.[11] Another, the Rev. Hugh Meade, rated Osborne for his passion and flair for the subject. Then there was Peter Pilkington, who was headmaster (or High Master, in the school's particular argot) for most of Osborne's time there. The future Chancellor was inspired by his teaching of the Glorious

Revolution, and the two kept in touch long after Osborne had left St Paul's. When Pilkington, who was later ennobled, died in 2011, Osborne gave a reading at his funeral.

His love of history did not stop at the classroom door. Paulines were given two-hour lunch breaks on the condition that some of the time was spent in clubs or societies. Allergic to the sports field, Osborne plumped for the history society, which was (and remains) named after John Churchill, the first Duke of Marlborough. Members were required to prepare and present essays; Osborne wrote papers on Dachau and the Katyn massacre. Perry was often there to lead the discussion. 'There was a bit of a *History Boys* feel to it,' remembers one of Osborne's peers, 'but without the gay undertones.' Osborne eventually ran the society and launched its own magazine, which featured interviews with the acclaimed historians J. C. D. Clark and Jeremy Blank. It would not be his last dalliance with journalism.

As a social being, the young Osborne was confident and well-adjusted, but never cool. He was drawn to quietly high-achieving types, quickly befriending Matthew Gould, now the British Ambassador to Israel, and Andrew Edgecliffe-Johnson, currently the media editor of the *Financial Times*. He remained close to Mungo Soggot, who followed him from Colet Court, but saw Ben Slotover head off to Westminster School instead.

In a group that was, according to one of its members, a 'pathetically straight bunch', Osborne stood out for his subversive sense of fun. Indeed, he became notorious beyond his group of friends as a provocateur. On his first day in the sixth form, he concocted a rumour that someone in the same year had got married over the summer. The entire school was convulsed by speculation over the identity of the (mythical) newly-wed 'within days, if not hours', marvels a classmate of Osborne's. 'It was absolute genius.' Sometimes his playfulness crossed the line of good taste. If a teacher was palpably out of his depth, Osborne would lead the class in assailing him with questions he could not answer. 'It was an unpleasant thing to do, and classic Pauline behaviour,' admits one of those who took part in these pitiless ambushes. The baser side of Osborne's mischievousness was an ability to 'put people down' and 'find their area of weakness'.

Time has not sapped Osborne of either his wit or his waspishness. There is a reason why successive Tory leaders have relied on him to coach them for Prime Minister's Questions, and why he is generally thought more compelling private company than David Cameron. 'He's got funny bones,' was the verdict of the comedian James Corden after an encounter with the Chancellor in 2011.[12] Photographs fail to capture the way Osborne's eyes widen and coruscate when he has mischief on the mind. Along with his capacity for cold calculation, playfulness is perhaps his distinguishing trait, and it was on show in his teenage years. 'When he walked into a room, you'd know something fun was going to happen,' says Edgecliffe-Johnson.[13] Another friend is even starker: 'Boys would talk about him more than anyone else.'

Notoriety, though, is not popularity. Some of Osborne's quirks and foibles as an adult – his ferocious networking, his desire for glamorous company – might be a reaction against his bookish teenage years. St Paul's has a reputation for being less cruelly riven by cliques and tribes than many private schools, but there was an 'in' group and Osborne was not a member of it. 'We were busy trying to finger girls,' admits one of the cool kids. Osborne's fingers were used strictly for all that typing and writing. His provocative wit gave him a presence in the school but it did not bring him social glory. He must have sometimes felt that life was taking place somewhere else.

Osborne achieved A grades in all of his O level exams, the forerunner of GCSEs. Such consistently outstanding marks were much less common in 1987 than they are now. 'Academically, I got better throughout my childhood,' he says.[14] Assiduous work, burgeoning confidence, superb teaching and a highly academic peer group fed this flowering. 'In a school of bright kids, he stood out as being among the brightest,' recalls Edgecliffe-Johnson.[15]

If he was slow to develop academically and socially, Osborne was early in attaining political consciousness. What began at Colet Court as a loose interest in 'current affairs' (a term he still uses interchangeably with politics) firmed up at St Paul's into an ambition for power. If he could not be Prime Minister, he said, he would like to be Foreign Secretary. He told a classmate that he envied defence secretaries for the high-tech planes and weaponry they get to handle.

He joined Policon, a society devoted to politics and economics that was chaired by his friend Matthew Gould. When guest speakers turned up, Osborne would escort them from the school gate to the Montgomery Room, where they addressed the society's members. He relished any fleeting encounter with a person of consequence. Guests included Rhodes Boyson MP, Terry Burns, the head of the Government Economic Service, and Jeffery Archer, who found Osborne waiting for him as he got out of his maroon Rolls-Royce in the school car park. The two would go on to encounter each other, not always happily, during William Hague's Conservative leadership many years later.

Osborne's zeal for politics also found an outlet in the debating society, where he matured from a reliable master of his script to a deftly extemporaneous speaker. An *Observer* profile of the Chancellor recounts a debate on nuclear weapons that Osborne won without being physically present; his argument in favour of the deterrent was strong enough to prevail even when read out by another boy.[16] His style, at turns forensic and pugilistic, has not changed. Now, when old classmates see the Chancellor on television taking questions in Parliament, the spectacle evokes lively afternoons spent arguing over the Cold War and the future of the monarchy in the St Paul's speaking chamber. 'It does bring it all flooding back,' says one.

Such was his interest in politics that Osborne even took the subject at A level. It was a recent addition to the curriculum. His two other choices were, more conventionally, History and Maths. 'Looking back, it doesn't surprise me he has got to where he has,' says a peer who was in all the same classes. 'He was driven and it always seemed to me he wanted to be in a position of influence. He liked being at the centre of things. I don't buy the idea that he ended up in politics by default.' Sam Bain, another contemporary, offered a similar testimony to *The Observer*: 'We were seventeen, and at that point he was grown-up in a way that no one else was in our year … He looked and behaved like a man who had already decided what he was going to do with his life.'[17]

His interest in politics was plainly more than academic. When Nigel Lawson delivered his radical tax-cutting Budget of 1988, Osborne was listening via a pocket radio as he and his friends took the number 9 bus home from school. As it crossed Hammersmith Bridge, he heard the Deputy Speaker of the House halt the session as opposition MPs barracked the Chancellor for scything the top rate of income tax. The cacophonous malcontents were led by a young Scottish Nationalist named Alex Salmond, who was suspended from the Commons for a week. Twenty-four years on, Osborne is more directly conversant with Salmond, and with the unpopularity of tax cuts for high-earners.

Osborne's prematurely political youth might evoke the adolescent, Hansard-reading William Hague, but it was not quite as intense. For one thing, Osborne retained broader interests, including a taste for the unconventional end of popular culture. Although he was 'very much a Madonna boy'[18] in his early teens, he came to adore the Canadian folk-rock band Cowboy Junkies, and implored friends to get into his favourite album of the period, the Talking Heads' *Naked*, which came out as he was studying his A levels. His brother Ben, a Beatlemaniac and voracious record-buyer, introduced him to new music.

Moreover, for all his absorption in politics, Osborne's actual views were tentative. He was never likely to give a free-market sermon to a Conservative Party conference at the age of sixteen, as Hague had done. As a school that was both well-off and metropolitan, St Paul's was ideologically eclectic. Its recent alumni included convinced conservatives such as Dean Godson, who would forge a path as a journalist and think-tanker, and Simon Milton, who served as Boris Johnson's deputy Mayor of London until his death in 2011. But there were also left-wingers among the pupils and the staff: one teacher would throw darts at a picture of Kenneth Baker, the Conservative Education Secretary at the time. Osborne was certainly not among them. 'In a sense, George was the rebel,' says Simon Heuberger, who, along with his fellow left-leaning South African Mungo Soggot, had good natured political disagreements with him.[19]

Nor, however, was he one of the school's young Thatcherites who would huddle around the newspapers and magazines in the library's anteroom. 'We'd sit there reading *The Times* and *The Economist*,' says a classmate, 'but George was fairly middle-of-the-road politically.' Osborne's aversion to ideology really hardened in his twenties as he saw the party he toiled for lose successive elections on strident platforms. The evidence, though, is that he was always of a pragmatic and doubting bent, even as a teenager in the Thatcherite zeitgeist of the '80s.

So, why the Conservative Party? His family's wealth might have nudged him towards the right but London abounds with privileged left-wingers, as Harriet Harman (who studied at St

Paul's Girls' School), *The Guardian*'s editorial staff and the good burghers of Hampstead and Highgate can attest. Osborne's own mother was a left-liberal who only voted for Thatcher because she was Britain's first female Prime Minister, so right-wingery was hardly forced upon him at home. The Tory party was, ultimately, a default recourse for a broadly centrist budding politico at a time when Labour was unelectably left-wing. Had Osborne been born a decade later and grown up in the mid-1990s, he might now be a Blairite Labour MP striving to catch Ed Miliband's eye for a frontbench promotion. Cameron was born into the Conservative Party. John Major chose it. Osborne fell into it. This lack of emotional or ideological ardour would later allow him, clear-headedly, to see that the party had to change.

Conservative ideologues curse Osborne for approaching politics as a game to be won, a craft to be mastered, rather than as a missionary calling. Insofar as he is an operator, his skills were first honed as a schoolboy. He knew how to talk to adults, always pitching himself as respectful but never obsequious. He got on with teachers, which gave him a status at St Paul's that was usually limited to outstanding young sportsmen. When the school came to decide which sixth-former would be appointed Captain, or head boy, Pilkington pressed the case for Osborne. This outraged staff who were steeped in the school's historic reverence for athletic achievers. Ultimately, their resistance was too vociferous to ignore and a more conventional candidate, the sporty and popular Ilya Colak-Antic, received the honour. Still, Osborne was made Vice Captain, a sufficiently august post to rattle the sporty types. 'I didn't feel he was a leader of people,' grumbles one, 'but he was in with the teachers.'

The burden of office did not weigh down Osborne's academic advance. His decision to study Maths will come as a surprise to some. Students in England, even at an academically ambitious place like St Paul's, tend to specialise in either humanities or sciences after the age of sixteen; to pursue a mix is more common in Scotland, where the Highers emphasise breadth. Moreover, Osborne is often assumed to be one of the less technical and numerate politicians to have held the Treasury brief in opposition or government in recent times. What this belief is based on has never been clear. An A level in Maths hardly makes him a 'quant' but he is no more ignorant of the discipline than Gordon Brown (a historian) or Alistair Darling and Ken Clarke (both lawyers).

Still, it was Osborne's history teachers who saw the best of him. Some of his A level essays were passable university efforts. Ironically for a man who is often said to be more of a Whig than a Tory, he wrote against the Whiggish view of history as a teleological journey towards ever greater freedom and reason. He was drawn to the new generation of High Tory scholars who were emerging, often via the *Salisbury Review*, in reaction to Thatcher's market liberalism. Especially influential on Osborne was J. C. D. Clark, then still in his thirties, who made his name by debunking Whig history from a sceptical, conservative angle. Until then, only Marxists had challenged Thomas Babington Macaulay and the other giants of liberal history.

Osborne's facility with the subject eventually brought him the school's ultimate honour. Each May, St Paul's holds a ceremony known as 'apposition'. A handful of the most able boys in the sixth form (which the school, in its peculiar way, insists on calling the eighth form) are chosen to present, or 'declaim', an academic paper. On the eve of his A level exams in 1989, Osborne was summoned for the ritual. He read out an essay he had written on Tudor anti-Papism called 'Why England hated the Catholics'. Beneath the characteristic bathos of the title was a 'really mature piece of prose', says another matriculating pupil. Osborne was commended by the Old Pauline Club for outstanding service to the school.

For five years, he had excelled in the classroom and contributed restlessly to the school's extracurricular life. The prizes accumulated in his final months at St Paul's. He won a Dean Rusk Scholarship to Davidson College in North Carolina, a six-month posting that was given to only three pupils at St Paul's and its school for girls annually. He also secured an offer to study Modern History at Oxford University. Then his A level results came through. He had scored A grades in History, Politics and Maths. The boy who struggled at prep school had gone through his O and A levels without lapsing into so much as a B grade. He did not choose his privileged schooling but he made the most of it.

Gnawing at Osborne, though, was the fear that all these baubles had come at a personal cost. He still lacked the bustling social life that some of his peers took for granted. Outside the school where he toiled over essays, debated the Cold War and curried the favour of his teachers, real life was taking place. In the beatific summer of 1989, a new kind of British youth culture was stirring. Acid house music boomed in illegal warehouse raves across London. Ecstasy, the movement's drug of choice, loosened limbs and attitudes. The media called it the 'second summer of love'. It was never going to be Osborne's scene, but the inescapable sense of a nation at play must have made the contrast with his own self-denying studiousness sting just a little bit. He was excelling at life. It was time to enjoy it too.

3.

Desert Brats

'One of my most hauntingly beautiful experiences.'

Among the prizes collected by Osborne in his closing year at St Paul's, the most important would turn out to be the Dean Rusk Scholarship to Davidson College in North Carolina. His time there was not especially dramatic but he could only fulfil the six-month placement, which was to start at the turn of 1990, by taking a year out before going to university. This period would see him, almost by accident, falling into the bigger, wider world. His character would grow more in this year, especially during a single month in the Sahara sands, than it did in a punctiliously academic half-decade at St Paul's.

The gap year remains a minority pursuit among British students, and it tends to come in two forms. For the privileged, there is the 'gap yaah' of popular derision: a period of travel, usually taking in the southern hemisphere, often paid for by the intrepid youngster's parents. Such expeditions are evocative of the 'grand tour' that a young man of means (including, famously, Lord Byron) would take in the eighteenth and early nineteenth centuries. Then there are gap years devoted to work: either structured internships with major employers or ordinary jobs taken to help with the student's university costs.

Surprisingly for such a fortunate eighteen-year-old, Osborne's gap year was a blend of these two formats. With a few months to kill before going to America, he went to a high-street recruitment agency and took whatever run-of-the-mill jobs were on offer. The first was as a data-entry clerk in an NHS office in Kensal Rise. He then moved to another bureau in Westbourne Grove. It was his grim duty to feed into a computer database the details of people who had died in London in the previous few days. He also worked as a waiter, which he hated, and as a sales assistant at Selfridges, which he tolerated well enough. Anyone who went shopping for bathroom accessories in the venerable department store in the autumn of 1989 might have been served by the future Chancellor.

He then enjoyed a stint at the revered independent bookshop Foyles on the Charing Cross Road. Appropriately for a politician whose bookshelves are now dominated by accounts of great men, he worked in the biography section, which was located on the ground floor. Bookshops were his natural setting. As a younger teenager, he and Ben Slotover would spend weekend afternoons perusing the neighbouring (and radically left-wing) outlet Collets, which is no longer there. There was a drawback to his time at Foyles, though. The job detained him while friends from school travelled to Germany to witness the fall of the Berlin Wall, an event Osborne had to watch on television. Not tasting the spectacle first-hand remains one of the biggest regrets of this historian and Cold War buff.

Osborne's brush with quotidian employment did not last, however. Ever alert to an opportunity, he discovered that a group of boys he had known at St Paul's were planning a voyage of Byronic ambition. Mungo Soggot, Simon Heuberger, Cameron Timmis and Adrian Montague wanted to drive from north Africa to Johannesburg via the Sahara desert. With money earned from part-time work, they had acquired a spluttering old Land Rover that had once been deployed by the Royal Ulster Constabulary. Heuberger led the way in organising the trip. He had come to Britain from South Africa at the age of fifteen and spent a year at a college converting his qualifications into O levels before joining St Paul's. Like Timmis and Montague, he knew Osborne through Soggot.

Weeks before the quartet set off, Montague announced that he would not be able to join the trip until it reached Nigeria. This created a vacancy for the first leg of the journey, which Osborne volunteered to fill. Timmis and Heuberger were initially wary. For them, Osborne was a conspicuously conservative friend-of-a-friend. Their interactions with him were usually limited to good-spirited political squabbles. He was enthusiastic, though, and helped to squeeze some additional travelling funds from the school, which was enough to win his way onto the trip.

The group set off in November 1989. Heuberger drove the Land Rover to Marseille, and then took the car onto a ferry to Algiers. There he met up with Osborne and Soggot, who had flown in together the previous day. Timmis joined them soon after. Arriving in Algeria directly was unusual; sour diplomatic relations with the UK meant that British travellers generally had to make their way into the country from neighbouring Morocco. Once they were united in Algiers, the foursome headed south via well-maintained tar roads to an oasis town in the Sahara called Tamanrasset, where some of the highest temperatures ever known have been recorded. Heuberger plotted the route through the desert while Soggot assisted him with the map.

The Sahara's arid, impersonal vastness confounded the ken of a lifelong urbanite like Osborne, who remains captivated by what he saw there. Only in places does the desert bear the smoothly sandy contours of popular imagination. Elsewhere, it is a mosaic of jagged mountains, red rock plains and unnavigable, boulder-strewn valleys. Osborne and his friends slept under the stars. By day, they sought out the most spectacular vistas at hand. When they encountered the Hoggar Mountains, which rise very suddenly out of the desert, they resolved to climb them. They woke up in the small hours of Christmas morning, when the desert was enveloped in darkness, and began the nine-kilometre trek up the peak. 'We reached the summit just in time to see dawn breaking over the mountains and desert, which stretched for hundreds of miles in every direction,' Osborne recalled in 2006.[20]

Later in the day he attended Mass in a tiny French monastery in Assekrem, at the top of the mountains, which consisted of just two monks. Osborne, a man of the arched eyebrow and the dismissive smirk, is the least sentimental of politicians. But he once recalled his visit to Assekrem as 'one of my most hauntingly beautiful experiences', and named the site as the place in the world where he would most like to be stranded.[21]

People travelling through the Sahara are encouraged to join with others and form a convoy. As they headed south on increasingly tricky roads, Osborne and his friends linked up with a party of New Zealanders who were also driving a Land Rover. Together, they would stop at designated campsites, unpack the sleeping bags and supplies they stored on their roof racks, and cook dinner while listening to the BBC World Service. Sometimes, Osborne and his friends stayed in cheap hotels in oasis towns, where locals helped them fix their struggling vehicle. Upon arrival in one town, Osborne introduced himself and his gang as members of the England under-21 football team. The ruse, cheekily aimed at securing new levels of Arabian hospitality from the townsfolk, got out of hand. A match was quickly arranged between the travellers and the locals, who were bemused when it became obvious that Osborne could not kick a ball. His outfit should have been the clue; English footballers tend to eschew rimmed hats and Barbour jackets.

Amid the japes, there was one serious conversation in the desert that sticks in the mind of all three of Osborne's companions. Their on-board radio kept them informed of the democratic upheaval taking place behind the Iron Curtain (the Berlin Wall had fallen just before they began their trip). For the South African boys, it was a galling reminder of the lack of progress in their own country. Heuberger was especially vociferous in lamenting apartheid's vile durability, insisting that there was no prospect of change. Soggot concurred that Nelson Mandela would probably die in jail. Only Osborne disagreed. He told them that apartheid would unravel as quickly as the eastern bloc. 'In the space of three months, he was proved right,' says Heuberger, for in February, 1990 the crumbling regime released Mandela.[22]

The journey went on to Zinder, in Niger, from where Osborne was to fly back to London while the others set off for another six months that would take them through Burkina Faso, Ivory Coast, Ghana, Togo, Benin, Nigeria, the Central African Republic, Zaire and then to the east coast of Africa before heading south. The boys held a farewell party for Osborne in a louche Zinder bar.

'The reason we came through the trip unscathed was the wonderful naivety and awe with which we approached it,' says Heuberger of the seven-month voyage.[23] Locals looked after them. Border guards who stopped more grizzled travellers let them pass and even educated them in the etiquette of giving a bribe (enclose some cash in a passport before handing it over for checking,). For Heuberger, who now works for Médecins Sans Frontières, organising a trip so tricky and dangerous (Soggot's father, who knew the continent well, advised against the central African leg) was more transformative than the experience itself.

The same was not true of Osborne. For him, being there was the point. Africa took him out of the narrow path to power that he seemed to be following at St Paul's. There was no professional utility or strategic advantage to be had in the trip, just its innate value as a mind-widening experience. It threw him out of his comfort zone by confronting him with challenges that could not be surmounted through diligent study and the taking of copious notes. He was already a confident student; he was now closer to becoming a confident person. More than twenty years later, he recalls his time in Africa with a faraway look in his eye. He chose to spend his honeymoon in the continent.

Osborne spent the rest of his gap year in the comparatively bland setting of a modern American campus. The Dean Rusk Scholarship (named after John F. Kennedy's Secretary of State, who had studied at Davidson College) allowed him a deeper immersion in a country that he had only visited on holiday. His growing sense of independence craved a sustained period away from home; the scholarship remains to this day his longest stretch outside Britain. America's higher-education system delivers small liberal arts colleges like Davidson as adroitly as the more famous behemoths of research, such as Harvard and Stanford. With fewer than 2,000 students in a gentle southern town whose population is only five times that size, Davidson was unintimidating, and almost quaint, for an eighteen-year-old from London.

When he arrived at Charlotte International Airport in January 1990, the official despatched by the college to greet him was waiting on the wrong floor. The two failed to find each other. Reluctant to hang around, Osborne took a taxi to the campus, which was twenty miles northwest of Charlotte. His first conversation at Davidson was with a kind stranger who offered to help him carry his giant suitcase, which contained half a year's worth of clothes and supplies. So began an effortlessly social six months for Osborne. The warmth and openness of his American peers was a compelling novelty for someone used to (and skilled at) the aloofness and snarky banter of London. It was a welcome change. He opened up and made friends effortlessly.

Newspaper profiles of the Chancellor allude to his love of America, but there is more to it than a political junkie's fascination with Washington. True, he is one of the few Tories who endeavour to maintain links with the Republican Party. He cultivates relationships with the likes of Mayor Michael Bloomberg and keeps a mental record of emerging congressmen. He took an interest in Paul Ryan, now the powerful chairman of the House Budget Committee and Mitt Romney's running mate in the US presidential election, long before he acquired his current eminence. For all this, though, it is America's wider culture that really draws him. Even now, as a political and economic potentate, he is likelier to holiday in California than the power centres on the eastern seaboard. During a visit to America as part of a parliamentary delegation a decade ago, he ducked out, travelled to Memphis and spent a joyous day buying records in the city's celebrated music stores.

At Davidson, Osborne elected to take classes in subjects he would not be studying in his history course at Oxford. He especially enjoyed philosophy and creative writing, both strengths of this liberal arts college. He also kept in touch with events abroad, watching Nelson Mandela walk from prison, as he had told his friends he would, in February 1990. However, it was his social flowering that was the real story of his time at Davidson and, indeed, of his whole gap year.

4.

Gorgeous George

'He was an Oscar Wilde character, a type of dandy.'

After Africa and America, George Osborne settled in for three years at the unmistakably English Magdalen College, Oxford. His admission interview, which took place in his final year at St Paul's, had gone badly. The interrogation was at the hands of two academics; one of them recalls the other 'really giving him a hard time ... he was being turned over.' Osborne's personal statement had claimed an interest in art, so the fearsome don asked him for his appraisal of the Wallace Collection in central London. Upon confessing that he had never visited it, Osborne endured a scolding for his indifference to a cultural treasure so close to his home. The interview remains infamous at the college.

What Osborne did not know was that he was only being ambushed like this because every other aspect of his application was regarded by the college as immaculate. His grades were perfect, his headmaster's report nearly evangelical in its praise and the essays he submitted improbably mature. Professor Laurence Brockliss, who oversaw applications for the History course, remembers reading Osborne's work. 'The reason George was under attack in this way was that he had done such an amazingly good entrance script that if he had come in and stood on his head and said nothing, he would have got in.'[24]

Osborne was drawn to Magdalen's beauty. The college has its own deer park and a river on its flank. It is also one of Oxford's posher institutions, though the political outlook of the students and the fellowship was generally leftish. It was, in that sense, much like St Paul's. In his first week there, he met another fresher who became and remains his closest friend, Peter Davies. They had in common a playful manner allied to an essentially serious commitment to personal success. Osborne was a historian. He preferred facts to ideas. Davies was a philosopher, more comfortable with the abstract. Perhaps counter-intuitively, it was Davies who pursued a career in finance and Osborne who embarked on politics. Both did so successfully.

As he had done at school, Osborne naturally gravitated towards cerebral high-achievers. As well as Davies, he befriended Julian Kenny, now a barrister, Raj Dutta, who has made his way in finance, and Sasha Slater, a journalist. 'They were the *jeunesse dorée* of their intake,' recalls a contemporary who has followed Osborne into Parliament, 'a self-consciously intellectual group of people. They had had a lot of opportunities in life but they had made the most of them.' Another agrees that 'he ran with a cool and clever crowd'.

Inspired by such company, it was unsurprising that Osborne applied himself academically, at least initially. He excelled in his first-year exams, which consisted of four papers, and was made a demy scholar, a Magdalen prize that had previously gone to the likes of Niall Ferguson and (fittingly, given Osborne's gap-year travels) T. E. Lawrence. He grew less industrious thereafter but his work remained 'incredibly consistent', says Brockliss.[25] He became a nineteenth-century specialist, focusing on the relationship between church and society and, in a nod to the career that awaited him, modern political theory.

Although Osborne is fascinated by the medieval period,

and chose Henry VII, who marked the end of that era, as his favourite historical figure in an episode of Radio 4's *Great Lives* in 2008, at university he was 'definitely a modernist', according to Brockliss.[26] He was close to John Nightingale, who taught him medieval history, but even closer to Angus Macintyre, who taught the modern British period and died in a car accident the year after Osborne graduated. In a delicate allusion to the intellectual confidence that Osborne brought with him to university, Macintyre once wrote in a report that the young man had gradually learned to tolerate those less clever than himself.

'I would love to have seen London at the end of the seventeenth century,' Osborne once told the *Daily Telegraph*, when asked in which period of history he would like to have been born.

> It was the age of Locke, Newton, Halley, Boyle and Purcell, when Wren's cathedral rose above the city skyline. Our understanding of the physical world was undergoing a transformation. And the Glorious Revolution laid the foundations of our parliamentary democracy. Quite a time to be alive.

It is difficult to imagine Osborne being as lyrical about any other subject. Years later, as shadow Chancellor, businessmen and financiers who encountered Osborne suspected that he was much less interested in economics than in politics. They were right, but he loved history more than both.

The political consciousness that Osborne had evinced at St Paul's receded during these years. He flirted tentatively with student politics before retreating in the face of its grating pomposity. He only attended a few Oxford Union debates, where he met Mark Reckless, who, along with Jo Johnson and Rory Stewart, is one of the student contemporaries who followed Osborne into Parliament. Reckless tried to recruit him as a college secretary for the university's Conservative Association but he declined. The closest Osborne got to the kind of machine politics that famously gripped his future boss (and Magdalen predecessor) William Hague was a failed bid to be elected the entertainment secretary at his college. His campaign was accused by rivals of playing fast and loose with electoral rules but his Tammany Hall skulduggery amounted to putting posters on doors rather than designated noticeboards and electioneering in the junior common room.[27]

Osborne was a Conservative, but not a very demonstrative one. A few years earlier, Oxford had teemed with 'punk Tories' – young men, usually from state school backgrounds, who favoured the meritocratic vigour of Thatcher over Old Labour's cloying statism. Ferguson, Hague and the journalist Andrew Sullivan were among them. By the early 1990s, however, Thatcherism was less an insurgent creed than common sense. Osborne and his friends did not feel any urge to evangelise on behalf of ideas that had plainly prevailed. 'We were quite relaxed about the whole thing,' says a friend. 'The punk Tory thing had kind of been done.' This ideological reticence remains a point of difference between Osborne and Conservative friends who are just a few years older, such as Rachel Whetstone and Steve Hilton. Having seen Thatcherism being fought for against implacable and some-times violent opponents, they are more inclined to proselytise.

Osborne did not completely detach himself from real-world politics. He watched Margaret Thatcher's resignation on the television in his room at Magdalen's Waynfleet building in November 1990. She had been Prime Minister for most of his life but her departure barely moved him. He was more engaged with the 1992 general election, which he followed with Peter Davies in the house they shared at 32 Cowley Road. They had both voted Tory in Oxford East, and watched the party's surprising fourth consecutive victory in the company of Labour supporters. Osborne was pleased by the result but, again, 'not too emotionally attached to it'.[28]

He found international politics much more compelling. He and Davies paid more attention to the Gulf War and Bill Clinton's election as US President, which took place in their first and last years at university respectively, than to anything happening in Britain at the time. On the day after Clinton's victory, Osborne was rambling along Oxford High Street when he saw University College, where the President had spent time as a Rhodes Scholar, flying the American flag. When Osborne and Davies are together, they are still likelier to discuss foreign affairs than Osborne's Westminster work.

'He voiced no particular interest in politics in tutorials,' Brockliss recalls.[29] Reckless confirms that he 'largely kept his head down politically'.[30] But Osborne did fill his time outside of the library. He sought an outlet for his interest in journalism, and initially found one in *Rumpus*, a bawdy magazine put together by fellow students Christopher Coleridge and Robert Norton. The rag pedalled 'dirty jokes and public schoolboy humour' according to one bored reader. The future Chancellor served as business manager and, on one occasion, cover star. He was wearing a wizard's outfit.

Coleridge and Norton then spotted that *Isis*, the venerable termly newspaper, was struggling financially and staged a putsch to take it over. Osborne assumed the editorship from them in his second year. Suitably for a man connected by blood to the world of high-end gambling, the first edition he oversaw featured a cover story on Britain's best poker players. The second led on an essay about cannabis (written by someone else, Osborne is quick to point out) and was printed on hemp paper. Osborne's own contribution to that edition was a piece about MI5's recruitment process; the research took him to the Home Office to interview the intelligence agency's headhunter. He then handed the newspaper over to Jo Johnson and Philip Delves Broughton, another friend. Both issues of *Isis* that Osborne edited are now framed and displayed in his Downing Street flat.

Emboldened by his year out, Osborne also became something of a socialite. He threw 'legendary parties', according to one peer, where the sound of the Happy Mondays, Osborne's favourite band at the time, boomed. (There has probably never been a bigger cultural gap between artist and audience than that dividing the Pauline heir to a baronetcy and the feral bacchanals of Manchester's music scene.) He let his hair grow long and curly, added aristocratic friends to his merely privileged ones, slept around a bit (though not as much as David Cameron had done at Oxford) and joined exclusive student societies such as the Grid and the Canning Club. 'He was an Oscar Wilde character,' remembers a peer, 'a type of dandy'.

Notoriously, he also made his way into the Bullingdon Club, the raucous blue-blooded dining society whose alumni included Cameron and Boris Johnson. Perhaps nothing has wounded Osborne's public image as much as his association with the 'Buller'. A murky and obscure institution that was once unknown even in much of Oxford has become popular shorthand for Conservative elitism. In the infamous photograph of his Bullingdon cohort taken in 1992, Osborne wears a golden waistcoat and an imperious countenance.

A kind of aristocratic *omertà* keeps the Buller's doings opaque to outside investigation, but it seems that Osborne did little of note or sensation there.[31] The club had calmed down a bit since the decadent mid '80s. The onset of recession and a grim jobs market for graduates meant that Oxford was a bleaker place, less tolerant of the hedonistic depredations of an over-privileged cult who would live their lives in comfort regardless. Ostentatious inebriation, rather than casual violence, was the club's way.

Moreover, Osborne was often a cowed bit-player. In the most sensational accounts of excess that have emerged of his time in the club, such as an alleged cocaine binge on top of a speeding bus and a series of skirmishes with local diners, Osborne is either a cringing presence on the sidelines or not present at all.[32] More to the point, even these stories are contested by some Bullingdon members. 'Certainly while I was there, no one was hurt or insulted,' asserts one. The closest Osborne got to a brush with authority in his three years as a student was his tardiness in paying his 'battels', the fees charged by his college for general upkeep and maintenance.

During Osborne's membership, the Buller's activities amounted to two big events a year. 'A breakfast and a dinner, that's all there was,' says someone who was a member at the time. 'It was just another way of getting drunk, really.' Osborne is certainly keen to play down his involvement. 'I have spent more time talking about it after the event than I spent doing anything in the Bullingdon Club,' he says. 'It has all been mythologised.'[33] One of Osborne's Magdalen peers found him 'frivolous' and 'not entirely welcoming of outside company' but 'not malign'.

It is the motive behind Osborne's entry to the club that is more telling. Contemporaries agree that he had no interest in the aristocratic lifestyle in and of itself, and only a little in alcoholic excess. He was drawn to the Bullingdon simply because it was such a challenge to get into. He regarded admittance as 'a form of success', says a fellow student. A contemporary recalls him being turned down at first. Having gone to St Paul's rather than somewhere even more exclusive, such as Eton or Harrow, he was at a disadvantage. 'A Pauline being a member of the Bullingdon does not compute,' says someone who went to the same school. His determination to get in paid off, however, and vestiges of that hunger for social eminence lives on in his industrial-scale networking and his membership of the hyper-exclusive Bilderberg Group. 'George loves being well-connected,' says a friend.

If Osborne maintained two distinct social circles at university – the scholarly crowd he met early on and the braying set he later befriended – he was by temperament a more natural fit in the former. These studious sorts also saw the best side of his character. When his friend Peter Davies ran out of money and was reluctant to ask his parents for help, Osborne immediately lent him some cash. Tutors also found him polite and thought-ful. It is likely that his showier side was an affectation borne out of insecurity. People often try on a new persona at university. Osborne's cloak of choice was the arch, almost self-parodying decadence of *Brideshead Revisited*. He still dons it from time to time, but his underlying character is shyer, straighter, squarer.

Academically, Osborne ended up slightly under-achieving. Dons expected him to get a first-class degree but he did not work especially hard in his final year, occasionally missing deadlines. He scored a 'very solid upper second', according to Brockliss, though he was not especially close to getting a first. 'He was someone who could write perfectly competent essays, time after time after time.'[34] Perhaps the result (which did not acutely disap-point Osborne as he had no interest in an academic career) was the inevitable conclusion of the personal journey he began in his gap year. At St Paul's he excelled academically but at the cost of his social life. Three years later, he was popular enough to throw a twenty-first birthday party in Soho's Quo Vadis with friends as glamorous as Amelia Gentleman, a university contemporary who has gone on to become a journalist (and Jo Johnson's wife).

But some of his academic lustre had been lost along the way. All in all, he regarded it as a price worth paying.

More to the point, Osborne was unlikely to struggle in the outside world. He was equipped with a formidable education. He had a galaxy of friends and useful contacts. He had been given opportunities that are unknown to all but a minority within a sliver within an elite of the overall British population. The economy was, by 1993, recovering steadily from recession. Above all, he possessed a searing ambition to be a person of consequence. The only uncertainty was exactly where his talents would be deployed. He had shown up at the 'milk round' of recruitment events that major employers stage at Russell Group universities but, according to a friend, corporate life was 'too predictable and impersonal to appeal to him'. Brockliss thought he might become a lawyer, as many of his history graduates did. However, it was another career demanding guile, ruthlessness and presentational flair that lured Osborne. Despite his apolitical time at Oxford, he was drawn to the world of professional politics, or what he would come to know as the 'guild'.

Emergence

1993–2005

'Regimes may fall and fail, but I do not.'
Charles Maurice de Talleyrand

5.

Joining the Guild

'He could not have embarked on a less cool thing to do.'

Politics was not Osborne's favoured career path. Having enjoyed his experience of journalism as a student, he tried to make a living out of it. It seemed the most stimulating way of involving himself in his beloved 'current affairs', and it held the lure of a foreign posting one day. He liked the idea of 'wearing a white suit and sitting behind a typewriter in a hotel room in Saigon'.[35] Asked for his dream job outside politics, he plumps for war correspondent.

He applied for the graduate scheme at *The Times* but failed at the final stage. Characteristically persistent, he asked the newspaper whether he could come in and write the occasional piece for freelance rates. They gave him permission and soon he was covering anti-BNP marches in east London and advising readers on the best toys to buy their children for Christmas. Contrary to rumour, he was never employed by the *Daily Telegraph*'s diary column *Peterborough*, though he had friends there and pitched the occasional story. Had he persisted with journalism, his break would have come. He had a fluent pen, an instinctive feel for a story and a gift for cultivating relationships. His friends always suspected, however, that he yearned to be the subject and not the author.

It was a chance meeting with another George that diverted him from the journalistic path. George Bridges, one of the Conservative Party's most able and genial operatives in recent decades, has been indispensable to Osborne's life and career. In 1996, he would introduce him to his future wife. In 1994, he introduced him to Tory politics. Bridges was leaving his job in the Political Section at Conservative Central Office to start work in John Major's Downing Street. Although he had met his younger namesake before, their first serious conversation took place at the end of 1993 during a pub outing with their mutual friend Philip Delves Broughton. Bridges, immediately impressed by Osborne's political insights and palpable ambition, suggested that he apply for his old role at Central Office. He did and, with Bridges's recommendation, got the job.

For the ensuing decade, Osborne's lot was one of personal success in a failing party. In the period between Britain's exit from the European Exchange Rate Mechanism (ERM) in 1992 and the resignation of Iain Duncan Smith as Leader of the Opposition in 2003, and perhaps all the way through to the Conservatives' third successive electoral defeat two years after that, the Tories were a bitterly riven and splenetically detested party. Unlike David Cameron, who left Westminster for Carlton Communications between 1994 and 2001, Osborne was there for almost all of this period. He did not even have the consoling experience of working on the 1992 election victory. His time as a back-room adviser was an unremittingly brutal education that shaped the politician he became: pugilistic, averse to vote-losing ideology and almost neurotically fixated on public opinion.

In a glimpse of horrors to come, Osborne arrived at Conservative Central Office in Smith Square during the week in January 1994 that John Major's exhortation to go 'back to basics' began to sour. Coined as a plea for traditional methods in education and policing, the slogan was mis-briefed to journalists as a moralising injunction. From that moment, any Tory MP who fell short of the most chaste standards of personal conduct would bring charges of hypocrisy onto his party. Osborne began work just after Tim Yeo, a minister who had deplored broken marriages, resigned over revelations that he had sired a love child with a Tory councillor. The scandal smudged the image of a party already seen as venal, inept and uncomprehending of modern Britain. 'He could not have embarked on a less cool thing to do,' says a university friend of Osborne's decision to toil for the Tories.

Central Office had become synonymous with slick profes-sionalism over the course of four election victories, and the unexpected triumph of 1992 in particular. Its most prestigious section was the Conservative Research Department, an incu-bator of Tory talent whose alumni included David Cameron, Chris Patten and Michael Portillo, who had just entered the Cabinet. CRD served as a think tank, a civil service and a political assault unit. It developed policies, briefed ministers and launched attacks on other parties while rebutting those directed at the Tories. It had teams of researchers devoted to specific policy areas, including home affairs and economics, but its most important branch was the Political Section, an Orwellian euphemism for what was in truth an attack machine. When Osborne arrived, it was headed by Rachel Whetstone. CRD was run by Andrew Lansley, and Smith Square's overlord was Norman Fowler, who had taken over as party chairman from the languidly gifted, Hong Kong-bound Chris Patten.

Smith Square's reputation for space-age modernity was out of date, however. By the time Osborne joined, it was an 'unimagi-nably terrible' office, according to someone who worked there in the mid-1990s. Its hideous bombproof curtains blocked out

natural light while dust from ancient files percolated the atmosphere. The technology was hopelessly antiquated. Everyone
worked in poky offices other than the press team, who were
located in the open-plan second floor. CRD was on the fourth,
spread out across a series of cubbyholes, with Lansley's office
at the end of a corridor. The availability of nooks and crannies
allowed for gossip and plotting. There was a cultural gap, and no
little enmity, between the press officers and the CRD members,
who were usually younger and posher.

It will amuse, or perhaps perturb, Osborne's current coalition
partners to know that his first job in the Political Section – and
indeed in politics – was to set about the Liberal Democrats.
Handling the Lib Dem portfolio meant exposing the third party's
policies as sloppily conceived and unaffordable, a job he did with
enough vigour to end up compiling a compendious dossier that
was 'launched' at a drinks party organised by Alistair Cooke,
a venerable Smith Square fixture who was ennobled by David
Cameron in 2010. Osborne's obvious talent saw him quickly
outgrow the Lib Dem silo and acquire a roving role as an all-
purpose attack dog. Like every other member of CRD, he would
identify individual Labour frontbenchers and painstakingly
gather information – usually no more scurrilous than embarrassing quotes about policy – that could be used against them.
It was frothy work, but also a practical grounding in the martial
discipline of politics. Osborne relished it.

CRD, which also employed Kate Fall, who would go on to briefly
date Osborne and now serves as the Prime Minister's deputy
chief of staff, and Gavin Barwell, who is now an MP, was fairly
orthodox in its right-wingery. Major's Cabinet was split between
Thatcherite Eurosceptics, such as Portillo, and Europhiles from
the left of the party, namely Ken Clarke and Michael Heseltine.
As dutiful party staff, the researchers in CRD served the Prime

Minister's strategy of marginally favouring the second group, but their personal sympathies were often elsewhere. Some cursed Major for signing the integrationist Maastricht Treaty in 1991, whose tortuous passage through Parliament exposed the party's rancid fissiparousness. CRD's right-wingers gravitated around Cameron's former boss Norman Lamont, who had lost his job as Chancellor in the aftermath of Black Wednesday.

Osborne, by contrast, 'cut a more metropolitan figure', according to a contemporary. He avoided dogma and seemed amused by his colleagues' Thatcherite certainties. The more they despaired of his political flexibility, the more he hammed it up. But his pragmatism was more than droll affectation. It was a commitment to rigour and analysis; he disdained colleagues who allowed ideological fervour to cloud their judgement as what would actually work as a line of political attack or defence. Despite being younger, he was, at least when it came to politics, worldlier.

Neither was he much taken with his peers' wishful thinking about the Labour Party, whose opinion-poll lead was dismissed by many in Smith Square as a mid-term chimera. Having managed to win a fourth election in the wake of a recession – and with a strapping margin in the popular vote – the Conservative government, by now in its fifteenth year, doubted its own mortality. Osborne didn't. Having observed the 1992 election half-interestedly as a student, instead of tasting it at first hand in the heady micro-culture of Smith Square, he did not read much into it beyond Neil Kinnock's hopeless implausibility as an alternative Prime Minister. John Smith, his replacement, who was stolid and credible in a Morningside bank manager kind of way, would be harder to brush aside.

On 12 May, Smith died of a heart attack. Within six weeks, Tony Blair – the smooth, southern shadow Home Secretary

– was elected as his successor. Gordon Brown, the shadow Chancellor who had carried the status of future Labour leader since his undergraduate days, was persuaded not to challenge his friend and fellow 'moderniser', as the party's centrist reformers had come to be known. Osborne was hardly alone in taking the Tories' new opponent seriously (across Westminster, Cameron told colleagues that he saw no way the government could beat Blair) but he was quicker to grasp the import of what had just happened than anyone at CRD bar Whetstone herself. Together, they wrote a memorandum to the party leadership refuting the alarmingly prevalent appraisal of Blair (at least among Tories) as a light, shallow, transient figure.

Weeks later, Whetstone was offered a job as a special adviser to Michael Howard, the Home Secretary who was overseeing a revolutionary hardening of criminal justice. She would replace Cameron, who was off to try his hand at corporate public relations. Her departure created a vacancy at the top of the Political Section, and Lansley gave the role to Osborne. It was an exalted post for such a young man. Previous incumbents had included not only Whetstone herself, but also Cameron and Guy (now Lord) Black. 'Anyone doing that job was seen as a hotshot who was going to be a special adviser and eventually an MP,' says a former and current colleague who has done both jobs. Osborne worked as hard as anyone in CRD but it was his cold, dispassionate guile that marked him out.

Osborne grew increasingly assertive in his loftier position. He was, according to a Tory staffer at the time, 'almost a mini-me of Cameron … They were uncannily similar in their build and manner.' He also shared with the future party leader a 'very high estimation of his own worth ... he could be quite short with people and didn't like being contradicted.' Perhaps Osborne was consciously emulating Cameron, who was venerated as the superstar of the Tory back rooms. More likely, he was donning a veil of exaggerated confidence to substitute for the kind of authority that only comes with age.

Either way, he loved the job. He was invited to important meetings and despatched to brief Cabinet members before major television appearances. This was his first sustained exposure to top-flight politicians. He worked hard when Parliament was in session but enjoyed a more convivial schedule during the summer recess, often finding the time to play backgammon for money in the office. (Having mastered the game as a schoolboy – there were gambling genes in the Osborne family – he left many of his Smith Square colleagues out of pocket.) He had a secretary, Philippa Rudkin, who still works for him at the Treasury. Men more than twice his age, with red boxes and ministerial cars to their name, relied upon him. He was twenty-three.

Osborne enjoyed his social life no less, carousing with old university friends who were making their way in London. As the *News of the World* would reveal more than decade later, he even crossed paths with a professional dominatrix named Natalie Rowe, the partner of William Sinclair, a friend of Osborne's whose gilded life was sent wayward by drugs. Rumours that Osborne himself partook in illegal substances and erotic derring-do have never been proven. Friends say that while he 'enjoyed what London has to offer', he was 'never at the bacchanalian end of things, no way'.

The scurrilous speculation misses a more interesting quirk in Osborne's character that had been evident since his time in the Bullingdon Club: he did not appear to be a natural libertine so much as a rather straight individual who sometimes wished he was. Quieter, coyer and less blue-blooded than many in his gang, he often found himself slipping to the sidelines. Friends found him 'endearingly stiff' and racked with a 'shyness that manifested as exaggerated confidence'. Rowe's own account of this period, given to the press again in 2011, has him as a well-meaning wallflower. Those who knew both Osborne and Cameron in their twenties theorise that they were actually social opposites: Osborne a retiring soul who liked to be thought of as wild, and Cameron an innately laddish character who was happy to be considered inoffensively middle-of-the-road.

If Osborne was a somewhat ersatz playboy, he was an utter natural at work. One humdrum duty that came with his promotion would turn out to be transformative. As head of the Political Section, he was required to attend the Labour Party's annual conference as the official Tory observer. Held in Blackpool, it was his first party conference of any kind, and two rather profound things happened to him there. He befriended a policy wonk and former Social Democratic Party activist called Danny Finkelstein, who would go on to become perhaps his closest political friend. He was also confronted by the near-existential menace that Blair posed to the Conservatives.

Osborne left his grotty bed and breakfast hotel on 4 October to attend the new leader's first conference speech. He found a seat near Finkelstein in the gaudy splendour of the Empress Ballroom. They knew of each other only vaguely through Julian Kenny, a friend of Osborne's who worked for Finkelstein's think tank, the Social Market Foundation. The two listened as Blair began his speech with a predictable excoriation of the government, and a moving eulogy to John Smith. Then the oration took a rather arresting turn. Blair essentially deplored the Conservatives for not being conservative enough. 'They are no more the party of the family than they are the party of law and order,' he declared, before accusing them of neglecting entrepreneurs. He championed 'social-ism', by which he meant a belief in community, rather than statist socialism.

This was followed by his most daring gesture. It was time for a 'clear and up-to-date' statement of Labour's mission, he said. Osborne and Finkelstein, both of whom had followed Labour politics closely over the summer, knew what this meant. Blair's first major act as leader was going to be a change to Clause Four, the section of the party's constitution that notionally committed it to common ownership of the means of production – or, to put it simply and toxically, nationalisation. In one speech, Blair had shown that his appeal to the swing voters who had ignored Labour since the 1970s lay in more than his charisma and southern, middle-class identity. His actual policies and political strategy were pitched unwaveringly to the centre ground.

Stunned, Osborne and Finkelstein repaired to a nearby burger bar to talk. 'At that moment, we agreed that the Conservative Party would never win another election until it found an answer to what we had just heard,' recalls Finkelstein, now a columnist for *The Times* and perhaps the shrewdest analyst of the party in the media. 'We knew it was very profound, that it was going to change British politics. Our friendship was forged out of our common ability to see that.'[36]

The epiphany was not that the Conservatives would lose the next election; the opinion polls, which gave Labour colossal leads, had long made that obvious. The point was that there would be no quick and easy return to power. The word 'modernisation' was yet to enter Conservative parlance and its meaning remains contested. However, if a moderniser is someone who attributed the Tories' unpopularity to something deeper than the wear and tear of a prolonged stint in office – to something more basic about the party's ideas and identity – then Osborne became a moderniser on 4 October 1994. It would take others, including Cameron, much longer to catch up.

The government, it has to be said, ably assisted Blair in his remorseless ascent to the premiership. Its divisions deepened and its scandals multiplied even as the winter of 1994 brightened into the spring of 1995. Donors deserted the Tories, the right-leaning press brutalised Major for supposed pusillanimity in the face of Europe, backbench MPs openly implored him to step aside while Cabinet members such as Portillo, Heseltine and John Redwood manoeuvred for a succession that could happen at any day. The 21-seat parliamentary majority that Major had secured in 1992 was whittled away to vanishing point by defections and by-election defeats. The government was deplored for a lack of vision while gaining no credit for a steady, growing economy. 'In office but not in power', was Lamont's elegantly caustic verdict from the back benches. It is unlikely that working in the Political Section has ever been tougher than it was in the mid-1990s, when the only relief was 'gallows humour', according to Malcolm Gooderham, who joined in 1995.[37] Osborne's work was industrious, supple but ultimately Sisyphean in its pointlessness.

Some kind of rupture was inevitable: perhaps Major's departure, or a cull of malcontents and dissenters. In the end, something halfway between the two took place. On the radiant afternoon of 22 June 1995, Major summoned the press to the Downing Street rose garden and announced that he would step down as Conservative leader – but stand in the subsequent contest to elect a new one. The idea was to reaffirm his authority and prevent any more challenges to his position until after the general election. He gambled that the rivals who had the best hope of beating him, Michaels Portillo and Heseltine, would not run. He was right. Heseltine was too Europhile to unite a burgeoningly Eurosceptic party and too old to plausibly represent its future.

Portillo, by contrast, was young and ravishingly right-wing. The Defence Secretary was also clever and cultured, with a following among journalists and parliamentary colleagues. He had the bearing and countenance of a man of power, and bore the mark of conservative institutions such as Peterhouse, Cambridge's most Tory college, and CRD. Margaret Thatcher, by then a semi-divine authority for disgruntled Conservatives, was mad about the boy. The thing he lacked was the most important asset a politician can have: judgement. He was undisguisedly keen to replace Major that summer but hoped that another candidate would make the running, allowing him to enter in the second ballot. This lowly vacillation took a bathetic twist when his supporters were caught installing telephone lines in readiness for a leadership campaign. They would never be needed.

Major's only opponent, therefore, was John Redwood, the intelligent, ascetic and Thatcherite Welsh Secretary. During the last leadership election, in 1990, Central Office had observed a policy of scrupulous neutrality. This time, much of its resources and manpower were commandeered by Major's campaign. Nevertheless, Osborne caused a minor fuss by being one of the earliest and most zealous volunteers. His alacrity came from a mixture of common sense (he knew a Redwood-led Tory party was unelectable) and personal ambition, for there was a prospect of coming to the attention of the Prime Minister and winning his favour. He secured a role on the campaign by calling Jonathan Hill, Downing Street's political secretary. With Lansley's blessing, he resigned from CRD and started working out of Major's campaign headquarters at 13 Cowley Street. His name lived on in CRD, where new recruits talked of Osborne as someone who had 'done well for himself' by 'breaking the unwritten rule of impartiality' as soon as the leadership race began.

The contest was no contest. Major had learned from Thatcher's fatal arrogance during her own leadership struggle five years earlier. Far from taking MPs for granted, he wooed them diligently. Meanwhile, his opponent failed to shed an image of extremism and other-worldliness. A press conference to which Redwood turned up with a gaggle of eccentric, chalkstripe-suited supporters seemed to capture the unelectability of a man the tabloids cruelly dubbed 'the Vulcan'.

The atmosphere at Cowley Street was serious but collegial. After long days crafting press releases and gauging the mood of MPs, Osborne would enjoy a buffet dinner with other workers in the garden. Campaigns have a way of compressing hierarchies; staff who are leagues apart in status in the normal run of things suddenly find themselves brushing up against each other. Osborne was able to observe seasoned operators like Howell James and Jonathan Hill at close quarters. He saw them work under stress, make important decisions in seconds, and coax and cajole the best out of colleagues and underlings. The education was not wasted on Osborne, who would go on to run perhaps Westminster's tightest political operation as shadow Chancellor.

Osborne's background in professional politics is unique in its extent. Even others of his generation who are thought to have 'never done a proper job' have at least left Westminster for a while, even if it has usually been for a related pursuit. Cameron worked in corporate public relations for seven years. Ed Miliband spent a year studying at the London School of Economics, and another one teaching at Harvard. Ed Balls was a journalist at the *Financial Times*. Aside from a few months as a freelance reporter just after graduating, Osborne's entire career has taken place within earshot of Big Ben.

This narrow background has marked his view of politics. In private, Osborne refers to professional politicians collectively as the 'guild'. Ostensibly, the phrase is a joke: 'We must make sure we look after our fellow guild members,' he will playfully intone when colleagues suggest recruiting giants of industry and other outsiders to fill political posts. But underneath the flippancy,

Osborne sincerely believes that politics is a trade with its own skills and codes that can only be learned on the job. It is not an amateur vocation for talented people from other fields, and he is never surprised when businessmen who have coined fortunes in the outside world flail and founder in Westminster.

When Alan Johnson was mooted as Gordon Brown's successor in the dying years of the last Labour government, Osborne discounted the idea. The mod-turned-minister had lived a remarkable and rather inspiring life before entering Parliament at the relatively advanced age of forty-seven, but Osborne saw his immersion in the real world as something of a disadvantage. He did not possess a lived knowledge of Westminster's sinuous ways, unlike the Miliband brothers, or Ed Balls, or Andy Burnham, all former special advisers who graduated smoothly to the Cabinet. The success of another Johnson – Boris – confounds and sometimes aggravates Osborne, who is unable to resist observing that the Mayor of London's career in Westminster, where he had never served time as an adviser, flopped ignominiously.

Major was re-elected as Conservative leader on 4 July. Two hundred and eighteen MPs had voted for him, compared to just eighty-nine who backed Redwood. In the garden of Cowley Street the day before, Major's campaign workers held a sweepstake on the result. Most of them wildly overestimated the Prime Minister's margin of victory. Osborne, who had studied the parliamentary party MP by MP, made a more cautious prediction and finished runner-up in the competition. The experience taught him what he still regards as the first rule of politics: 'you have to be able to count'.

The Prime Minister was now safe in his job until his inevitable evisceration at the hands of the electorate, which was still the best part of two years away. For his supporters, there were the spoils of victory. Loyal Cabinet members were rewarded with promotions, including Heseltine, and so were back-room staff.

The customary route out of CRD for its brighter members was to become a special adviser. 'Spads' are employed by the government rather than their party, and provide the kind of political advice to their minister that nominally objective civil servants cannot. Few in number – there are usually only one or two per Cabinet member – they carry more prestige, access and influence than many MPs. Just as he had hoped when he quit CRD for Cowley Street, Osborne was to be rewarded with one of these precious advisory roles. The question was where he would be deployed.

There were three vacancies for special advisers that summer: one at the Department for Transport, one at the Cabinet Office and one at the Ministry of Agriculture, Fisheries and Food (MAFF), now headed by the dutiful Douglas Hogg. MAFF was an incongruous home for Osborne, a Londoner with little feel for the countryside. It was also a relative backwater in Whitehall, though the developing saga of mad cow disease was changing that. Still, at twenty-four, he was thought too young for the other vacancies. He had also befriended Sarah Hogg, the minister's wife and a senior adviser in Downing Street, during his time on the Major campaign. Any spad job was a promotion from CRD so, after consulting Bridges for advice, he seized it.

Back at Smith Square, Lansley held a leaving party for Osborne. Among the guests was Cameron, by now ensconced in the frenzied but better-remunerated world of corporate public relations. Divided by half a decade in age, the pair only knew each other loosely and many years would elapse before they were vaunted as both a coherent political partnership and the future of Conservatism. Lansley, however, was already sure that his two most gifted alumni were the right's answer to Blair and Brown. 'When you two are running the country,' he said to Cameron and

Osborne in front of the other guests, 'please make me Governor of Bermuda.'

The milieu to Osborne's personal success was a brightening, flourishing country. Decades of economic upheaval were giving way to consistent growth and low inflation, while British music, art and football began to stir after several fallow years. If either politics or life were fair, the Conservatives might have won some credit for all this national ebullience; the painful structural reforms of the '80s had helped to make Britain a more dynamic and less class-bound society. Instead, the government was seen as the grey, grouchy exception to it all. It was Blair, with his personal flair and subversive take on Britain as a 'young country', who basked in the sunny zeitgeist.

Astonishingly, this wasn't the worst of it for the Tories. Major's renewed mandate staved off internal challengers but his other blights – ministerial scandal, administrative crises, the malicious hostility of the right-wing press – actually got worse in his last two years in power. Having observed the government's decay from the relative remove of Smith Square, Osborne would now taste it directly. 'I have not faced personal adversity,' he would say years later, 'but on professional adversity I've got a record second to none.'[38]

6.

Belly of the Beast

'He seemed more of a 40-year-old than a 25-year-old.'

George Osborne was following the news more attentively than most fifteen-year-olds in 1986 but one story was too esoterically pastoral to pique his metropolitan ken. In November, the government announced that its Central Veterinary Laboratory had discovered a neuro-degenerative disease that was killing cattle. Bovine spongiform encephalopathy, or BSE, was a gruesome affliction that slowly wasted away a cow's brain and spine. It was probably caused by the practice of feeding these herbivores the infected remains of other cows. Television footage of stricken cattle stumbling and meandering gave rise to BSE's tabloid shorthand: mad cow disease.

By the time Osborne began work at MAFF, almost a decade had elapsed and BSE had mutated from an agricultural blight into a political saga. The government had ordered the slaughter of infected cattle and regulated the feeding of cows. It insisted, however, that BSE could not be passed on to humans. This was despite the emergence of new variant Creutzfeld-Jakob disease (CJD), a condition that bore similarities to BSE. In the spring of 1995, a teenager called Stephen Churchill became CJD's first casualty. He would not be its last.

This looming crisis was not the only worry troubling Osborne as he started life in government. He covets prestige and power, and MAFF had less of each than perhaps any other corner of Whitehall. Then there was his new boss, Douglas Hogg, who was other-worldly even compared to his predecessors John Gummer, who shared a burger with his daughter on national television to underscore his faith in British beef, and William Waldegrave, a cerebral blue blood who perhaps missed his true calling in academia. Hywel Williams, a waspish adviser to John Redwood in the mid-1990s, described Hogg as 'an amalgam of cleverness and foolishness' who 'confronted Britain's democratic masses with a pinched, self-righteous irritability'.[39] Of all the parliamentary expense claims revealed by the *Daily Telegraph* during its notorious exposé of 2009, Hogg's gardening upkeep, including a mole catcher, remains among the most notorious.

It is remarkable, therefore, that Osborne enjoyed his time as a special adviser more than any job he had before becoming shadow Chancellor. Proximity to power compensated for the grimmer aspects of the appointment, he confesses. 'You get thrown into these meetings with senior officials and Cabinet ministers and the like, which you would never get the chance to be in unless you were twenty years older.'[40] He had his own office and secretary, as well as privileged access to Cabinet minutes and government papers. It was also during his time as a spad that Osborne attracted his first press notices. In April 1996, a *Times* diary story reported that the young adviser had used his membership of the Tate Gallery to get the visiting EU Agriculture Commissioner into an over-subscribed Cézanne exhibition.[41] Five months later, the same diary column mentioned that the 'Gucci-clad' Osborne was the nephew of not one but two Tory parliamentary candidates, John Aspinall and James Osborne.[42]

Something else attracted Osborne to the job. For all its remoteness from the full swim of Westminster life, MAFF was actually a place of growing political import – even aside from the cattle crisis. Fisheries and the European Union's Common Agricultural Policy had both become proxies for the vituperative issue of European integration. Newspapers chronicled the apparent victimisation of British fishermen at the hands of Brussels, while condemning the munificent subsidies given to French farmers. Osborne was not working at a great office of state, but the pure politics of his berth were deceptively interesting. It was an instructive exposure to Tory Euroscepticism for someone whose views on the matter oscillated between indifference and ambivalence.

As well as immersing himself in agriculture policy, Osborne's job was to serve his master in ways too political and partisan for a civil servant to contemplate. He would defend the government to journalists, brief Hogg before media appearances and help him get his way with his ministry's mandarins without alienating them. Spads must possess supple personal wiles as well as intellectual capacity and a tolerance of being on-call more or less permanently. The best ones are to politics what investment bankers are to finance – talented all-rounders who link the distinct elements of the overall system in the service of their particular client. David Cameron, who worked for both Norman Lamont and Michael Howard, was the outstanding exponent of the craft in his generation of advisers.

If Osborne never acquired the same renown, it was largely because he did not serve in as grand a department as the Home Office or the Treasury. He was about as highly rated as a MAFF spad could be. 'You can tell a lot about a politician by the kind of special adviser they employ,' says Richard Packer, who was then Permanent Secretary (the top civil servant) at the ministry. 'What you want is competent, clever, hard-working, civil, positive. That's what Osborne was like. He was more of a 40-year-old than a 25-year-old.'[43] Mandarins were particularly taken with his adamantine calm under pressure, while ministers noticed his dynamism. Stephen Dorrell, who as Health Secretary had regular dealings with MAFF, recalls that the young Osborne 'was clearly going places'.[44]

It was Dorrell who would inaugurate the most traumatic period in British agriculture since the war, and Osborne's most testing time as a spad. On 20 March 1996, it fell to the Health Secretary to announce that a probable link between BSE and CJD had been established. He stressed that all known CJD cases were most likely caused by exposure to beef before the banning of offal-feeding in 1989. In other words, all British beef currently on sale was safe. Inevitably, though, the panic was immediate and overwhelming.

Osborne was one of those who learned of the discovery ten days before it was announced. He was present at a briefing for MAFF ministers and officials by Professor John Paterson, a scientific specialist who advised the government. After he revealed the link to the gathering, the chief medical officer presented a paper suggesting that up to 2 million people could die from CJD. This was not a prediction or even an estimate but an absolute maximum figure that could not be ruled out on the basis of available data. The rather critical distinction was lost on his horrified audience in the room – and subsequently the British press.

Following Dorrell's statement, BSE became the dominant political story for much of 1996. It had implications for health, agriculture, the economy and, above all, Britain's relations with Europe. Within a week the EU banned all exports of British beef, prompting outrage from the government, which nevertheless ordered a new round of cow-culling to assert its safety credentials. While ministers battled with Europe and a sensationalist press, they also fought among themselves. Hogg was briefed against by Cabinet colleagues for arguing against a futile 'beef war' with Brussels. Despite the provocation, he ordered Osborne not to counter-brief against his tormentors. The young man obeyed dutifully.

To paraphrase Rahm Emanuel, President Obama's pugilistic former chief of staff, Osborne did not let the crisis go to waste. He became increasingly indispensable to an overworked Ministry. He, Hogg and Packer, besieged by the outside world and much of the rest of government, began to operate as something of a unit. He was no longer sought after by lowly lobby hacks but by the most eminent journalists in Westminster; Michael Brunson, the political editor of ITN, took him out for lunch. Crucially, he also had more exposure to the very centre of power. A rare consolation for crisis-stricken departments is that Downing Street is forced to take an interest in them. The BSE saga meant more meetings with No. 10 staff for Osborne, and more opportunities to impress them.

The impeccable access came with limited responsibility. Downing Street toyed capriciously with the careers of Hogg and Packer, at one point telling them that they had only survived because replacements had been hard to find. As a spad, Osborne faced no such pressure. 'No one expected George to fix the whole thing,' recalls a colleague. Had his boss been sacked, Osborne would have most likely remained at MAFF or transferred to another Whitehall department. His equanimity struck some as insouciance. 'He knew his boss was fucked so he treated the job as a staging post in his career,' says a spad who worked in another department at the time. Urban and urbane, Osborne was always unlikely to become an authority on rural affairs, but some sceptics doubt that he even tried. 'If you're a spad, you get to know your subject,' says one. 'George never bottomed out the epidemiology of CJD.'

If Osborne was less than mono-maniacal in his focus on work, he had a good excuse. Away from Westminster, his personal life was increasingly rich and satisfying. He shared a flat with his best friend, Peter Davies, in Haldane Road in Fulham. He was young enough to enjoy the brashly hedonistic national mood that had stirred the previous year but which really peaked in the summer of 1996, when England hosted the European Championships of football (a few games of which Osborne attended) and Oasis became the biggest British band since The Beatles, playing in front of colossal audiences at Maine Road and Knebworth (where Steve Hilton, a future colleague and occasional adversary of Osborne's, stood among 165,000 others).

Good-looking and impeccably connected, Osborne was also becoming something of a catch. He had already dated Kate Fall, his former CRD comrade, when, in July, George Bridges invited a group of friends to a dinner party at his parents' home in Surrey. Among them were Osborne and a financial analyst named Frances Howell, whose father David had served as a Cabinet member under Margaret Thatcher. They were a pretty pair and formed a connection over dinner, as Howell, who yearned to write for a living, found Osborne reading animatedly to her from a newspaper.

She was taken by his passion for the life he was building for himself; he by her spark and maturity. Although Osborne harboured a juvenile streak – even challenging another Magdalen alumnus to a wasabi-eating contest at a Japanese restaurant that summer, emerging victorious but doubled-over in agony – he was actually drawn to 'intellectually self-made women', says a peer. His female friends, such as the historian Amanda Foreman, were 'more Bloomsbury than Knightsbridge'. Howell was two years older than Osborne and at least as clever. She also had an even wider circle of friends, including Catherine Ostler, a former flatmate who would go on to edit *Tatler*, and Simone Finn, now a special adviser in the government and a one-time girlfriend of Michael Gove, Osborne's future Cabinet colleague. Osborne and Howell began dating seriously. Within two years, they would marry.

Towards the end of 1996, John Major's advisers were allocating jobs for the forthcoming general election campaign. His inner circle – Howell James, Jonathan Hill, Sheila Gunn and Lord Cranborne – would accompany the Prime Minister as he toured the country. In Smith Square, Brian Mawhinney, the party chairman, would oversee the campaign. Under him were the likes of Charles Lewington, Andrew Cooper and Danny Finkelstein ('who was always ahead of the game', according to Lewington),[45] who were respectively in charge of media, polling and research. Age and experience were furnished by Tim Bell and Maurice Saatchi, youthful vigour by the likes of Bridges and CRD stars such as Malcolm Gooderham and Michael Simmonds. Yet nowhere in this great unwieldy organogram was there anyone to provide Major with his morning briefing, which would comprise a summary of the newspapers and the party's official line on the day's stories. It was a chore performed by the young Michael Portillo for Margaret Thatcher in 1979.

Tom O'Malley, the head of the Political Section, was the natural candidate. Osborne, though, sensed that his service to Major in the summer of 1995, and then again during the BSE crisis, might give him a competitive advantage. He approached Howell James to press his case. He enjoyed the endorsement of his friend Danny Finkelstein, who had been put in charge of CRD after Major's re-election as Tory leader two years earlier. James was persuaded. At the age of twenty-five, Osborne was handed a role entailing a daily one-to-one meeting with the Prime Minister. He started work in March 1997, two months before the election.

His schedule was onerous. In a typical day, Osborne would turn up at Smith Square at 3 a.m. to read the first editions of the newspapers. When his senior colleagues arrived two hours later, they would draw up the party's response to each of the day's main stories. Then, at 6 a.m., Osborne would walk across a deserted Westminster to Downing Street to brief the Prime Minister in the flat where he himself now lives as Chancellor. In his underwear or pyjamas, with his wife Norma soundly asleep in the next room, Major would listen stoically enough as Osborne read out the unbroken litany of scorn and contumely heaped upon him by the press. On one occasion, the young man had to inform the Prime Minister that even his own sister had told a tabloid that he could not win the election. He would then return to Smith Square, where he would continue to monitor the media and help rebut Labour's remorseless assaults on the government. On quieter days, he took an afternoon nap in the flat on Horseferry Road where the party had put him up. More often, he would remain working until 11 p.m.

Osborne hungered for personal advancement, not an easy life, so he did not begrudge the toil. But he knew that the only uncertainty about the impending election was the margin of Labour's victory. The Tories wore the scars of eighteen years in power, including the self-inflicted wounds of disunity over Europe. The right-leaning press had brutalised Major for ideological impurity; MPs who rebelled over Maastricht in 1992 continued to hound him from the back benches. The party was also marked by the stain of sexual and financial impropriety. One misdemeanour would turn out to have profound implications for Osborne's career. Neil Hamilton, a colourful former minister, was dogged by allegations that he had taken money from Mohamed Al Fayed, the owner of Harrods, to ask questions on his behalf in the Commons. In his previously safe seat of Tatton, a former BBC journalist named Martin Bell had decided to stand against him on an anti-sleaze ticket.

Exploiting all these agonies was perhaps the best opposition British politics had seen since the war. Headquartered in the open-plan modernity of Millbank Tower, Labour were ruthless, disciplined, professional, unwavering in their devotion to the centre ground, and fronted by a politician who was without peer in grasping and expressing the national mood. The Tories had no answer to Blair. As Osborne now points out in private, they would never find one. The day before the election, Osborne arrived at No. 10 to find the Majors' possessions packed away in boxes awaiting removal. The Prime Minister understood his fate. Thirteen years would elapse before Osborne himself saw the inside of Downing Street again.

The great Conservative imperium, which ran across three decades and refashioned Britain unrecognisably, finally fell on 1 May 1997. On the day, Smith Square despatched staff to marginal constituencies for some last-ditch campaigning. Osborne was sent to Hammersmith & Fulham, where he chaired the Eel Brook Ward of the local Conservative Association. Enjoying his first day out in two months, he found himself being interviewed for Italian television outside a polling station on the Fulham Broadway. He then headed to Orso, a restaurant in Covent Garden, for dinner with senior campaign staff including Howell James and Jonathan Hill. In such venerable company, Osborne felt that he had made it as a political adviser. His personal rise had been stunning, even if it was taking place against the backdrop of his party's obliteration.

At 10 p.m., the voting ceased and the exit polls were published. There was no mobile phone reception in the basement restaurant so Hill scurried upstairs to receive news of an expected Labour landslide. After sharing the projections with his colleagues, they scrambled to Smith Square, where a forlorn 'party' of sorts was taking place for the staff while televisions beamed in the dismal results from across the country. Osborne had to navigate his way in through a mob outside Central Office who were, it has to be said, shrieking the sentiments of much of the country: 'Tories! Tories! Tories! Out! Out! Out!' Inside, tense and shattered campaign workers clutched their wine glasses close, as if holding on to the last rung of power. Many would lose their jobs as the indebted party machine cut its cloth, and all knew MPs who were being pitilessly cashiered by the electorate.

Tom O'Malley, beaten by Osborne to the plum job of briefing the Prime Minister during the campaign, circulated a list of Cabinet members who were likely to lose their seats under various swings to Labour. Michael Portillo was at the foot of the page; only something seismic would deprive the Tories of their leader-in-waiting. In the room were two not even remotely threatened by eviction: Michael Heseltine, who had come back from his Henley seat, and William Hague, the 36-year-old Welsh Secretary whose constituency in Yorkshire would not conduct its count until the following day. At around 2 a.m., Portillo's north London constituency declared its result. He was, unbelievably, gone. As plausible successors, both Hague and Heseltine drew the beseeching glares of everyone else in Smith Square. The younger man in particular was already being softened up for a leadership run by campaign staff and donors.

Osborne was not among those who approached Hague that night, but he knew that the Welsh Secretary's mix of youth and mainstream Conservatism gave him a good chance of winning a leadership contest. At 5 a.m., Osborne took a taxi home to Fulham with his girlfriend Frances. The government – his government – had been eviscerated. It had won just 31 per cent of the vote, 12 percentage points fewer than Labour, which now boasted an indecently gargantuan majority of 179 seats. The Tories had lost more MPs (170) than it now fielded in Parliament.

Not one represented a Scottish or Welsh constituency. Barring calamity, Labour could expect at least two terms in office.

Osborne, however, was far from distraught. Indeed, he was taken by the palpable sense of occasion. He awoke to television images of Tony Blair that now radiate a kind of prelapsarian innocence: his car journey from his Islington home to Buckingham Palace, his deftly curated arrival at Downing Street. Such equanimity, even perkiness, in the aftermath of his own party's humiliation will stoke the suspicion that Osborne is not much of a Conservative at all. It is truer to say that Blair in 1997 was something approximating a culturally cosmopolitan Tory, and that Osborne identified with that wing of his party. He also admired the Labour leader's sparkling gifts as a political performer. His ardour would intensify in the ensuing years but that is true of many Tories of his generation, even if not all of them went to the extent of privately referring to Blair as 'the master' and 'our real leader'.

Osborne is not moved emotionally by political events but he is alive to them intellectually. He does not scar easily, but he learns rapidly. For him, the lesson of the Major years was the primacy of politics over policy. After all, by any reasonable standard, Major led one of the more effective post-war governments. The first five years of what would turn out to be a fifteen-year economic expansion took place under his premiership. The British curse of inflation was finally exorcised. Crime, whose rise since the 1960s had come to be accepted by political and judicial elites as an inexorable function of modernity, began to fall after Michael Howard's radical toughening-up of home affairs policy. The monoliths of the state, especially the NHS and welfare, underwent reform. His Citizen's Charter envisaged the kind of choice, competition and transparency in public services that Blair and Cameron would later make their driving creed. Neither has ever acknowledged the debt. In a final rally at the Docklands Arena, the Prime Minister gave a speech largely devoted to public services. 'That was the real Major coming out,' says Lewington.[46]

Major's ultimate service to his country, though, was rendered in Europe. He kept Britain out of the single currency, the continent's most ruinous misadventure since the war, without tipping his nation out of the EU altogether. He achieved all this under the most hellish conditions any recent Prime Minister has known: a sliver of a Commons majority (itself outrageous short-change for what was an easy victory in the popular vote in 1992), a poisonously riven Cabinet and parliamentary party, a 'Tory' press of quite stupefying cruelty, and a pitilessly effective opposition. In the ensuing decade, Blair would govern in propitious circumstances and achieve less.

Yet for all this, Major's reward was the largest defeat endured by any party during his lifetime. His shrewd judgement and quiet competence – some polls put the Tories ahead of Labour on economic trust on the eve of the election – mattered less than his party's repellent reputation. The Conservatives were despised as cruel, complacent and corrupt. The word 'Tory' regained its original coinage as an insult to be spat out with disgust. By 1997, Britain was prosperous and governable in a way it was not in 1979, but voters had banked these achievements. They were now worried about the state of public services. Culturally, Britain was on its way to becoming perhaps the world's first post-modern country: Godless, classless, consumerist and hedonistic, with London as a kind of cacophonous Babel. The Tories had inad-vertently wrought this transformation with their radical reforms in the '80s, but they were barely comprehending of the society they bequeathed to Blair. Osborne, by contrast, was utterly at ease in it. He could stay and strive to acquaint his party with contemporary Britain – to *modernise* it – or he could take his leave of the guild.

7.

Hague's Apprentice

'He can walk into a room and immediately identify who the
three most important people are, and how to talk to them.'

Osborne's first full day in Blair's Britain was spent empty-
ing his office at MAFF. Cushioned by the six months'
pay that came as part of a special adviser's severance
package, he could contemplate his future in some repose. He was
about to turn twenty-six. Business held no lure for someone so
animated by public life, and the indifference was mutual. With
the exception of lobbyists and public-affairs outfits, corporate
employers tend to shun politicos out of a forgivable confusion
over what they actually do. The nascent Tory leadership race,
and William Hague's mooted candidacy in particular, intrigued
Osborne – but if the electoral annihilation of the Conservative
party was not the cue for him to try life outside Westminster,
whatever would be?

Two years of dealing with journalists on behalf of Douglas
Hogg had not diminished Osborne's interest in their trade. He
applied to become a leader writer at *The Times*, where he had
freelanced in 1993. Meanwhile Sarah Hogg, who had begun her
career at *The Economist*, suggested to old colleagues there that
they consider hiring him. There was a vacancy for a correspondent in the venerable weekly's Britain section and Osborne was

summoned for an interview by Gideon Rachman, who had just started editing those pages.

Rachman, new to the business of interviewing potential recruits, began by telling Osborne that he would probably not get the job. The younger man's pique would have worsened had he known that the role was earmarked for another former spad, Peter Barnes, who was older and had worked for the Social Security Secretary Peter Lilley. The iciness thawed quickly, however, and not only because Osborne and Rachman had been given the same first name at birth, gone to the same school and spent part of their youth in the same street (St Petersburg Place in Bayswater). They also shared a dry and sardonic manner. Osborne explained that his job at CRD had been to 'destroy Blair'. 'I obviously didn't do a very good job of it,' he dead-panned. When Rachman asked him why he favoured Hague for the Tory leadership, Osborne replied obliquely that 'he is the one I know least about'.[47]

Despite the awkward start, Osborne could sense that Rachman was being won over by his intellect and self-deprecation. With characteristic chutzpah, he implored his fellow Pauline to 'give a young guy a chance'.[48] Before either *The Economist* or *The Times* got back to him, William Hague did exactly that.

Hague's history of almost unblemished personal success – a first at university, a star turn at McKinsey, a precocious entry to Parliament and then the Cabinet – suggested that he could lead the Conservatives one day. But at just thirty-six, that day was expected to be at least four years away. Had Michael Portillo survived the election, Hague was himself minded to back his inevitable campaign for the leadership. Even with the hero of the right gone, he initially pledged to serve as running mate to Michael Howard. The game plan (and the ambitious Hague always had one of those) was obvious: the outgoing Home

Secretary would stabilise and unify the party before leading it to defeat, just as he would end up doing between 2003 and 2005, at which point a more seasoned Hague could take over with a realistic prospect of winning power.

However, it is fiendishly difficult, even unnatural, for a politician to walk away from the prospect of immediate eminence. Osborne would manage it in 2005, when he turned down invitations to stand for the Tory leadership. Perhaps he learned from Hague's failure to do the same in the summer of 1997. Hague yielded to pressure from MPs and party elders to renege on his deal with Howard. Their confidence in him was understandable. Hague was fresh enough to represent the future and barely tainted by association with the Major years. Neither was true of Howard. He was also in the party's ideological mainstream: staunchly Eurosceptic and broadly Thatcherite in his economics. A divided party was likelier to find unity under Hague than Ken Clarke or Stephen Dorrell, both running from the party's vanishing left, and it had little hope of softening its hard-faced image under Howard or Redwood, who were standing as rather orthodox right-wingers. Peter Lilley, another candidate from the right, was quicker to grasp the party's hideous image problem but he was ultimately a less dynamic version of Hague.

Fourteen years later, when Hague spoke at Osborne's fortieth birthday party in Dorneywood, he mischievously expounded his old apprentice's 'four laws of political success'. The first is to work out before others who will be the next party leader, inveigle yourself into their court and become indispensable to them. It was said jokingly but it was not a joke. Just as Osborne manoeuvred his way into the vicinity of the Prime Minister two summers earlier, so he thrust himself upon Hague, calculating that the fragmentation of the right-wing vote, along with the determination of most Tory MPs to back anyone but Clarke, would hand victory to the contest's youngest hopeful.

He asked Alan Duncan, an MP and one of Hague's best friends from university, for a place on the campaign in its Stafford Place headquarters, which buzzed with around fifty other volunteers. 'What happens in that situation, where there is no immediate structure, is that talent quickly rises to the top,' remembers Hague. Although Osborne began by doing odd jobs, his aptitude as a writer of speeches and newspaper articles allowed him to quickly displace more established staff such as Barnaby Towns, the candidate's former special adviser. 'He became my main scribe,' says Hague.[49] Osborne turned the back room of the building into 'his place, the writers' place', according to another volunteer on the campaign. 'He just glided in.'

The thrill of politics was dimming his interest in journalism, as was the prospect of victory. A quixotic alliance of convenience between Clarke and Redwood, perhaps the least compatible individuals in the whole of the Tory party, merely drew attention to the inoffensive common sense of Hague's candidacy. His prospects were gilded by the endorsement of Margaret Thatcher, who preferred to see her party led by a neophyte than a Europhile. Osborne turned out speech after deft speech for Hague, who says: 'In six weeks, I went from not knowing him to having a lot of confidence in him.'[50]

On 19 June, Hague was in the shadow Cabinet room in Parliament with another of his campaign team, Mark Fox, when he was telephoned with the news that he had become the youngest Tory leader since Pitt the Younger. Clarke and then Howard, who had forgiven Hague's opportunism, came in to congratulate him. Within the hour, the new Leader of the Opposition gave a speech to his MPs and party staff at Smith Square that was largely authored by Osborne. 'The days of disunity, of factions and wings, and groups within groups, and parties within parties, must now come to an end,' he warned his querulous flock. 'If anyone doubts I mean it, I say this to them – just try me.' They would.

For Osborne, the summer of 1997 evoked the summer of 1995: another campaign, another SW1 townhouse, another victory, and another sinecure by way of reward. Of all the dozens of volunteers who had worked on Hague's campaign, only a handful would make it into his leadership team. Osborne was always going to be one of them. Hague appointed him as his political secretary, exactly the kind of nebulous title that abounds in professional politics. The few specific duties it entailed included serving as a messenger between Hague and his shadow Cabinet and writing the leader's speeches. Otherwise, these jobs are whatever their occupants make of them. The lure for Osborne was access to the very summit of the Conservative Party, not on the provisional basis he enjoyed in the closing months of Major's leadership but indefinitely and as of right. Another who graduated to Hague's team recalls Osborne as a 'kid in a candy store', so happy was he to have not only survived the Tory collapse but to emerge with a more prestigious job. 'He had been at the scene of disasters like BSE. I did think "What are you doing here?"'

His first duty was to reconnoitre the parliamentary offices set aside for the new opposition. For eighteen years, Conservatives had enjoyed Whitehall departments and all their trappings: tastefully appointed rooms, uncountable reserves of staff, a Downing Street switchboard that can purportedly connect its patrons to anyone on Earth. Osborne was the first Tory to glimpse the party's dismal new circumstances: poky offices with fraying furniture and little in the way of administrative support or technological capacity. Thousands of unopened letters, including some from the American government and international royalty, tottered in piles on the floor. 'There was literally no apparatus, no structure for opposition at all,' he recalls.[51] He still recounts the story to younger staff as a lesson in the glory of power and the ignominy of opposition.

As he silently took in the desolation, he heard someone enter the office. It was Major. He had turned up with words of counsel for Hague but left them with Osborne instead. 'William must not be captured by the party,' he said softly, cutting a bleak but dignified figure. 'He must be his own man.' The incongruous pair, separated by a generation and several tiers of social class, shook hands and bade farewell.

Folklore has divided Hague's leadership into distinct halves: a plucky effort at moving his party to the centre ground, or 'modernising' it, until 1999, followed by a dunderheaded appeal to the Conservative core vote. This overrates the coherence of the first phase and fails to reckon with the redeeming aspects of the second. His early reforms were more technical than ideological. Although Hague's leadership is now known for tragicomic haplessness, the former management consultant was initially vaunted as the only Tory at ease with the professionalisation of politics. He assembled his political court as painstakingly as he had once put together McKinsey project teams, or his gang of student hacks at the Oxford Union.

He brought in Danny Finkelstein as his head of policy. Gregor Mackay, another friend of Osborne's, joined from Smith Square as press secretary. Seb Coe, the Olympian-turned-parliamentarian who had lost his seat in May, became Hague's chief of staff. Outside this inner circle, of which Osborne himself was a member, were the likes of Rick Nye, who had taken charge of CRD, Andrew Cooper, a pollster and student friend of Finkelstein's who probably has the best claim to being the first Tory moderniser, and Tina (now Baroness) Stowell, the dominant organisational force in the office.

Hague simultaneously applied his technocrat's mind to the Conservative party itself, which has rarely been a party at all so much as a loose confederation of distinct and sometimes warring bodies, including the parliamentary party, Central Office, the leader's operation and the little platoons of local constituency associations. Hague commissioned Archie Norman, a sublimely able corporate executive who had recently left business for politics, to bring coherence to the Tory machine, remodel Central Office and chisel away at the party's £14 million debt. As a way of imposing his authority on Smith Square's den of intrigue, Hague took an office there instead of relying exclusively on his parliamentary bunker. Osborne sat nearby. In a provocative coup, Hague then changed the rules governing Tory leadership elections so that ordinary members would have the final say, thus ending the MPs' immemorial right to decide their chieftain among themselves. Had the rules been in place for the contest that summer, Clarke would have won handily.

Osborne believes Hague is entitled to more credit than he has been afforded for restoring a laughably dishevelled party to some kind of working order, just as Neil Kinnock enjoys a lofty perch in Labour folklore for doing the same. Institutional reform is not substantive change, however, as both leaders learned at the polls. Hague's early efforts to improve his party's reputation were largely symbolic: a visit to the Notting Hill carnival was meant to signal his comfort with multi-ethnic modernity, a campaign tour named 'Listening to Britain' was supposed to convey humility. His speech to the Tory conference in October 1997, again largely written by Osborne, was not even the most substantial call for change heard in Blackpool that week. At a fringe event organised by the Centre for Policy Studies, a chastened Portillo gave a dense lecture on the future of Conservatism that inspired, among others, the restless, ornery Cooper, who is now Downing Street's director of strategy.

The ultimate expression of Hague's tentative approach to modernisation was his first shadow Cabinet, which saw the Treasury, trade and foreign portfolios in the hands of Lilley, Redwood and Howard respectively, as well as the emergence of a Catholic conservative and former army major called Iain Duncan Smith. Such appointments were hard to avoid from the moment the country returned a shrunken and almost uniformly right-wing Tory parliamentary party. Clarke had declined to serve and avowed modernisers were rare; Francis Maude, who was made shadow Culture Secretary, was still halfway through his personal conversion to the cause. Still, there were other, deeper reasons for Hague's equivocation about change.

One was his own ambiguous political soul. Yes, he was liberal-minded on matters of race and sexuality, even provoking euphemistic whispers about the 'bachelor boys' who worked on his leadership campaign. His time as Minister for Disabled People also stirred the undemonstrative compassion that distinguishes both himself and the average Tory member, who is likelier to be an elderly churchgoing widow than the plutocratic chauvinist of caricature. This product of a Yorkshire comprehensive was also sincere in his passion for social mobility. Despite all these credentials, however, Hague was at core a technocrat whose few fervent views were conventionally right-wing. He simply was not very fervent about remaking Conservatism.

He had a good excuse: modernisation itself lacked shape and content as an idea. Its champions were not only few in number but vague in thought, quicker to urge change than to itemise its meaning. This said less about them than about the Tories' confusing predicament. Labour's plight in the '80s was easy to grasp: its policies were too left-wing for swing voters. Nothing so simple was true of the Conservatives. Thatcherism, once an insurgent creed, had attained the status of common sense by

1997. Indeed, Blair had been elected on a platform of retaining its fundamentals, from low marginal tax rates and flexible labour laws to privatised utilities and fiscal thrift. If the Tories' image was a greater curse than its ideas, then which of its myriad image problems were most pressing? Arrogance? Sleaze? Fogeyishness? Bigotry? In any case, how does a party go about changing something as intangible as its image? All these puzzles still grip Tories in 2012. In 1997, they were utterly confounding. Modernisation was, at most, an embryonic movement.

Of course, the muddiness of Hague's message was a secondary concern. He was not being listened to in the first place. As he knew when he struck his original deal with Howard, voters had effectively given Labour a two-term mandate and were utterly indifferent to anything the Tories had to say about anything for the foreseeable future. If this structural problem was eminently predictable, his personal unpopularity was less so. Although Hague had carried a reputation for geeky oddness since addressing the Conservative Party conference at the age of sixteen, the sheer speed and force with which voters concluded he was not a plausible Prime Minister remains stunning.

His aides struggle to recall any time at which he was taken seriously in focus groups or opinion polls. Satirists lampooned him as a schoolboy in shorts while cartoonists had fun with his balding pate and cherubic features. His accent, bizarrely mid-Atlantic for a son of Rotherham, only added to the sense of strangeness. When he responded to Lady Diana's death with measured stoicism, he was derided for emotional illiteracy. It was cruel treatment for a man of ability and decency but, as Osborne observes whenever life's unfairness is lamented, there is no point pretending the world is anything other than it is.

Osborne helped to supply Hague's sole source of relief, but it ended up doing more for his own career than his boss's. Prime

Minister's Questions was the making of the young adviser. The Tory leader consistently wounded Blair in their Wednesday showdowns across the despatch box. Much of this was down to his own gifts as a parliamentarian but the coaching he received from his aides was indispensable to his performances. Finkelstein furnished the jokes, CRD's Haldenby took notes, and Duncan would provide an MP's perspective, but it was Osborne who really sparkled.

He parsed dense arguments into one-liners. He could intuit which topics would play best in the Commons. He was also an eerily good mimic, able to not only emulate Blair's voice and manner but to accurately predict his answer to any question. Hague would use this insight to draw up McKinsey-style 'decision trees' that set out his question, then a menu of likely prime ministerial responses, and then the best follow-up question to each of those responses. Such fastidious preparation, allied to the force and fluency of Hague's delivery, kept him on top of Blair in the chamber. This may have girded his leadership by denying his enemies any momentum. Backbenchers would arrive in Westminster each week grumbling about his shortcomings and go back to their constituencies on Thursday roused by his latest besting of Blair.

That was the limit of any advantage that Hague accrued from PMQs. The few voters who tuned in found his pat point-scoring more becoming of a student debater than a potential Prime Minister, and Blair learned to brush him off. For Osborne, though, it was transformative. Word percolated about his political wiles. 'You kept being told about this guy,' remembers Keith Simpson, a frontbencher at the time and now Hague's Parliamentary Private Secretary.[52] He piqued the interest of journalists, received invitations to exclusive Whips Office parties attended by Major and other party grandees, and socialised with Hague and his wife Ffion. 'He used his position to build his network,' says a colleague who admired his gifts as an opera-tor. 'He can walk into a room and immediately identify who the three most important people are, and how to talk to them.'

Every Tory leader since Hague has called on Osborne's counsel before PMQs. Compared to summoning great thoughts about policy, this seems like a frivolous service to render, but the first step to political advancement is simply being in the room. Week after week, for hours at a time, Osborne was eyeball to eyeball with Hague, and then Duncan Smith, and then Howard. Few frontbenchers, let alone advisers, had such intimate oppor-tunities to impress. 'He made his career at PMQs,' says a friend.

Osborne's deft mimicry in those PMQs sessions offered glimpses of a much deeper personal quality. He is a perspica-cious analyst of people, including himself. He studies humans as assiduously as more conventional politicians study ideas. The bookshelves in Osborne's Tatton home are dominated by biog-raphies, not works of political theory or economics. The second of his laws of political success, as cheekily itemised by Hague at his fortieth birthday party, is to get inside an opponent's mind and soul. Only by grasping their motives, insecurities, impulses and habits of thought can their future moves be fore-seen. It is a pugilistic take on empathy, and would later equip Osborne to rattle Gordon Brown in a way no other shadow Chancellor had managed.

His gifts as a psychological seer were less integral, but not irrelevant, to the other great service he performed for Hague. From the day he commandeered Stafford Place's back room during the leadership campaign, Osborne had excelled as a speechwriter, a job he sometimes shared with Finkelstein. Indeed, the friendship between this odd couple – the baronet-in-waiting and the football-mad immigrants' son, almost a decade older

– deepened during these collaborations. They would work late in Smith Square, nourished by Finkelstein's beloved Diet Coke and takeaway dinners ordered by young David Gold, Hague's diary manager. The banter between the two was and remains something to behold. 'You could have sold tickets for it,' chuckles Hague, more than a decade on.[53]

Osborne 'wrote beautifully', according to Coe, and approached each speech with Hague's own instincts and idiom in mind.[54] That was how, in May 1998, this agnostic on matters European came to author an incendiary lecture at Fontainebleau warning that the single currency could bring civil unrest – an intervention pithily immortalised as the 'boulevards and blood' speech by sections of the press. Adopting Hague's style of speech was harder. The leader, steeped in parliamentary tradition, preferred lyrical orations so his writers had to suppress their more utilitarian urges. To this day, Osborne and Cameron's own speechwriters lament their aversion to rhetorical flourishes.

Those who encountered Osborne in these years disagree about whether his ego grew with his eminence. MPs visiting the leader's office took offence at the unelected twenty-something's lack of deference, and were doubtless responsible for some of the disparaging quotes that began to appear about him in the press. 'Vain' and 'disgustingly smug' were among the choicest, though the anonymous author somewhat undercut his or her credibility by introducing Osborne to readers as an 'Old Etonian'. Nevertheless, Osborne did genuinely rankle with some who crossed his path. The offending behaviour was never outright boastfulness so much as a supercilious mien and an unadvisedly provocative sense of humour that consciously played up his image as a Lord Snooty character. On one occasion, Jeffrey Archer, disappointed with Osborne's performance of some chore or another, told the youngster that he did not have what it took to make money in the real world. 'You are obviously unaware of my personal circumstances,' he shot back, asking for trouble. (Archer might have been soothed had he known that Osborne's favourite book as a teenager was his *First Among Equals*, which he read obsessively after discovering an old copy in a holiday chalet his family was staying in.)

Most of Hague's team, however, remember a benign Osborne. Coe found him 'a very gentle soul, actually'.[55] Stowell liked him and, as the daughter of a painter and decorator, she would playfully insist that their fathers were in the same line of work. Nye found him 'very generous when he didn't have to be', on one occasion taking the blame for a sloppily researched speech about the Metropolitan Police that was actually the fault of a junior member of CRD.[56] David Gold, one of the lower ranking members of the Hague team, marvelled at the interest Osborne took in him. 'He never became aloof or cocky,' he insists.[57] Another Hague adviser is more vivid in his praise: 'If we'd had his privilege, we'd be twenty times the wanker that he is, and he's not a wanker at all.'

Although Osborne's closest political relationship was with Finkelstein, he grew more devoted to Hague than he ever expected when he rather calculatingly joined his campaign. The Tory leader was as stoutly Yorkshire as Osborne was metropolitan, but they had both been politically obsessed adolescents with entrepreneurial fathers. Friends say that Osborne 'enjoys the company of older people', relishing any opportunity to impress them, but Hague is one of the few to have actually influenced him. His Zen-like equanimity left its mark (judging by the off-the-record testimonies of those who have worked under either Hague or Osborne, it is possible that neither man has ever sworn or shouted at an underling). Osborne also learned from the seriousness with which Hague took the mechanics of management: delineating responsibilities, chairing meetings, planning for contingencies. Despite never having run anything before, Osborne would oversee a purring Bentley of a private office as shadow Chancellor. Hague's tutelage was instrumental.

Such is the mutual fondness that some of Osborne's frontbench colleagues suspect him of going easy on Hague in opposition. As Cameron's number two, the shadow Chancellor acquired an informal role as a kind of line manager for the shadow Cabinet, empowered to scold, harry and reward frontbenchers according to their performance. In 2008, he even intervened to fix Boris Johnson's flagging campaign to become London Mayor. Hague was unique in being left alone, despite doubts about his commitment and criticism of his condemnation of Israel's retaliatory strikes on Hezbollah in Lebanon during the summer of 2006. It might be, as some allege, that Osborne simply could not summon the nerve to challenge his old boss. But it is likelier that he did not think Hague was doing much wrong. Hague himself is equally admiring of Osborne, and remembers him as less of an underling than a near-equal: 'He was always a good political companion for a leader, able to talk at a young age about every issue, every complication.'[58]

On 4 April 1998, Osborne married Frances Howell. The wedding took place in St Margaret's Church, next to Westminster Abbey. This ancient grandeur then gave way to the most modern of receptions at the newly revived Oxo Tower on the South Bank, then one of London's more modish venues. The event was a vast affair replete with politicos, but Osborne's best man was his old university friend Peter Davies, who had worked alongside the bride at Mercury Asset Management. Independent-minded and stunningly successful in her own right as an author, she remains about as far removed from the caricature of a Tory wife as a woman can be. 'Frances helped George come into his own,' says a friend of the couple, who testifies that she shimmered more natural confidence than Osborne at the time of their marriage.

Osborne's professional life was changing no less than his personal circumstances. The autumn of 1998 convinced Hague that modernisation was the wrong strategy, at least at that time and under his leadership. Polls put his party around 30 percentage points behind Labour, and his personal ratings were no more cheering. Aware that seditious whispers were audible in corners of Smith Square, he would set aside fifteen-minute segments in his diary to 'spontaneously' tour the office and charm the staff. The situation was so bleak that his team found themselves hoping that an economic downturn provoked by financial rumblings in Asia would turn into an outright recession. After a particularly ineffectual party conference in October, *The Sun*, the Thatcherite tabloid that had converted to New Labour, pronounced the Tories an 'ex-party' over a Pythonesque image of Hague as an expired parrot. Were he to endure heavy losses at the European elections the following May, his leadership would likely be over. It was time to change strategy. If he could not compete with Blair for mastery of the centre ground, he could at least pitch for a distinctively Conservative audience.

To that end, he hired two journalists who were immersed in the uncomplicated right-wingery of the mid-market tabloids. Nick Wood was a wily, raffish chain-smoker who replaced Mackay as Hague's press man. (In 2005, at the age of just thirty-six, Mackay, to whom Osborne was close, would tragically lose his life to cancer.) Amanda Platell, a self-starting Australian who had thrived in Fleet Street, was asked to direct the broader media strategy. So began the hardening of Hague's image and message. With what was left of his hair shorn to a few millimetres in length, this creature of the boardroom was increasingly pictured in the rugged outdoors or on the judo mat. Fatefully, he also began to say stridently Tory things about predictably Tory issues. He deplored the apparent influx of 'bogus' asylum seekers, the limpness of the criminal justice system and Blair's enthusiasm for the euro. He evoked Nixon's 'silent majority' by siding with the unglamorous masses against the 'liberal elite'. In exactly the kind of gesture that Osborne would repudiate forever when he became shadow Chancellor, he even 'guaranteed' to cut taxes.

Hague did not expect any of this to win him the next election. His hope was merely to consolidate his party's natural support, enthuse the right-leaning press and shore up his position as leader. These limited aims were met – the party ended up over-achieving in the European elections of 1999, for example – but at some cost. According to a popular theory in modernising circles, the most grievous damage to the Tory brand was done after, not before, the party lost power in 1997. Under Major, so this argument runs, Conservatives were seen as corrupt and haplessly uncomprehending of modern Britain, but not bigoted or brutish. That stain came with the tub-thumping of the Hague years.

Bizarrely, the ignominies endured by Hague, and before him Hogg, did not deter their apprentice from following them to the political frontline. Having nearly left Westminster for journalism in 1997, Osborne was, with Hague's approval, actively seeking to become a parliamentary candidate by the end of 1998. Andrew Mitchell, a former Tory MP who would later return to the Commons and enter the Cabinet, encouraged him to acquire some business experience first, but he found the young man immovable. Osborne wanted to become an MP while the Conservatives were at their nadir: it would be easier to rise to the top and, by the time he arrived there, the party would be on the precipice of power. 'I'm buying at the bottom of the market,' was his mantra, delivered reflexively whenever friends questioned his eagerness to become enter Parliament at such a young age and at such a bleak time for his party.

At the turn of 1999, Osborne made his move. Two years ahead of the likely general election, the Conservative Association in Leominster, a market town near the Welsh border not far from where his wife had grown up, began looking for a candidate to take on Peter Temple-Morris, a left-wing Tory who had defected to Labour at the end of 1997. Osborne, just twenty-seven, was one of ninety-six applicants. He also went for Tatton, in Cheshire, which had been represented by the independent Martin Bell since his ousting of Neil Hamilton, the personification of sleaze, two years earlier. Michael Portillo, eager for political resurrection, preferred to wait for a by-election to come along rather than defer his parliamentary comeback to the next general election. Chris Patten also declined to apply for either seat. Their absence meant that, in both constituencies, Osborne was the candidate with the strongest claim to insider clout.

Sure enough, when the Leominster Association whittled the hopefuls down to a final four, he was one of them, along with Hugo Swire, a former candidate who would grow close to Osborne and Cameron over time, Patrick Mercer, an army colonel and local, and Bill Wiggin, son of the former Tory MP Jerry Wiggin. When the selection hustings took place in a local sports hall on 5 March, around 650 members turned out. Mercer's speech was well-judged but for its Thatcherite denunciation of Heseltine and Clarke, which failed to electrify what was one of the less ideological Tory Associations. Swire, who followed him, said some cannily inoffensive things but spoke with less command. Then came Osborne. He was plainly the insider, effortlessly fluent on matters of high politics but too conspicuous a sophisticate for such a doggedly pastoral corner of England.

'George was shooting too high,' according to one of his rivals for the nomination. 'Everyone recognised that this was a guy who was going to go somewhere, just not there.' He came within a few votes of victory but Wiggin, who mixed self-deprecation with righteous dismay at Blair's ban on fox hunting, did enough to win.

In many ways, Tatton was an even less propitious seat for Osborne. This affluent collection of villages and small towns, populated by retirees, commuters and a smattering of professional footballers, was as removed from his London life as the rural Welsh border. He had no history in the area, not even the kind of tenuous link afforded by his wife's family background in Leominster. Most worryingly of all, the politics of the seat were dangerously fraught. The Conservative Association was riven: a hardy band of Hamilton loyalists endeavoured to get the former MP to stand again. Worse, Bell, who had promised to serve for only one term, was implored by locals to renege on his commitment. He was proving a popular MP and enjoyed the job. Were he to run again, he would win at a stroll.

Tatton represented an enormous risk for Osborne. Although Hague encouraged him to stand, other colleagues argued that he would be at the mercy of Bell's whim and forfeit his peace of mind. For the two years until polling day, he could never be entirely free of the fear that this ageing, white-suited crusader would stand again. But Osborne knew that precisely because of this hazard, high-calibre Tories were not putting themselves forward for the seat. He would face little competition for what was, in the normal run of things, an impenetrably Conservative constituency. He was right. The final four candidates were Osborne himself, Richard Ashworth, a local businessman, Peter Fleet, a Ford manager who had previously contested Southampton Itchen, and Chris Grayling, another former candidate who, like,

Bell, had been a BBC journalist. Although Grayling would go on to hold ministerial office, Osborne was the only candidate with any lustre about him.

The selection hustings were held on 18 March in the village of Knutsford. Osborne's speech was so well-received that he won over 50 per cent of the votes on the first ballot, claiming the contest immediately. He still shows the speech to budding MPs as a lesson in how to win over a selection meeting. The address should consist, he believes, of a couple of self-deprecating jokes followed by passages explaining that Conservatism is a commitment to freedom (denoting low taxes), a duty to others (meaning public services) and pride in Britain (a subtle hint at Euro-scepticism).

Osborne's eagerness to become an MP suggests that his ultimate interest was not politics or current affairs, in which he was amply immersed already, but power. However much influence he might accrue as an adviser, the formal prerogative to make decisions and run things would always be limited to ministers. He saw that even Peter Mandelson, New Labour's *eminence grise*, had plumped for a parliamentary berth in 1992. Finkelstein, too, was contesting a seat: Harrow West. 'Politics is the only career in which you can actually get stuff done,' Osborne would tell friends. This seems to argue against his reputation as a dilettante, amused enough by the sport of politics but bored by the actual business of government. It also explains why journalism piqued his interest without ever truly captivating him. Something about his view of business comes through in the quote, too. Osborne has never believed the rhetoric about 'captains of industry' and 'masters of the universe' – even the mightiest businessmen, he points out, must operate in a framework of laws and taxes set by governments. The ultimate power is political power.

Back in Westminster, Hague's change of strategy was rupturing a party that had threatened to achieve some kind of unity. The *Tory Wars* chronicled by the journalist Simon Walters began innocuously enough in Hague's kitchen Cabinet, where modernisers such as Finkelstein, Nye and Cooper worried about the more orthodox designs of Wood and Platell, but also Tim Collins, a leftover from the Major team, and sometimes Coe. The disagreements then spread to the shadow Cabinet. In March 1999, Cooper unveiled 'kitchen table Conservatism', a strategy document that might be the first meaningful codification of the modernising creed. It urged the party to talk about public services without invoking the market, to moderate its criticisms of the government and to humbly acknowledge the misjudgements of previous Tory administrations. Hague summoned his shadow Cabinet to announce that they would each be promoted and demoted according to their implementation of Cooper's strategy. Most nodded along without ever intending to obey this injunction.

An exception was Peter Lilley, who had been moved from the Treasury brief to the deputy leadership. In April 1999, he gave a thoughtful speech exploring the limits of Thatcherism in public services. It showed impeccable fealty to kitchen table Conservatism, but colleagues cursed his heresy. Howard, usually a cool customer, found himself shouting irately during a shadow Cabinet meeting. Lilley lost his job and an exasperated Cooper left to set up his own polling firm, Populus. The ascendancy of the right was unmistakable. For Professor Tim Bale, author of an acclaimed study of the Conservatives since Thatcher, the treatment of Lilley was 'what academics call "a critical juncture"'.[59]

Lilley's departure crystallised not only the party's reluctance to modernise, but also its loss of basic professionalism. He had stuck to the agreed strategy, and was punished for it. Meanwhile, those who ignored the strategy suffered no sanction. Sure enough, the shadow Cabinet degenerated into a kind of Babel in which frontbenchers pursued their own ideological hobbies without any reference to a central message. Some of the blame belonged to Hague, who 'behaved like a chairman' and provided 'no strategic direction', according to one of the right-wing figures in his team.[60] But there was only so much he could do to impose order on such recalcitrant colleagues.

Indeed, it was the right's cacophonous indiscipline, far more than its actual worldview, that really irked the likes of Osborne and Finkelstein. They craved the professionalism with which New Labour did politics, and had no quarrel with the one right-winger in the shadow Cabinet who sought to change rather than blithely override Hague's modernising message: Michael Howard. When the shadow Foreign Secretary took Finkelstein to lunch at the Carlton Club to persuade him that kitchen table Conservatism was wrong-headed, the strategist appreciated the gesture. 'What most people did was ignore it. Howard actually believed in political strategy and discipline.'[61] To this day, the highest praise Osborne can bestow upon a politico is 'professional'. He reveres professionalism because he has witnessed its absence.

The chaos really deepened when Michael Portillo returned to Parliament in November as MP for Kensington & Chelsea, a vacancy left by the death of the famously fleshly Alan Clark. Hague quickly made him his third shadow Chancellor, displacing Maude. Although Portillo's sheer talent warranted the promotion, Hague seemed only faintly aware of his conversion to modernisation during his time in exile. The party now had a leader and shadow Chancellor who disagreed on the basics of strategy. Whereas Portillo regarded the 'tax guarantee' as dogmatic and incredible, Hague insisted that the Tories were a tax-cutting party or nothing. While Portillo, a Belgravian opera buff of continental provenance, self-identified as a member of the liberal elite, Hague, who would grumble that 'I hate this bloody place' as he drove into London from a weekend in Yorkshire, employed ever tougher rhetoric.

Maude, by now shadow Foreign Secretary, was Portillo's staunchest ally, but they were outnumbered by a deeply conservative caucus in the shadow Cabinet that included Ann Widdecombe, the 'blue nun', Bernard Jenkin, the suave face of the Thatcherite No Turning Back group, and Andrew 'Landslide' Lansley, architect of the punchily right-wing European election campaign. Platell, convinced that Portillo was scheming to topple Hague, guarded her man much too aggressively for some tastes.

Where was Osborne in all this? Modernisation's early adopter might have been expected to resist Hague's rightward drift, but Osborne is also the ultimate realist. 'We are getting nowhere with this strategy,' he would sigh to Finkelstein, who was sympathetic but willing to give it more time. Even if Osborne had felt differently, he lacked the clout to prevail over the teeming, tenacious right. 'He would have seen the way the wind was blowing,' says Wood. 'He was not a man to stand against the crowd.'[62] He shuddered at Hague's defence of Section 28, which constrained what schools could teach about homosexuality, and at the force of his rhetoric against asylum seekers. 'One or two of us started to think "this is not what we signed up for",' remembers another liberal-minded colleague. But Osborne knew that fighting all this would not only be futile, it would also mean taking sides with the shadow Chancellor against his own beleaguered boss. 'George was never particularly close to Portillo,' says Finkelstein, despite their shared glossy metropolitanism. 'He worked for William Hague.'[63]

As the fault line between 'mods' and 'rockers' widened, Osborne maintained cordial ties with both – even Platell, who usually read malice into any doubts about the direction Hague was taking. 'They had something of a mother and son relationship,' says one member of the team. Wood himself found the young man 'charming'.[64] In short, Osborne was a good political secretary: preserving channels of communication, cooling hotter heads, serving his leader rather than a particular cause. Silently, though, he was pocketing the lessons of the disorder around him. One was that modernisation had to be more than a list of grievances about the Conservative Party, delivered with the lordly disdain of a Portillo or a Maude. The right was influential because it offered concrete ideas and bold gestures, however misconceived. 'George's frustration with modernisation was that it was all diagnostic,' remembers a colleague. 'He could see that this aloof, "Graham Brady is an idiot" approach wasn't enough,' an allusion to the vigorously Conservative MP who now chairs the 1922 Committee of backbenchers.

If there was a blueprint of what modern Conservatism might look like, it was on show in America in the summer of 2000. George W. Bush was sauntering towards the Republican nomination for President, and polls suggested that he would beat Al Gore, the serving Vice President and likely Democrat candidate, in November's election. As fanciful as it now seems, his popularity derived from a 'compassionate conservatism' that cooled the anti-government fervour gripping the Grand Old Party. Far from abolishing the federal Department of Education, as once proposed by Newt Gingrich, the Republican Speaker of the House, Bush wanted to strengthen its powers to hold school boards to account. He said he would not 'balance the Budget on the backs of the poor'. He invoked his Christian faith as inspiration for his sense of social justice, and not as justification for censorious laws on moral and sexual conduct.

Osborne and Finkelstein were rather taken by the Texas

governor, and not merely because American politics grips them both (a wall of Finkelstein's office at *The Times* is adorned with pin badges from presidential elections going back half a century). They knew that a victory for Bush in November would help them to persuade fellow Tories to emulate his broad, generous creed. Along with Rick Nye, they were despatched to the Republican National Convention in Philadelphia that August.

Osborne was deliriously in his element. As observers from an opposition party in another country, the Tories were peripheral players at the event, but Osborne's chutzpah ensured that they were not stuck in dismal barbecue parties thrown by the Louisiana delegation. He gatecrashed a reception held for former President Gerald Ford and ambushed Jeb Bush for an autograph after hiding in an anteroom until he came out of a rally. His ultimate coup, though, came just before George Bush's speech to the convention. He somehow persuaded a friend who knew the venerable columnist Peggy Noonan to get the Tory gaggle into Bush's box high up in the auditorium. Osborne and Finkelstein watched the presidential hopeful's speech from the best seat in the venue in the company of Karl Rove and Karen Hughes, two of Bush's closest aides, and his wife Laura. 'It was the sort of thing that only happens to you when you're with George,' says Finkelstein.[65]

By the time he returned to London, Osborne was a fading presence in Hague's team. He was campaigning industriously in Tatton, which the party was treating as a marginal despite its history as a Conservative redoubt. Having planned to devote only his weekends to the constituency, he followed Coe's advice to also go up on regular weekdays to visit schools and workplaces. Each trip was a little liberation from the deepening enmities in London, where Portillo and Maude would beseech Hague to dismiss Platell, who in turn would brutally suppress plots both real and imagined. On one occasion, Nye complained to Osborne that the Australian was briefing against him. Osborne took the grievance to Coe, and soon the vicious whispers against Nye stopped. Osborne was happy to protect his friend but village life in Cheshire was a pleasingly bucolic relief from such stresses. Colleagues sensed another kind of equanimity in Osborne from the moment he won his nomination: he knew that his career would no longer depend on Hague's fortunes at the coming election.

Osborne adapted his wiles as an operator to the provincial setting. Robert Meakin, then a young journalist for the *Manchester Evening News*, found him to be 'charm personified' when he met him in a café in Alderley Edge in 2000.[66] Radiating clubbable accessibility, Osborne seemed to belong to a different species to local MPs such as Ivan Lewis and the cartoonishly solipsistic Nick Winterton. But his charm was, as it often is, strategic. Sensing Meakin's talent and ambition, he encouraged him to take his career to London, even arranging for him to attend a shadow Cabinet meeting and talk to Hague. The result was a special edition of the *Manchester Evening News* devoted to Westminster, which not only enhanced Osborne's profile in the north-west but also aroused Fleet Street's interest in Meakin. At the start of 2002, the *Daily Telegraph* hired him as a diary reporter. Osborne, a new MP, now had a well-placed journalist to whom he could leak stories, usually detrimental to Labour. Osborne told Meakin that he was happy to supply material as long as he never turned his pen on him. When, at the insistence of his superiors, Meakin finally did, relations cooled. (Soon after moving to the *Telegraph*, Meakin met Tom Watson for a drink on the House of Commons' riverside café. 'That's the future Tory leader,' said the newly elected Labour MP, pointing to a faintly rumpled figure enjoying a cigarette across the terrace. His name was David Cameron.)

Another target of Osborne's rather purposeful warmth was Martin Bell. During the pair's occasional lunches, the younger man was respectful, ingratiating – but not above reminding his companion of the 'messy' consequences of standing again. He also applied pressure indirectly by telling local journalists that Bell had 'personally reassured' him that he would honour his pledge. Such vigilance turned out to be unnecessary. Although Bell was lobbied endlessly to renew his parliamentary career – 'There aren't many MPs whose constituents urge them to break a promise,' he says now – a man who had been elected on the single issue of integrity could not go back on such a hard and fast commitment.[67]

The best and worst moments of Hague's leadership took place within a few weeks of each other in the autumn of 2000. The first came when hauliers and others aggrieved by rising petrol prices started blockading fuel depots. The obstruction of supply created shortages, panic and fury at a government that seemed both indifferent to the grievances and thrown by the crisis. After initially hesitating, Hague publicly sympathised with what Wood and Platell argued was a 'C1 uprising'. Portillo reluctantly went along. The Tories gained a lead in the polls for the first time in the parliament, though it dissipated quickly. With Nelson Mandela in attendance, Tony Blair, sweat-stained and righteous, gave one of his best, though least vaunted, conference speeches soon after. 'The test of leadership in politics is not how eloquently you say yes,' he thundered, alluding to Hague's indulgence of the protestors' demands. Only in recent years, through the memoirs of Blair's chief of staff Jonathan Powell, has it been established exactly how close the country came to effectively shutting down.

Then came the Tories' own conference, and perhaps the most naked exhibition of the party's dividedness since Major challenged right-wing rebels to 'put up or shut up' in 1995. This time, the fault line was culture rather than Europe. Portillo perturbed the right with a proto-modernising speech in which he conspicuously pronounced his name the Castillian way (Porgh-tee-yo) and wondered why gay people and ethnic minorities should 'respect us when we withhold respect from them?' The following day, Widdecombe was equally voluble on behalf of the traditionalist right, and even suggested imposing a criminal record on anyone caught in possession of cannabis. It was as if the conference had been deliberately staged to dramatise the majestic distance dividing shadow spokesman from shadow spokesman. That both politicians were positioning themselves to replace Hague as leader was not lost on the media. When frontbenchers openly derided Widdecombe, breezily confessing that they themselves had smoked pot as students, her humiliation was complete – as was the party's reputation for comical indiscipline.

Osborne was never particularly demonstrative about his social liberalism in Hague's office. He would do what he could to cool the rhetoric of the campaign to retain Section 28, but he picked no fights with the rockers, much less with the leader. Hague recognised that he was 'naturally on the side of modernisation' but encountered little resistance from him.[68] 'He was too willing to pander to Hague rather than challenge him,' grumbles another of the team's liberals. Years later, as an MP, he emphatically announced to a reunion dinner of the Hague team that he was a proud liberal on both economic and social issues. The likes of Wood had never guessed. His circumspection as Hague's political secretary might have been evidence of his supple skills as an operator, but Wood puts it down to a youthful lack of confidence.

Hague's stridency grew as the election approached and seemed to cross the line of good taste at his party's spring conference in Harrogate. However, just as Major's exhortation to go back to basics had been calamitously mis-briefed to journalists as some kind of call to chastity, something similar was true of Hague's 'foreign land' speech. In what was virtually his last contribution before focusing on Tatton, Osborne wrote much of the draft. He found that a passage warning of the consequences of European integration needed livening up, particularly its invitation to 'come with me to Britain in five years' time'.

In Hague's hotel suite on Saturday 3 March, the eve of the speech, either Wood or Finkelstein (both claim responsibility) suggested that Osborne replace the line with: 'Come with me to a foreign land – to Britain after a second term of Tony Blair.' By Wood's account, Osborne reacted warily to the idea but relented when he secured Hague's approval. Where Finkelstein and Wood agree is that it was the subsequent briefing of the speech to Sunday newspaper journalists that gave the phrase its notoriety. It seems likely that Wood went to reporters with the extract about Europe and a separate one about immigration. The press interpreted 'foreign land' as applying to both. He was disappointed with the lurid coverage of the speech. Finkelstein, a son of immigrants, was more than disappointed.

This furore inaugurated a general election campaign that posterity regards as one of the oddest ever waged by a major political party. At the start of 2001, the Tories had compromised with the electorate by commissioning a series of posters about the most salient issue in the country: public services. The campaign, designed by Nye, asked voters, 'You've paid the tax, so where are the nurses?' (or 'teachers' or 'police'). By the spring, however, the core vote strategy had reasserted itself. A foot-and-mouth epidemic in the countryside had delayed the election until 7 June. When Parliament was eventually dissolved for the campaign, Hague took it as his cue to tour marginal seats on a flatbed lorry heralding the election as 'the last chance to save the pound'. Tory candidates menaced locally by strong support for the UK Independence Party were covertly permitted to rule out the euro forever, rather than just Hague's avowed horizon of the next parliament. He also visited Dover to propose 'secure reception centres' for asylum seekers. He managed just one trip to a school, and one to a hospital, during the campaign.

As well as dwelling esoterically on Europe and immigration, the Conservatives offered tax cuts to an electorate that craved more spending on public services. This was to be funded by £8 billion of slower expenditure growth but Oliver Letwin, the shadow Chief Secretary, left a delegation of interviewees from the *Financial Times* with the impression that the figure he really had in mind was £20 billion. In the kind of farce that had become all too run-of-the-mill for the Tories, Central Office put him in hiding while Labour and the press demanded the release of 'the Dorset one'. The party's economic and fiscal message was paralysed by the chaos.

Assessed purely on its electoral wisdom, Hague's campaign was unforgivably bad. It neglected the most pressing concerns of voters in favour of narrowly Conservative themes, and said such strident things about those that the party's most precious possession – its reputation, its 'brand' as it would come to be known – suffered grievously. Even when the Tories addressed a truly salient topic, namely tax and spend, it did so with a tin ear to the electorate's preferences. When Labour unveiled a poster showing Thatcher's bouffant grafted onto Hague's head, a devastating visual expression was given to the suspicion that four years of opposition had changed the Tories very little. The scale of the resultant cataclysm remains scarcely believable: a gain of one per cent in the popular vote and one seat in Parliament.

However, the electoral test is not the only one of value. Seen with over a decade's hindsight, Hague's 2001 campaign is striking as much for its prescience as its stridency. Consider the three themes of the campaign: Europe, asylum and fiscal policy. To describe Hague's opposition to the euro as vindicated is to butcher him with understatement. His description of the single currency as a 'burning building with no exits', deplored by establishment opinion at the time as distinctly non-U, has become the most exquisitely apt metaphor for the unfolding eurozone crisis of today. Joining the single currency might have ruined Britain in the wake of the great recession of 2008–09 by paralysing its ability to loosen its interest and exchange rates. Blair wanted to join, and often regretted his promise to put the issue to a referendum. Gordon Brown, his obstinate Chancellor, can claim the greater share of the credit for frustrating this whim but the relentless pressure applied by the Leader of the Opposition, which peaked in the run-up to the election, was also a factor.

On immigration, too, Hague's 2001 posture has aged well. He could not have foreseen that the decade would bring the greatest wave of immigration Britain had ever known, largely from central and eastern European countries that joined the EU in 2004. Neither is it obvious that this influx was a bad thing. Nevertheless, immigration rose from a minority gripe in 2001 to the third biggest issue for voters in 2010. More to the point, it became increasingly acceptable for the subject to be discussed in politics and the higher quarters of the media. Hague's broaching of the topic helped to nudge elites out of their comfort zone.

Posterity has afforded Hague some credit for his position on the euro, much less for his line on immigration and virtually none for his fiscal platform. Yet his plan to expand government spending more slowly than the growth of the economy was, in retrospect, more than mere common sense. Such budgetary caution might have ensured that Britain went into the crash years later in more robust fiscal condition – that is, without a structural deficit. The country would have been better able afford a fiscal stimulus and a bailout of endangered banks. Its overall debt would have swelled less prodigiously. Its fight for credibility in global financial markets – which still continues – would have been less fraught. Indeed, the most powerful criticism of the Tories' fiscal policy in 2001 was that it was not conservative *enough*. It went along with the splurge of spending on public services that Brown had inaugurated the previous year, and sought only trimmings at the margins of overall expenditure. Yet Hague was on the right side of the argument, economically if not politically.

Major's electoral evisceration against the backdrop of a goldilocks economy had taught Osborne the difference between economics and politics. Four years on, he at least had the consolation of a personal victory. In the early hours of 8 June, as his boss's adolescent ambition to become Prime Minister was dematerialising, Osborne fulfilled his own childhood dream. He was elected to Parliament. He won 19,860 votes in Tatton, 8,611 more than the runner-up, Labour's Steve Conquest. 'In 1997 Tatton was a symbol of what had gone wrong nationally,' he told the audience at his count. 'It was my responsibility to show what is now going right for the Conservatives in the north-west.' He was 'elated' with the victory. Now thirty years old, he was also about to become a father. He had served his time as a back-room boy.

8.

Through the Portcullis

'George realised way, way before Dave
that the party had to change.'

'**N**o man or woman is indispensable and no individual
is more important than the party.' Blinking in early
morning sunshine outside Smith Square, an address
that once served as a byword for electoral invincibility, William
Hague was renouncing the job he had coveted since adolescence.
'I've therefore decided to step down as leader of the Conservative
party when a successor can be elected in the coming months.'

Who that successor should be was Osborne's first major
decision as an MP. He and his parliamentary colleagues would
whittle down the field of candidates in successive rounds of voting
until they arrived at a final pair, who would then go before Tory
members in the country. 'George made great play of the fact that
he was the youngest of the intake,' remembers another member
of the 2001 cohort, but his approach to the leadership election
was anything but jejune. There was no perfidy or prevarication.
He had made his mind up before the general election.

Of all the candidates who emerged in the ensuing weeks, Ken
Clarke could boast the broadest national appeal and a virtually
unblemished record as Chancellor. However, he also espoused
an intolerable fealty to the EU (and open-mindedness about the

single currency) for what was now an overwhelmingly Eurosceptic parliamentary party. His victory would not so much risk division as guarantee it. Osborne grasped this cold reality when Clarke spoke to a Tatton Association dinner before the election. 'I don't want George Osborne to be like Roy Hattersley,' he told the crowd, who waited warily to discover what their candidate might have in common with Labour's deputy leader in the '80s. 'A talented man who spent the best years of his career in opposition.' The roughly 500 members were warming to the garrulous big beast – until one of their number asked him about Europe. Clarke embarked on a fervently Europhile monologue and lost his audience. Osborne did not forget the evening.

Meanwhile, most of the other hopefuls were plainly not good enough to trouble, much less defeat, an imperious and emboldened Blair. Michael Ancram, the party chairman, was a politely ineffectual aristocrat. Iain Duncan Smith, the shadow Defence Secretary, barely seemed frontbench material to some of his colleagues. The best of these stragglers, David Davis, had shone as chairman of the Public Accounts Committee, but his candidacy seemed little more than a registration of interest for a future race. It would turn out to be exactly that.

So, with the same alacrity that he had backed Hague four summers earlier, Osborne endorsed Michael Portillo. Both men were metropolitan liberals with cultural hinterlands. Both were professional politicians who had passed through CRD and briefed a Tory leader during a general election. They even shared a reputation for outward arrogance and private warmth. For all this, Osborne was not one of the troublesome 'Portillistas' who orbited the shadow Chancellor. As an adviser in the Major years, he had witnessed Portillo's capacity for misjudgement: the failure to either conclusively support or challenge Major in the summer of 1995, the irking of the generals with a crassly vainglorious speech that invoked the SAS a few months later. Then, under Hague, Osborne had seen him fail to leave a mark on Gordon Brown in Parliament, and to control the troublemaking of his acolytes. He knew Portillo was a flawed politician.

In a poor field, though, the former Defence Secretary offered a promising blend of Clarke's political talent and the reassuring Euroscepticism of, say, Davis. Tantalisingly for Osborne, he had also become as evangelical a moderniser as he had once been a Thatcherite. In 1997, Osborne supported Hague largely because he expected him to win. In 2001, he endorsed Portillo primarily because he thought he would be good for the Conservatives. 'I couldn't imagine him backing anyone else,' says Mark MacGregor, who worked on the Portillo campaign.[69]

In fact, Osborne was among the first of the Tory MPs to declare his support for the shadow Chancellor. 'David Cameron played hard to get by comparison,' says a Portillo supporter, although the newly elected member for Witney did eventually sign up. The campaign, which was being run by Francis Maude, made some play of the fact that a former Hague adviser was zealously backing their candidate. After all, Hague and Portillo had fought over political strategy in the shadow Cabinet and would not speak again for seven years. Aside from being the subject of this pleasing little coup, however, Osborne was given a marginal role in the campaign. This turned out be a rather important oversight by Maude. 'Had I known what a good operator he is, I would have got him more involved,' admits a senior campaign figure now.[70]

Osborne was happy not to be involved, preoccupied as he was with the birth of his first child, Luke Benedict, who arrived on 15 June, a week after the election. There was also the bureaucratic hassle of setting up a parliamentary office. To that end he hired Philippa Rudkin, his secretary at CRD and still a part of his Treasury team. He already possessed an insider's facility with the geography and protocol of the Commons – 'He knew more about Parliament when he entered it than I did when I left,' says Bell – and found his way onto the Public Accounts Committee, where Davis had coined his reputation.[71] Still, he attended induction meetings organised by the Commons authorities, where he and Cameron gravitated towards each other. Before that, they were acquainted rather than close. Apart from a few months in 1994, they had never actually worked in Westminster at the same time. Throughout their tenuous relationship, Cameron, the elder by five years, was of effortlessly superior status and renown: a more senior spad, a more coveted social presence, a man with real world experience (of sorts) at Carlton Communications. Now they were equals: Members of Parliament, and nothing more.

On 2 July, during a debate on Europe, Osborne gave his maiden speech in the Commons. After the customary praise for his predecessor, and the equally traditional eulogy to his constituency, he did something uncharacteristic. He invoked his own continental ties in a way he has seldom done since. Putting his Euroscepticism in a personal context, Osborne delivered his peroration:

> I am part-Hungarian. My grandmother's family fled to Britain from Budapest just after the war because they had lived through the devastation of the Nazi tyranny, and wanted to escape the tyranny of Soviet rule. In 1956, their house in London became a home for refugees from the Hungarian uprising.
>
> The lessons that I learn from my family's past are these: one must not impose political systems on peoples who are unwilling to accept them; one should not allow a gap to open up between the governed and the governing; and one cannot afford to stop listening.[72]

The mere fact of this autobiographical detour is novel enough – what renders it doubly intriguing is its ambiguity about Osborne's broader view of foreign policy. He privately describes himself as a 'neo-conservative' and supported Blair's military activism, including the invasion of Iraq. In the current Cabinet, perhaps only Michael Gove has a stronger reputation as a liberal interventionist. Sure enough, there are hints of this worldview in the speech's invocations of uprisings and tyrannies, of people fighting for freedom. However, the words also betray a wariness of utopian projects, especially any attempt to 'impose' a political order on a society. Anyone judging Osborne by this speech alone would not be able to guess whether he was generally minded to support or oppose wars of choice and nation-building. This inscrutability encourages the suspicion that his neo-conservatism is actually (and some would say wisely) shallow: an instinctive sympathy for free countries such as America and Israel rather than a belief in pre-emptive wars to remake rogue autocracies.

So poor was the party's showing at the election that many of its ablest candidates failed to get elected, clearing the way for Osborne to advance. So far, he had prospered through his own talent and opportunism, but he was now also profiting from circumstance. Aside from Cameron, it was Paul Goodman, a former leader writer for the *Telegraph*, and Boris Johnson, the chaotically charismatic editor of *The Spectator*, who represented the most serious competition.

Daniel Finkelstein was one of those who did not make it in. His personal loss was limited: a career in journalism beckoned, and he now wields more influence for better pay than most ministers. The real significance of his absence was for his friend. Although Cameron was always vaunted as the leading Tory of his generation, it is far from obvious that Osborne would have established himself as his partner and second-in-command had

Finkelstein been there to compete with him. Finkelstein had a similar intellect, nearly identical views, greater experience and, crucially, a relatively ordinary social background. With his London vowels and mania for football, voters might have found him less jarringly rarefied than Osborne. In the argot of American politics, a Cameron–Finkelstein partnership would have been a more 'balanced ticket' than the gilded duopoly that emerged. Had the editor fielding graduate job applications at Wapping made a different decision in 1993, Osborne might now be doing Finkelstein's job. Had the good people of Harrow voted differently in 2001, Finkelstein might now be doing Osborne's.

Finkelstein would have doubtless supported Portillo, too, and the shadow Chancellor needed every vote he could find. Although upwards of a hundred MPs were favourable to his candidacy, his talk of a rupture with the past was diminishing this number every week. 'Portillo was not willing to say things to win the leadership election that would restrict his ability to take whatever actions he thought might be necessary to reposition the party afterwards,' says MacGregor.[73] MPs who sought reassurances on traditional Tory concerns – support for marriage, opposition to all-women shortlists in constituency selections – were airily rebuffed. The cultural openness Portillo espoused in his conference speech the previous year was now his manifesto. He craved not mere victory but an explicit and overwhelming mandate for modernisation.

Compounding this inflexibility was Portillo's aloofness, which allowed the flesh of ordinary backbenchers to go unpressed. The price was paid in a disappointing first ballot on 10 July. He won forty-nine votes, the most of any candidate but nowhere near as many as his team had planned for. Like Thatcher's aides in the days before her fall in 1990, they were unforgivably sloppy in keeping numbers and distinguishing committed supporters from perfidious flirts. The first rule of politics, as Osborne could have told them, is that you must be able to count. Duncan Smith, who overshot expectations with thirty-nine votes, was now likely to attract many of the right-wing backers of Davis and Ancram, who secured just twenty-one votes each. Clarke had thirty-six. Portillo's closest advisers agree that it was at this point that their man lost interest. If the best he could hope for was a narrow victory among his parliamentary colleagues, he would not have a mandate to remake the party.

Two days later, the second ballot gave Portillo just one more vote. With fifty supporters, he was only eight ahead of Duncan Smith and eleven ahead of Clarke. Ancram was eliminated, and Davis withdrew voluntarily. Then, on Tuesday 17 July, Portillo's compelling career in frontline politics came to a whimpering end. By a solitary vote, he was edged out by Duncan Smith to take on Clarke in the membership ballot. He was sincerely relieved to lose, and not only because he desired a commanding personal mandate or nothing. His time away from politics had also reacquainted him with his real passions: culture, travel, a life of a contemplation. To this day, one of his most senior advisers (and now a colleague of Osborne's) believes that Portillo did not vote for himself in the final round.

The son of a Republican intellectual exiled from Franco's fascist Spain, Portillo was perhaps the most captivating Tory of his generation. His upbringing in suburban north London was comfortable enough but his father, who struggled to master English, never reprised the scholarly status he had known in the old country. His frustrated ambition stirred his son, who soared through grammar school, Cambridge and then a political career which seemed so certain to culminate in the ultimate glory that his biography, authored by Michael Gove in 1995, was quite reasonably titled *The Future of the Right*. Instead, his stint as

Defence Secretary would turn out to be the loftiest position he would ever hold in public life.

Why did Portillo underachieve? Osborne was anxious to derive the lessons. One was that a politician's ultimate asset, far above intellect and charisma, is judgement. Analysis alone, however sophisticated, cannot gauge the mood of an electorate, or sense how a speech might play to a particular audience, or distinguish between a chance to strike for personal gain and a moment that calls for demure patience. Indeed, too much analysis brings paralysis. It is a politician's animal instincts, his sense of smell, that really empowers him to make the right call. Blair, with his supernatural feel for every last contour of the national mood, had peerless judgement. Portillo's was at best erratic. Osborne fancied his own well enough.

There was something else, though. Portillo's take on modernisation was, if not vacuous, then certainly unsatisfying. It boiled down to an esoteric preoccupation with cultural cosmopolitanism. While it was true that Conservatives had to shed the aroma of bigotry, voters seemed more turned off by the party's perceived indifference to public services. Liberalism was a necessary but nowhere near sufficient electoral strategy; the basic distributional questions of political economy had to be addressed too. Instead, the Portillo campaign contrived to blend cultural liberalism with an apparent celebration of luxury metropolitan living. His supporters came from the fashionable end of the Tory establishment. He launched his campaign at Avenue, a slick restaurant in Mayfair, perhaps the wealthiest urban district in the world. He argued his case in the way an advertising man might pitch for a Benetton contract: 'We must adopt a tone that is moderate and...' – pausing as if to savour the modishness of the next word – '...*understanding*.'

Osborne was wide awake to these mistakes. 'It was not enough to get the social issues right,' he says now.[74] The Tories had to show their commitment to state schools, the NHS and a measure of income redistribution. An unacknowledged irony is that Duncan Smith understood this better than Portillo. For all his Chingford right-wingery, his campaign trialled the conscientious themes of his eventual leadership: the state of public services, the social blights of poverty, worklessness and addiction. If any prominent Tory was emulating the compassionate conservatism Osborne had witnessed in Philadelphia the previous summer, it was the balding army major. He was a man of limited ability but considerable social conscience. Portillo was a man of immense talent but rather narrow political sensibilities.

On 13 September, it was announced that Duncan Smith had defeated Clarke by 156,000 votes to 101,000 in the ballot of members. The declaration had been due two days earlier, but history intervened.

On 10 September 2001, Osborne and his wife flew back to London from a wedding they had attended in Rhode Island. As they made their way through the checks at Boston Logan airport, they remarked to each other at how lax the security seemed to be. The next day, two passenger jets leaving that same airport were hijacked by terrorists attached to al Qaeda, an Islamic fundamentalist group led by the Saudi exile Osama bin Laden. They flew the planes, loaded with fuel, into the twin towers of New York's World Trade Center during the morning of a working day. Similar attacks in Washington and Pennsylvania brought the total death toll to almost 3,000.

The worst act of international terrorism ever committed was watched by Osborne on television at home. The London of his youth had suffered the spasmodic blight of bomb attacks by the Irish Republican Army, but those depredations were contained. There was usually an anonymous phone call to warn of the bomb's location and civilian casualties were limited: the aim was to intimidate the British state out of Northern Ireland rather than to rack up the highest body count possible. These 'rules', if they deserved that name, had now given way to another, more nihilistic kind of terrorism – one that was unrestrained in its means and impossibly millenarian in its ends.

9/11 would eventually draw Western armies into Afghanistan and then Iraq, and presage other terrorist strikes on London, Madrid, Bali and elsewhere. Among its more immediate political effects was the elevation of Blair from an electorally untouchable but somewhat inconsequential Prime Minister to the unofficial spokesman of the international alliance waging war on terror. President Bush could not match his poise or prose, and Duncan Smith was consigned to irrelevance for the opening months of his leadership. '9/11 shut down domestic politics for the first year of that parliament,' recalls Osborne.[75] There was a perverse advantage for Duncan Smith: his shortcomings were not given the chance to show.

The new leader's first shadow Cabinet was impeccably conventional. Howard, Ancram and Letwin were given the Treasury, foreign and home portfolios, while Davis's combative-ness was harnessed as party chairman. Although Osborne had voted for 'IDS' as an ordinary party member in his run-off with Clarke, he was not in the first wave of promotions lower down the hierarchy. Neither was Cameron.

Among the lesser known political by-products of the war on terror was the deepening of relations between the two brightest Tory MPs of the 2001 intake. Osborne and Cameron would sit together for hours in Commons debates about anti-terror legisla-tion. They both lauded Blair's leadership, though Osborne was more voluble in his praise for Bush. 'He is not the fool, the redneck or the coward that some people imply,' he told the Commons, citing his own contact with the former Texas governor. 'He is an intelligent and thoughtful politician and is surrounded by some of the wisest advisers ever to be assembled in an American administration.'[76] After these late night sessions, Osborne would drive Cameron back to west London in his car. When Osborne decided to start cycling instead, Cameron was briefly without a lift. He eventually relented and began cycling too. Another of their intake found Osborne 'more overtly ambitious than David but also more relaxed and sociable'.

'Just the right size,' was Lyndon Johnson's verdict on the Senate when he entered it for the first time. Ninety-nine other legislators would be easier to lobby, bully and charm than the 434 he worked with in the House of Representatives. The House of Commons has fully 650 MPs. No individual can network his way up its ranks. Popularity with other MPs might ease one's path onto a committee, but these are not especially powerful or prestigious. The only meaningful status is a frontbench berth. To get one, a new MP must win the favour of his party's leaders. His relationship with a few people at the top is more important than his popularity among his hundreds of peers.

As guild members with a lived knowledge of politics, Osborne and Cameron understood all this. They spent very little time cultivating fellow backbenchers. Their insider status allowed them to mix in more rarefied company, and their talent as political advisers earned them roles in Duncan Smith's PMQs preparation sessions. 'They were identifiable from the rest of us,' recalls one MP elected in 2001. 'They didn't go out of their way to ingratiate themselves with backbenchers,' says another. Tellingly, few of the 2001 cohort would vote for Cameron in the leadership election four years later.

The new member for Tatton was happy to risk alienating his colleagues if it meant catching the eye of those who held the power of patronage. Sure enough, Osborne's first major media intervention was incendiary. On 19 July 2002, he wrote a column for the *Daily Mail* deploring the recent rise in parliamentary pensions that MPs had voted for themselves. The screed, titled 'Why I am so embarrassed to be an MP', enraged many Tory backbenchers, especially older ones who could not fall back on inherited wealth.[77] To each resentful grumble in the tea room, however, Osborne had an unanswerable reply: 'It's been years since Tory MPs were getting op-eds published in the *Mail*.' Paul Dacre, the newspaper's exacting editor, usually commissions many more pieces than he publishes. Competition for space is of Darwinian intensity, and submissions by mere MPs from a ragged and ravaged party rarely made the cut. Osborne had pulled off a small coup. At the top of the party, it was not overlooked.

Meanwhile, a few hundred yards from the Commons, something more high-minded was stirring. The scarred veterans of the Portillo campaign had not shed their zeal to remake Conservatism. If they could not run the party from the inside, they could influence it from the outside. One option was to launch a magazine but this came to nought. A better idea was a think tank. The acronymed citadels of right-wing thinking, such as the Institute for Economic Affairs (IEA) and the Centre for Policy Studies (CPS), had peaked in the 1970s. Their reputations were more impressive than their recent work, and their outlook was unreconstructedly Thatcherite. There was space on the centre-right for a think tank that specialised in rigorous, research-led policies rather than pamphleteering. It would also provide a congregational space for scattered and demoralised modernisers.

In the spring of 2002, Francis Maude, Portillo's old ally and campaign chief, set up Policy Exchange. Michael Gove, the cerebral *Times* columnist who had chronicled Portillo's life and career, was appointed as its chairman. The job of director went to Nicholas Boles, a former Westminster councillor who had studied public policy at Harvard and once shared a flat with Gove. They also set up an adjacent body called C-Change to campaign for modernisation within the party. Policy Exchange would expand from a two-person operation in the gloomy innards of Methodist Central Hall to become the largest and most influential think tank on the right (physically, though, it has moved only a few metres along Storey's Gate).

Policy Exchange served modernisation by finally giving a well-meaning but vacuous movement some kind of intellectual definition. Its animating conviction was that the size of the state was less important than the distribution of power within it. The Western world's most centralised country should devolve power to local government and below; public services should be opened up to competition and consumer choice. To this day, giving away power (or, to use Cameron's favourite word, 'responsibility') is the governing mission of Tory modernisers. Policy Exchange's first report, which called for elected police commissioners, is government policy. Its paper on schools reform, authored in 2005 by James O'Shaughnessy (who ran Cameron's policy team in No. 10 for a while) and Charlotte Leslie (now an ascending MP), has informed Michael Gove's education policies.

However, Osborne himself has an ambiguous relationship with ideas. He regards intellectualism as a naive distraction from the worldly priority of winning votes; in meetings, he shuts down any abstract discussion much faster than Cameron, who is himself hardly a philosopher, and tends to roll his eyes when a Letwin or a Willetts waxes cerebral. He has never been particularly taken with localism, wondering why a politician would strive to win power only to give it away, and fretting about the electoral consequences of empowering hated local councils. 'A fourth-term priority' is how he used to private describe the idea of local income tax. This hard-headedness provoked tension with Cameron's most fecund source of ideas, Steve Hilton. 'If Steve had a motto, it would be: "It's the right thing to do,"' says a Tory who knows them both. 'George's would be: "We're here to win an election."'

Yet Osborne is also hyper-conscious of the political utility of ideas. He knows that parties that tap into the latest thinking tend to impress the commentariat, and radiate a sense of owning the future. He recalls with a shudder the Conservatives' utter intellectual exhaustion during much of their time in opposition. As shadow Chancellor, he deputed one of his advisers, Rohan Silva, to develop policy in emerging areas, including technology and behavioural economics, and to cultivate relationships with acclaimed American thinkers such as Robert Schiller and Robert Cialdini. If Cameron is somewhat more of an ideas man than his unpretentious Englishness is willing to let on, Osborne is the opposite: a flinty sceptic who often likes to be seen on the intellectual avant-garde.

Duncan Smith's politics were informed more by his Catholic social conscience than by the quasi-Blairite technocracy of Policy Exchange. The modernisers could not fault his initial determination to broaden the Conservatives' appeal, but his approach was very different. At the prodding of Dominic Cummings, a young Eurosceptic activist who joined Smith Square as a strategist in the spring of 2002, the leader launched a series of campaigns on public services. He made 'Helping the vulnerable' the theme of the party's spring conference in Harrogate, which marked progress from the narrowly Eurosceptic speech Hague had given there the previous year. He visited Easterhouse and Gallowgate, two Glasgow council estates blighted by unemployment and drug addiction. Osborne saw the wisdom in all this, even if it challenged his own rather dry and secular habit of mind.

Other Tories were less impressed. Much of the shadow Cabinet favoured a more punchily Thatcherite message, and claimed vindication when the opinion polls failed to move in the Tories' direction. The right-leaning press also lamented the absence of a clear commitment to tax cuts and Euroscepticism. Like Cooper under Hague, Cummings grew restless as front-benchers assented to his strategy memos without ever intending to act upon them. MacGregor, who had been made chief executive of Conservative Central Office just before Cummings was hired, was equally frustrated. The pair worried that Wood, retained by IDS as his press aide, was spinning his own tub-thumping lines rather than the agreed messages. They watched as shadow Cabinet members simply refused to believe evidence of the party's unpopularity. 'However many times Nye rolled out the poll findings, they would find another way of interpreting them,' says MacGregor.[78]

However, the ultimate problem was the leader himself. He lacked grip on his own party (including Davis, who was removed as Chairman in the summer) and dulled the impact of each broad-minded campaign on poverty and public services with a reactionary gesture on Section 28 or immigration. The lesson of Portillo was that social liberalism was insufficient, not that it was unnecessary. IDS also frustrated Howard's attempts to emphasise public spending over tax cuts. Reservations about him went deeper than his strategic confusion, though. With each dismal speech and faltering interview, the sense grew that he was simply not good enough. He brought in Osborne, Cameron, Goodman and Johnson to help him prepare for PMQs but their combined wits – and Osborne's brilliance in particular, attested to by Goodman – could do nothing about his croaky voice and lack of poise.

Hague had repelled threats to his leadership with regular

displays of unanswerable rhetorical flair. By contrast, every public outing brought IDS closer to doom. At the Tory conference in October, his speechwriters tried make a virtue of their man's hopelessness as a communicator: 'Do not underestimate the determination of a quiet man,' he warned, unconvincingly. Osborne had doubted his underlying capacity to lead even as he cast his vote for him in the membership ballot. Within a year, those doubts had hardened.

The parallels between IDS and Hague were multiplying. Both began with tentative plans to soften the party's message. Both capitulated in the face of internal opposition, stubbornly bleak opinion polls and their own conservative impulses. Both failed to grasp exactly how far the country had moved on issues of race, sexuality and personal morality – or how the Tories' tin ear on those subjects was damaging the party's brand. Both struck the public as inherently implausible Prime Ministers. Even the specific events they had gone through were eerily alike. In 2000, Hague had endured a querulous conference in which a shadow Cabinet member (Portillo) confronted the party with its own ugly reputation. In 2002, IDS suffered something similar when Theresa May, who had replaced Davis as chairman, offered an arrestingly candid appraisal of the Tories:

> Our base is too narrow and so, occasionally, are our sympathies. You know what some people call us: 'the nasty party' ...We need to reach out to all areas of our society. I want us to be the party that represents the whole of Britain and not merely some mythical place called 'Middle England', but the truth is that as our country has become more diverse, our party has remained the same. We should not underestimate the extent of this problem. Ask yourselves: how can we truly claim to be the party of Britain, when we don't truly represent Britain in our party?

The speech, and especially the phrase 'nasty party', irked many activists and MPs. IDS put some distance between himself and his chairman. A decade on, however, May's words only stand out for their unerring good sense. The speech was a more grounded version of Portillo's confessional two years earlier, with as many nods to public services and 'active government' as to cultural cosmopolitanism. It was modernisation as done in Maidenhead (May's seat) rather than Mayfair.

She even previewed the anti-politics mood that would come to pervade cynical, post-modern Britain:

> Politicians are seen as untrustworthy and hypocritical. We talk a different language. We live in a different world. We seem to be scoring points, playing games and seeking personal advantage – while homeowners struggle to make ends meet and schoolchildren see years of hard work undermined by the stroke of a bureaucrat's pen.

May is not a modernising insider, or even particularly political. She is regarded by journalists as soporific company. However, it is hard to think of a Tory who has given a more perspicacious and prescient speech about the party since the fall of Thatcher.

With modernisers in place as Chairman, chief executive and chief strategist, their cause should have advanced, but real power lay in a parliamentary frontbench dotted with right-wingers such as Bernard Jenkin and Owen Paterson. IDS himself was, at best, fitful in his enthusiasm for change. In October 2002, just eight months after starting work at Smith Square, Cummings quit in frustration. MacGregor would leave soon after to join Steven Norris's campaign to become London mayor.

On 4 November 2002, an otherwise obscure parliamentary vote served to exhibit IDS's poor judgement – and give some definition to Osborne's ideological identity, which had remained stubbornly inscrutable to most observers. The government was legislating to allow gay couples to adopt children. The personal opposition of the Catholic Tory leader was unsurprising but rather than allow his colleagues to vote according to their consciences, he issued a three-line whip requiring them to resist the measure. As well as sullying his efforts to soften the party's reputation, the gesture erred tactically by provoking dissent at a time of peril for his leadership. Eight Tory MPs defied the whip by voting with the government, including Ken Clarke, Michael Portillo and Francis Maude. Fully thirty-five abstained, including Cameron, Johnson, Howard, Alan Duncan and Osborne himself.

The rookie MP for Tatton was summoned for a scolding by David Maclean, the Chief Whip. His abstention was a rare act of defiance from a pragmatist usually willing to genuflect before those who held the power of patronage. It was also a clarifying event for journalists who knew little of his views. Those who knew Osborne well had him down as a moderniser. But to the average lobby hack, there were few clues. He was cautious in conversation about ideas, he belonged to the most technocratic parliamentary committees (Public Accounts and, from 2002, Transport) and he generally avoided publically identifying himself with factions and wings. His violation of the whip over gay adoption was, perhaps, Osborne's official coming out as a moderniser.

The rebellion humiliated IDS, as did his handling of the dissent it provoked. MPs smirked wryly at the old Maastricht malcontent's exhortation to 'unite or die' the following day. He had contributed to a culture of disloyalty that was now slowly claiming his crown. The shallowness of his parliamentary support during the previous year's leadership election was also catching up with him. Only a third of Tory MPs had backed him to lead the party, and many of those only did so out of antipathy to Portillo and Clarke. By the turn of 2003, speculation about his leadership was inescapable in the parliamentary party. Around this time, Osborne told Mark Field MP that were IDS to be removed, his replacement would be neither Clarke nor Davis, the most fancied successors, but Michael Howard.

He would be proved right but not for several months. Respite for IDS came with the Iraq war, which effectively suspended domestic politics. Osborne, like his party, supported Blair's argument for invasion: that the prospect of a rogue state armed with weapons of mass destruction was intolerable in a post-9/11 world; that Saddam Hussein had defied the UN's efforts to examine his arsenal; that the very credibility of the West was on the line. Osborne's parliamentary interventions in the weeks leading up to the war are intriguing in their vigorous defence of the maligned American administration.

He challenged the *bien pensant* view of President Bush on 26 February, just as he had done after 9/11: 'On Iraq, does the Prime Minister agree that what lies behind some of the opposition to his policy is a caricature of President George W. Bush which is a gross distortion of the truth? Will he take this timely opportunity to set the record straight?' He used almost identical words for the logistical architect of the war a week later. 'Does the Defence Secretary agree that behind some of the opposition to the Government's policy on Iraq is a caricature of US Defense Secretary Donald Rumsfeld, which is a gross distortion of the truth?'[79]

It was not until 18 March, the date of Blair's compelling (and, for some, wilfully exaggerated) parliamentary argument for war, that Osborne made a substantive observation about the rights and wrongs of the invasion. 'Surely it was not the weapons inspectors' job to find the weapons but Saddam Hussein's job to show them where the weapons were?' he asked.[80] Two days later, he was practical and forensic:

It is clear from the action overnight that the military is targeting Saddam Hussein himself. Should Saddam Hussein be killed or overthrown, would military action cease immediately? If not, how would the Iraqi military bring the conflict to a close? What would it have to say to us to bring the conflict to an end?[81]

Perhaps the most revealing insight into Osborne's sentiments on foreign affairs came in a separate debate about terrorism on 11 March, in which he challenged the *realpolitik* of the left-wing Tory Andrew Tyrie:

Does my Hon. Friend claim that the sovereignty of nations should always take precedence over humanitarian concerns? Were we therefore wrong to intervene in Kosovo and right not to do so in Rwanda, where most people believed that we should have intervened? Should vile regimes always be left in place simply because that preserves the nation state?[82]

It is difficult to think of a more convinced liberal interventionist than Osborne on the Tory benches, though Michael Gove's arrival in Parliament two years later would change that.

Merely by supporting the government in measured and dignified fashion, Duncan Smith was having a good war. This was not enough to lift either his party's poll ratings, which often undershot the 31 per cent scored at the previous election, or his own, which were calamitously bad for a would-be Prime Minister. Then, at the Conservatives' spring conference in Harrogate, he inadvertently elucidated exactly what modernisers thought was wrong with his political strategy. He proclaimed the 'and' theory of conservatism. The party did not have to choose between its traditional themes and those favoured by modernisers, he contended. It could espouse both: economic conservatism but also a concern for social justice; a tough line on asylum but also a colour-blind celebration of all Britons. This made immaculate sense in theory, except for the obvious clash between low taxes and generous public spending. The practical problems with it, however, were thoroughly debilitating.

The ultimate wisdom in politics is the ability to grasp how little attention the public are paying. Their exposure to news rarely exceeds a few minutes of the evening television bulletins and a cursory scan of a newspaper. They will certainly not pause their harried schedules while a political party unfolds and exhibits the broad canvas of its worldview. They will only notice a few primary colours and it is up to parties to decide what those colours are. Political strategists face what economists call an opportunity cost: time and space devoted to denouncing immigration is time and space not given to, say, embracing the NHS. A political message can only consist of a few things at a time – politics very often is a matter of 'or' not 'and'.

Modernisers were beginning to understand all this. Finkelstein, ensconced at *The Times*, was evolving an analysis of politics that dwelt on the demand side (in other words, the perspective of voters) rather than the supply side of tactics and campaigns that grips Westminster villagers. Indeed, they were beginning to question whether the substance of the party's message was really the problem. The likes of C-Change and Populus, headed by modernisation's earliest prophet Andrew Cooper, were discovering evidence that policies popular with the public suddenly became unpopular when they were revealed to be espoused by the Tories. It was the underlying character of the Conservatives that voters did not trust, and this was poisoning almost everything the party said on any issue, no matter how objectively sensible. Image, brand, perception – the things fogeyish Tories disdained as shallow – really did matter.

In retrospect, it seems obvious that the party's basic identity could never be modernised without a modernising leader. Yet among this growing band of reforming Tories, which included Osborne, Gove, Boles and (less full-bloodedly) Cameron, the idea of seizing the leadership in the medium-term did not arise. They still saw the outer limits of their mission as persuading whichever conventional Conservative was leading the party – Hague, IDS, eventually Howard – to adopt more of their strategy. 'The obvious solution of taking the leadership did not come up,' says one of the modernisers. 'If it had come up, I think we would have agreed that it had to be David.'

As his party continued to falter, Osborne continued to rise. Hague once told him that he regretted never having served as a whip. The role bestows an intimate education in the anthropology of one's parliamentary party, and conveys an endearing appetite for unglamorous work. These benefits fell to Osborne in the summer of 2003 when he was made a junior whip in place of Cheryl Gillan. He was given a cohort of MPs to 'look after', a decorous euphemism for baser chores: cajoling them into voting with the party, ensuring their attendance at important debates, relaying any of their seditious grumbles to the Chief Whip. 'He was good at the job because he was a good gossip,' pronounces an MP who worked alongside him in the Whips Office. 'But he saw it as a management training course rather than a career choice.' Andrew Mitchell, who had been a whip in the 1990s, remembers Osborne for his 'colossal work rate' and 'good whip instincts'.[83]

Indeed, there is evidence to suggest that Osborne was already aiming for a Treasury post. He began reading up on economics in his spare time, as Gordon Brown had enjoyed doing in opposition, and even asked CRD for an academic bibliography. If he regarded the Whips' Office as a stepping stone to greater things, it was a fairly reliable one. Part of his job was to polish the silver goblets used during the whips' regular dinners. On each were engraved the names of former junior whips. One that attracted Osborne's eye was 'John Major'.

Osborne only served as a whip for a few months before his leader fell. IDS took to the stage at his party's conference in October beleaguered by dismal polls, overshadowed by Howard's commanding speech the previous day, and dogged by suggestions (later disproven) that he had used his parliamentary allowance to pay his wife Betsy for secretarial work that she did not do. Expectations for the speech were low, and he lived down to them with an intemperate rant at the government. 'The quiet man is here to stay and he is turning up the volume,' he insisted, excruciatingly.

When the new political season opened days later, the Parliamentary Commissioner for Standards announced that he would launch an inquiry into what had come to be called Betsygate. After that, usually circumspect Tory donors began to grumble about their leader. As the putsch grew closer, Osborne was uncharacteristically anguished. He shared the almost universally low estimation of Duncan Smith's ability but he had developed a relationship with him via PMQs. 'What am I going to say if he asks me whether I back him?' he wondered to other close friends. In the end, he was spared the conundrum. Duncan Smith never asked him the question.

The only remaining obstacle to Duncan Smith's removal was the practical hassle of a drawn-out contest but even this faded as MPs concurred, in the convivially discrete way that Tory leaders used to be chosen, that Howard should be elected without challenge. This was not because he was likely to be much more popular with the public – polls, if anything, suggested quite the opposite – but because he offered a basic competence that

Duncan Smith lacked. Osborne regarded Howard as 'a serious, proper politician', according to a friend. The party could stand losing, but it was tired of being humiliated.

Tory protocol required twenty-five MPs to write to the chairman of the backbench 1922 Committee to trigger a confidence motion in the leader. By 28 October, fully forty-one had done so. By lunchtime the following day, Duncan Smith was pleading for his job for in front of his parliamentary party in Committee Room 14 of the Commons. Just after 3 p.m., Osborne, in his role as a junior whip, brought a black ballot box into the room and plonked it down on a table in the middle, next to stacks of voting papers bearing the motion: 'I have confidence in Iain Duncan Smith as the leader of the Conservative Party'. Over the course of the afternoon, MPs marked either 'yes' or 'no' on their slip and dropped it into the box.

The result was announced at 7 p.m. Seventy-five MPs had backed Duncan Smith, and ninety had declared no confidence in him. Osborne, along with the other whips, was among the latter. The least convincing Tory leader since the war resigned with grace immediately after. Over dinner that evening with his chief of staff, Tim Montgomerie, he discussed how to ensure that his vision of a broad, conscientious Conservatism lived on. A think tank, the Centre for Social Justice, was the outcome. Today, Duncan Smith is said to wonder why he ever ran for the Tory leadership in the first place.

If there is a moment of take-off in Osborne's career, an instant in which his promising trajectory suddenly soared, it was the elevation of Michael Howard to the Conservative leadership. He was crowned uncontested, and therefore without going before the membership, on 6 November. The former Home Secretary is an immeasurably more complicated politician than his caricature suggests. His tenure at the Home Office was hard line but successful. Not only was the post-1960s rise in crime reversed, but the nature of the job was transformed. Home secretaries used to be patrician types, such as William Whitelaw and Douglas Hurd, who often seemed more perturbed by popular anger about crime than crime itself. Since Howard, all holders of the office have been more or less in his mould.

More to the point, Howard the crime-fighter was also a product of the 1960s with a taste for popular culture and a wife who had been divorced. He mixed toughness on crime and immigration with a liberal easiness on matters of sexuality and personal morality – a blend that characterises the typical contemporary Briton. This comfort with modernity endeared him to younger Tories, such as his former special advisers David Cameron and Rachel Whetstone, who remained in his orbit after they had ceased to work for him. It also allowed him to see with a clear eye that the Conservative Party needed to change, and that the change could only be credibly wrought by a generation untainted by association with the previous government. Indeed, he understood it before even they did.

To that end, he promoted Cameron and Osborne aggressively – first to his kitchen Cabinet, and then to the shadow Cabinet. They, along with Whetstone and Boles, helped to shape the modernising speech that launched Howard's leadership, with its renunciation of cultural conservatism and opposition for opposition's sake. He became the third consecutive Tory leader to rely upon Osborne for PMQs. In fact, it was under Howard that the court mimic crafted his best lines. On the issue of access to university for less privileged students, Howard relished being able to tell the Fettesian Prime Minister that: 'This grammar school boy isn't going to take any lessons from that public schoolboy.' The jibe was written by the expensively educated Osborne.

As Osborne expected, Howard restored basic competence to

the Conservative Party after the ignominies of the Duncan Smith period. He gave strong speeches and parliamentary performances, and surrounded himself within a fearsome platoon of professional political operators. Stephen Sherbourne, a former aide to Thatcher, became his chief of staff, and Whetstone his political secretary. He filled Conservative Central Office with the likes of Guy (now Lord) Black, a former head of the political section, Greg Clark, a policy wonk and now a minister of state, and, less wisely, the duopoly of Liam Fox and Maurice Saatchi, who ran the party as co-chairmen. Shrewdly, and symbolically, he curtailed the Tories' 45-year association with Smith Square by selling its lease and moving the party to more modern offices above Starbucks in Victoria Street.

Ideologically, however, Howard stumbled along the same path followed by Hague and Duncan Smith. He opened his leadership with modernising gestures, the most impressive of which was a speech extolling meritocracy, delivered at Policy Exchange in February 2004. Conjuring a 'British dream', he spoke of his Romanian-born father's rise from immigrant penury to respectable middle-class business ownership. He lauded the contribution that minority groups made to Britain with a fervour that his predecessors had never managed. But right-wing tropes survived – Howard yearned ideologically for a 'small state' – and he was already breaking his pledge to transcend partisan politics by opposing the government's plans for higher university tuition fees and foundation hospitals, both of which were impeccably conservative reforms. Osborne was privately appalled, partly out of ideological conviction but mainly because he knew the Tories were left looking shameless and bereft of vision. Howard compounded the error by intensifying his criticism of the government's handling of the Iraq war, which the Tories had supported.

Howard's modernisation was as hedged and as qualified as

Hague's in 1997/98 – but, to the extent that it did advance, the animating force came from Osborne and his generation. He and Cameron, who discussed the plight of the party as they cycled to and from Westminster, were leaders of a set that was rapidly congealing from a loose gaggle of acquaintances into a coherent political clique. The pair attended regular dinners which also featured Boles, Whetstone, Cooper, Finkelstein, Gove (whom Osborne was only just getting to know) and Steve Hilton, who was taking time out of Good Business, the consultancy he owned and ran, to advise Howard. The impressive cast might have made for some coruscatingly brilliant political discourse but the meetings, which were usually conducted over takeaway pizzas at Policy Exchange, rarely moved beyond weary, impotent grumbling at the status quo. The most interesting thing about the discussions was the identity of the least fervent moderniser. It was Cameron who questioned the need for radical change, and who harboured the most hope for the Tories at the next election. 'George realised way, way before Dave that the party had to change,' according to one of the gang.

The influence of the modernisers was rather predictably resented. In the summer of 2004, marginalised MPs grumbled to journalists about the gilded clique around Howard. Derek Conway, an ally of Davis, lampooned the 'Notting Hill set' as wine-drinking dilettantes with modish views and a mendacious habit of briefing against older, more traditionalist MPs. The media cited Osborne – who by now had the impressive-sounding non-job of shadow minister for economic affairs – and Cameron as ringleaders. That neither they nor many other members of the group actually lived in the faux-cool neighbourhood did not prevent Notting Hill becoming associated with modernising Tories in the way Islington was synonymous with New Labour.

If Conway misrepresented the modernisers, he was at least

right to portray them as an increasingly tight unit. Serving as social glue was a young member of the 2001 intake who did not show up in the newspaper profiles of the Notting Hill set. Greg Barker, who had been elected for Bexhill & Battle in Sussex, had befriended Cameron during parliamentary induction sessions and implored him to consider running for leader as early as 2003. He attended the moderniser's semi-regular dinners, which were beginning to migrate to Cameron's London home, and always left frustrated at their lack of an official frontman. He would earn the nickname 'Mystic Greg' by forecasting to friends in the summer of 2004 the series of events that could propel Cameron to the top of the party. His projection was eerily close to what transpired the following year. If Cooper was the original moderniser in thought and spirit, Barker was perhaps the first practical agitator – and the first to insist that the movement would go nowhere until it acquired a leader.

Osborne was not cowed by the summer's adverse publicity. Indeed, he went out of his way to court attention. He wrote a provocative column in *The Times* on 31 August that cited President Bush, by then reviled by many Britons, including Tory voters, as a master of political strategy and campaigning. Whatever the calamities of his administration, Osborne argued, the Texan was fusing Ronald Reagan's sunny disposition ('No electorate wants to be told their best days are behind them,' the young MP wrote) with brutally effective negative campaigning. He also blended rousing gestures for his core vote with major speeches about 'the things the uncommitted voters are interested in: jobs, education, healthcare and security'. In a rare public glimpse into his own modernising thoughts, Osborne conceded that the Tories had tried and failed to emulate Bush's compassionate conservatism in recent years. 'Perhaps the transplant was too crude,' he wrote, before hinting at what he really meant: 'Perhaps the patient didn't yet realise it needed treatment.'[84]

Osborne meant what he wrote, and he was right. Despite a gruesomely deteriorating occupation of Iraq, Bush was not only re-elected that year but became the first candidate since his father in 1988 to win more than 50 per cent of the popular vote. However, Osborne was unabashed about the real motive behind the column: to command the attention and respect of the Tory leadership. A reshuffle of the shadow Cabinet was likely before the run-up to the general election and he wanted to be among its winners. A brave op-ed in the *Mail* had burnished his reputation two years earlier, so an even bolder one for *The Times* might work the same spell.

Osborne's endeavours to raise his profile also included plans for a book. With Finkelstein, he wanted to author a history of great progressive events in British politics. Osborne wrote a draft chapter on the decriminalisation of homosexual acts in 1967, scouring the national archives in Kew like the history student he once was, while Finkelstein prepared a chapter on the Factory Acts of the nineteenth century. Other reforms covered in the book included the end of slavery and female suffrage. Osborne and Finkelstein wanted to show that high-minded politics did not belong exclusively to the left: the regulation of the factories was supported by aristocrats and opposed by the *Manchester Guardian*, which spoke for industrialists, while Emmeline Pankhurst ended her life as a Tory. It was a nakedly modernising book that attracted the interest of Simon & Schuster but, before they could go ahead with it, Osborne's career made another leap.

On 8 September, while voting in the Commons, Osborne took a mobile phone call from Howard, who immediately offered him the post of shadow Chief Secretary to the Treasury. Osborne accepted and the call abruptly ended, leaving him to absorb this vaulting promotion in the deathly hush of a now empty division lobby. At thirty-three, he was in the shadow Cabinet and carrying perhaps the most technical portfolio in politics. A Chief Secretary is the executioner of his Chancellor's fiscal strategy. He masters the arithmetical minutiae of revenue and expenditure, and harries ministers and mandarins on their departmental budgets line-by-line, number-by-number. Paul Boateng was doing the job for Gordon Brown. Osborne was to be his opposite number. 'It's now my job to make sure the sums add up,' he told a local newspaper in Cheshire. 'Tax and spending really are the heart of politics.'[85]

Howard's admiration for Cameron, whom he promoted to policy co-ordinator, was well-known and long-standing. He had told colleagues as early as 1994 that his young adviser would lead the party one day. Osborne, whom he had known less well, grew in his esteem during PMQs sparring sessions ('which were certainly more fun than PMQs itself', attests Howard). It was not his wit and cunning that impressed the leader so much as his toughness and, less obviously, his ideological core. Howard detected in him a 'framework of beliefs' without which 'you get blown about by every passing gust of political wind'. He was a 'man of steel', according to Howard, who admired as well as embodied that trait.[86] This appraisal is hard to reconcile with Osborne's reputation as a ducker and weaver, an exceptionally tactical and transactional politician even by modern standards – but others who knew Osborne and Cameron at this time agreed with Howard. One of the pair's closest friends and advisers found Osborne less 'squishy' than Cameron.

Osborne's elation at his new role cooled as he observed the demise of Howard's modernising mission that autumn. Confronted by polls that gave the Tories no more than 35 per cent of the vote, the leader emulated his two predecessors by concluding that modernisation's strategic logic was greater than his own ability to embody and communicate it. If voters still saw him as a brutal and cold politician, as the evidence suggested they did, turning that image into an asset might be wiser than toiling to refute it. So began a hardening of the Tory message in the run-up to the general election, with crime, immigration and Europe exhumed as the party's motifs. To give some strategic shape to what was in danger of becoming an amorphous populism, Lynton Crosby, an Australian political consultant who had helped to win elections for his own Prime Minister, John Howard, was recruited to run the Tory campaign towards the end of 2004. He was also given the brief of imposing order on a party headquarters that, even after its physical relocation and personnel overhaul, was still prone to chaos, leaks and intrigue.

Crosby's performance in the second of these missions still evokes unprompted praise from veterans of the 2005 campaign. He established a clear chain of command at CCO, which he renamed Conservative Campaign HQ, with himself at its summit. He clearly delineated roles for the rest of the staff, deftly managed myriad personalities and took decisions quickly, firmly and under intense pressure. He was, in short, exactly what the Conservatives would lack in their next general election campaign five years later.

When it came to the content of the campaign, however, Crosby's instincts compounded Howard's. It was the leader's decision to fight the election on predictably Tory themes, but the Australian then packaged and presented them in searingly strident fashion. He blew the 'dog whistle', his metaphor for any political message that slices through the cacophony of the news cycle to arouse voters' most visceral sentiments. Immigration is a dog whistle issue, as are crime and welfare. As the election approached, Conservative posters on these topics bore the insinuating tagline: 'Are you thinking what we're thinking?'

The question also adorned the party's rather thin manifesto, which had been drawn up by Cameron. There was nothing explicitly bigoted in this rhetoric, and the reaction of the liberal press betrayed a mix of acute sensitivity and feigned outrage. It is forgotten that the slogan also accompanied posters about school discipline, hospital cleanliness and other perfectly innocuous subjects. But the general aroma being emitted was pungent. As forensic polling studies would show in the aftermath of the election, swing voters, even those who shared the views expounded by the campaign, felt uneasy for doing so. The Conservatives were giving conservatism a bad name.

The most calamitous aspect of the campaign was, gallingly for Osborne, tax and spend. Despite the evidence of the previous election, many Tories insisted that the party go into the election offering an overall cut in taxation. Howard and Letwin, his shadow Chancellor, also wanted to match Labour's spending plans on the major public services. The mathematical tension between these competing priorities was resolved – very much in theory – by magicking up £35 billion of 'efficiency savings' that could be made in government expenditure. The figure was produced by David James, a City financier the party had commissioned to look into public sector waste. Letwin announced that £23 billion of the savings would be reinvested in services, £8 billion would ease government debt and the remaining £4 billion would fund tax cuts.

Owing to Letwin's perilously close fight with the Lib Dems to retain his Dorset constituency, but also because Crosby rated Osborne as the superior communicator, the shadow Chief Secretary served as the face and voice of Tory Treasury policy during the campaign. It was his job to sell the James Review and its attendant tax cuts to the electorate. He performed manfully, becoming a star of the Tory campaign and virtually assuring himself another promotion after the election. But the task was ultimately impossible. It was one of the great educational experiences of Osborne's career, and continues to colour his views on the politics of economics.

Part of the problem was the sheer complexity of the message. Compared to Labour's simple offer of more public spending, the Tory pitch was tortuous: cuts to waste but no loss of spending on frontline services, and a three-way division of the proceeds of efficiency. George Bridges, sharing a car journey with Osborne that spring, was struck by his friend's anguish at having to parse this intellectual mosaic into sound bites. 'It taught him the need for simplicity,' he says.[87] A deeper flaw was the ropiness of the numbers themselves. 'Back of a fag packet stuff,' is how another senior staffer on the campaign describes the James Review, with its optimistic calculations for the revenue-raising potential of abolishing quangos and other peripheral public bodies. Osborne had to master every last figure in a document that he himself found implausible. Then there was the odd timing of the tax cut pledge. Instead of painstakingly forming the argument for months and years, it was suddenly announced during the campaign itself. 'We failed to make the case long enough and hard enough for lower taxes,' concedes Bridges.[88]

But Osborne suspected that something more fundamental was at work. For him, the 2005 campaign completed an epiphany that began with the previous election four years earlier. In the aftermath of 2001, he and Finkelstein began to postulate the 'baseline' theory of election campaigns. Whatever the government's overall fiscal plan going into an election, so this goes, it will be treated by the media and voters as the baseline, or common sense position. Any proposed deviation from it by the opposition will be scrutinised remorselessly. If it is a Labour opposition proposing to veer off a Tory government's baseline, this will be presented as a plan for tax rises. John Major's devastating campaign against

Neil Kinnock's 'tax bombshell' in 1992 was just such an example. If, on the other hand, it is a Conservative opposition proposing to deviate from a Labour government's baseline, this will be equally vulnerable to attack as tantamount to spending cuts. 2001 was proof of this, and so was 2005.

The only route out of the trap is simply to accept the government's baseline, as Gordon Brown did in 1997 – the only election campaign in the past twenty years during which the opposition did not haemorrhage votes over its fiscal plans. Osborne resolved to follow Brown's example if he was ever in a position to design his party's economic policy in advance of an election.

As another certain election defeat approached, Osborne was not alone in being impatient to actually define what a modern, electable Conservatism might look like. At a pre-election gathering of the modernising crowd at Cameron's house, Hilton, who thought the dinners and pizza parties were going nowhere, gave a presentation setting out his vision for the party. Its themes – environmentalism, general well-being, voluntarism – would, under the stewardship of the evening's host, end up forming the Tory message over the next couple of years. Osborne, whose approach to politics always bore a sharper retail edge, was visibly unimpressed. He took Hilton aside and told him that his proposed message was too 'fluffy'. He argued for something more akin to Mayor Rudy Giuliani's muscular, metropolitan conservatism: a blend of economic and cultural liberalism with a tough line on crime. Indeed, he was urging Howard's aides to focus the party's general election campaign on law and order. It was the only issue, he pointed out, which voters regarded as both salient and better handled by the Tories.

The strengths and weaknesses of Osborne's argument stand out with several years' hindsight. There was wisdom in his demand for a clear and punchy political message. The Tories would lack exactly that five years later. Had his hawkishness on crime and security been heeded in the ensuing years, the party would not have attempted its eccentric ploy of seducing voters with soft-headed and unpopular nods to the civil liberties lobby. But his analysis – and, indeed, Hilton's – betrayed a lack of thought about issues of social justice. Voters doubted the Tories' commitment to easing poverty and improving public services, and these concerns were never going to be palliated by the economic dryness of a Giuliani. Four years after Portillo's culture-obsessed leadership campaign crashed and burned, even the most far-sighted Tory modernisers were only tentatively grappling with the basic distributional questions of politics.

For Osborne, who had endured 1997 and 2001, 2005 was a less forgivable result. Against a government enervated by war and eight years of power, the Conservatives never seriously threatened to win. Labour's popular vote had fallen by 5.5 percentage points over four years but the Tories had gained just 0.7. In other words, the public were open to a change of government but saw no plausible alternative. Tony Blair, now in the same thrice-elected company as Thatcher, sat atop a diminished but still comfortable majority of sixty-six seats.

In 1997, Osborne was captivated by the drama of Blair's victory. In 2001, he was elated to be an MP and a father-in-waiting. 2005 was the first of the Conservative defeats that truly wounded him. He told friends that he was trying to gird himself for another decade of opposition – with fewer than 200 MPs, the Tories would need to make an improbably prodigious leap to win a parliamentary majority at the next election. Under whose leadership that would be was the question that confronted the party for the fifth time since 1995.

Eminence

2005–2012

'I do understand power, whatever else may be said about
me. I know where to look for it and how to use it.'
Lyndon Baines Johnson

9.

Brown's Nemesis

'We did not, unfortunately, claim that there was anything
fundamentally wrong with the economy.'

The strangest twist in the long ordeal of Conservatism is that the man who fought the most pungently right-wing election campaign of recent decades then became the midwife to modernisation. More obvious candidates for the role had either taken their leave of Westminster, such as Chris Patten, or nursed leadership ambitions of their own, such as Ken Clarke, or registered utter indifference, as in the mercurial case of the departing Michael Portillo. Neither were any of these men particularly close to the modernisers.

Michael Howard, by contrast, counted them as friends and could use his leadership of the Conservative Party to ease their path ahead. Instead of resigning immediately after the election or obeying the exhortations of aides and donors to stay on until at least the middle of the parliament, he did something in between: he announced that he would stand down but not until a prolonged leadership race, perhaps one held under revised rules, produced a successor. This delay might allow time and space for a less established candidate to overhaul the favourite, David Davis, whose turn it seemed to be. In the meantime, Howard could elegantly curate the contest in favour of such a usurper. As a work of political craftsmanship, it was lethally effective.

His first gambit was to promote Osborne and Cameron in a shadow Cabinet reshuffle. Whetstone called Osborne on the day after the election to hint that he was to be offered one of the most eminent roles in the shadow Cabinet – without, contrary to some accounts, specifying that it would be shadow Chancellor. This coolest and most calculating of politicians was, for once, utterly thrown. He had expected a promotion, yes, but to shadow education, health or trade – nothing so dramatic as the burden of shadowing one of the great offices of state. He was, after all, a 33-year-old with just four years' experience in Parliament.

As he journeyed to his meeting with Howard later that day, Osborne expected to be appointed shadow Home Secretary. He shared the leader's tough instincts on crime; he had even urged him to make law and order the single dominating theme of the election campaign. His guess was half right. Howard actually gave him a choice of two posts: shadow Home Secretary or, astonishingly, shadow Chancellor. 'Think about it over the weekend,' said Howard, who then trumped even that offer by suggesting that Osborne also stand for the leadership. Osborne, already physically flagging after an arduous campaign, took some time to absorb what he was hearing. He had been nudged to consider running before, but by friends and peers such as Steve Hilton – not a party leader and former Cabinet titan who was older than his own father.

A weekend set aside for blissful repose was now clouded by pensive deliberation. Osborne and his wife went to see Nicholas Hytner's production of *Henry IV* at the National Theatre on London's South Bank, with its modernist architecture and strategic views of Parliament. Osborne identified with the political agonies playing out on stage: a weary king looking to his own succession, his son and heir slowly coming of age. He smiled wryly, and came to a view. Yes, Gordon Brown, who had presided over eight years of growth and low inflation, was the towering slayer of six shadow Chancellors. In the Commons he was, in Howard's words, 'dominant in a way I still struggle to understand'.[89] Were Osborne to flounder against him, as six older men had done before him, his political rise would be over in his mid-thirties. For all this, however, Osborne felt that it was better to try and fail than to spurn the chance and harbour eternal regret. Since his school days, Osborne had craved eminence. This was it.

He spoke to his wife, his parents and, fully four years after he had ceased to work for him, William Hague, before deciding that he would accept the job of shadow Chancellor. The leadership, however, struck him as a leap too far. He was five years younger than the most junior of all the mooted candidates, his friend David Cameron.

Indeed, that Sunday, Osborne hosted Greg Barker at his London home to discuss how to stop another candidate seizing the modernising tag before Cameron, who was relaxing in his Oxfordshire constituency, made his move. The idea of Osborne himself running did not occur in the conversation.

On the morning of 10 May, Osborne told Howard that he would like to become shadow Chancellor but was minded not to stand for the leadership. With needless grace, he said he would understand if Howard chose to withdraw the first offer in light of his reluctance to accept the second. Howard brushed this aside and confirmed him as shadow Chancellor. Upon hearing the news, Andrew Mitchell, an MP (and now a Cabinet member) whose office was in the same Commons corridor as Osborne's, invited him inside for some celebratory champagne. The new shadow Chancellor told Mitchell that his 'gambling streak' had drawn him to the job. 'Brown needs to get lucky all the time,' he said, in the manner of a plucky guerrilla taking on a ponderous army. 'I only need to get lucky some of the time.' He envisaged opposition politics as asymmetric war.

Cameron was simultaneously appointed shadow Education Secretary, having initially turned down the work and pensions brief. That Howard was happy to meet this request is a measure of his regard for Cameron but why, given this inordinate esteem for his former adviser, did the outgoing leader not offer him the shadow chancellorship, or ask him quite as directly to become his successor? Osborne's impressive public performances during the election campaign might have influenced his thinking; Cameron, the author of the manifesto, played a largely back-room role. There is also a theory, espoused by some of those close to Osborne, that Howard favoured Cameron all along but could not give him the shadow chancellorship as it would effectively be seen as an endorsement for the leadership. Osborne was too young and improbable a contender to attract the same suspicion.

Both of these explanations are plausible but many Tories who knew all three men also suspect that Howard nursed some reservations about Cameron. He had, it is said, spurned the chance to become party chairman the previous year. Then there was the 'squishiness' that irked even his closest political friends. Cameron was neither an unreconstructed right-winger – indeed, he had voiced worries about the party's tone on immigration that disappointed Howard's team – nor an especially vociferous moderniser. Since the mid-1990s, his gaggle of political peers – Whetstone, Fall, Bridges, Gove, Hilton, Osborne himself – had seen him as the most plausible future leader among them without ever knowing what a Cameron-led Tory party would be like.

Osborne, by contrast, had some definition and direction. He was plainly fixated on the centre ground. During a conversation that summer with John Glen, the young head of CRD, he drew a horizontal line on a scrap of paper to represent the political spectrum. He scribbled 'Tories' halfway along the right side of the line, 'Brown' some way to the left side, and 'Blair' in its very middle. 'That is where we have to be,' he said, jabbing insistently at the Prime Minister's name.

Osborne is not a worrier. Although he had not yet refused outright Howard's invitation to run, there were no long dark nights of the soul. 'That's just not how he thinks,' according to a friend. His state of mind blended indecision with equanimity. When he interviewed a Bank of England analyst called Matthew Hancock with a view to recruiting him as his adviser, the young economist asked his future boss whether he would go for the leadership. 'I honestly don't know but I suspect not,' was the reply. Others around Osborne picked up the same intimations. 'I got the feeling pretty early on that he wouldn't stand,' remembers Ed Staite, a press adviser who briefly worked for Osborne.[90]

During the ensuing week, this reluctance to run was hardened by two experiences. On 17 May he endured his first Commons showdown with Brown. He was confronted by an orchestrated wall of noise from the Labour benches and struggled to test his intimidating opponent. As he peered over the despatch box, he understood that his most pressing priority was simply to survive as shadow Chancellor. Combining the job with the burden of a leadership campaign would probably undermine both roles. This realisation then became a settled will when he talked to Cameron soon after. The new shadow Education Secretary was clear and direct: he wanted to run and, if Osborne did not, he would like him to manage his campaign. Osborne saw that Cameron possessed the certainty that a leadership hopeful needed, and that he himself lacked. His mind was now made up.

To avoid any scent of conspiracy or deal-making, Osborne did not inform Cameron of his decision before briefing journalists. The *Daily Telegraph* carried the story on 20 May that Osborne would not stand for the leadership after all. 'I have a big enough job being shadow Chancellor, opposing Gordon Brown and developing an economic policy that broadens the appeal of the Conservative Party,' he told the newspaper, in an unalloyed account of his genuine thoughts.[91] Although Osborne was now relieved of one burden, he had taken another upon himself. Running a leadership campaign is an onerous job, especially when the candidate is as much of an outsider as Cameron was in the summer of 2005. A YouGov poll published on 1 June showed that over half of party members regarded Davis as their first or second choice, compared to just a third who thought the same of Cameron, whose parliamentary support was even scanter.

In age and experience, Davis was neatly equidistant between the neophyte Cameron and the fading Ken Clarke. Ideologically, too, he offered more thoroughgoing Conservatism than either of those two without quite joining Liam Fox on the unelectable right. Anyone who doubted his loyalty was reminded of his role as a Maastricht whip, when he set aside personal ideology (and popularity) for the sake of his leader. Above all, his back-story as the son of a single mother on a council estate was one few senior politicians, let alone the Etonian Cameron, could match.

Against all this, Davis lacked a certain star quality – though he was a consistently solid communicator – and seemed to underestimate how much his party needed to change. He issued fragrant bromides about reform but did not grasp the kind of realities set out in *Smell the Coffee*, a polling study of the Tory predicament conducted by Andrew Cooper and Lord Ashcroft, a party donor who never allowed his own conservative instincts to cloud his analysis of public opinion. The report, published in the aftermath of the election, painstakingly dismantled the assumptions of the right. It found, for example, that the party's focus on immigration repelled prosperous, liberal-minded professionals without attracting poorer and tougher, working-class voters from Labour. It captured the hideousness of the Tory brand by show-ing that right-wing policies repelled voters only when they were revealed to be espoused by the party.

Davis also lacked the support of Howard, who had squabbled with him in recent years and almost shuddered at the prospect of handing over to him. As a result, Howard's efforts to shape the race did not stop at giving profile-raising portfolios to Cameron and Osborne. Francis Maude, modernisation's wizened elder, was made party chairman, confirming Central Office as a pro-Cameron redoubt. Staffers were required to be impartial but CRD offered covert help to both Davis and Cameron knowing that the latter was more likely to accept. Tim Chatwin, who had joined the Cameron team from CRD, served as a link. The donors who kept Central Office going were also ahead of MPs in taking the young candidate seriously. Michael Spencer, a City financier, was 'very, very persuaded' by Cameron and Osborne when they visited his ICAP office for lunch in June.[92]

Howard followed Maude's appointment with the delaying tactic of proposing reforms to the party's leadership elections. On 25 May he issued a consultation document, *A 21st Century Party*, which suggested that the final say over new leaders should go to MPs rather than members. Howard continues to insist that his motives were innocent but the proposals ultimately came to nothing, and conveniently stalled the formal start of the campaign until September. It also aggravated Davis's team, who were eager to exploit their man's frontrunner status while it lasted, and inaugurated a bizarre summer in which hopefuls as implausible as Alan Duncan, Bernard Jenkin and Andrew Lansley toyed with running. Lansley's modernising pitch – he suggested renaming the party 'Reform Conservatives' – piqued the interest of intellectually serious types such as Willetts and Letwin but never caught on.

Cameron made an unofficial declaration of his candidacy with a speech at Policy Exchange on 29 June. He and Osborne arrived as a pair. The speech was neither particularly good nor especially modernising, and featured a pledge to recognise marriage in the tax system as its most vivid idea. Afterwards, the gabbing think-tankers and like-minded guests, most of whom regarded Cameron as 'their' candidate, despaired of his flatness. Across Parliament Square, MPs were not flocking to his campaign either. In a preview of the social narrowness that still defines Cameron, his parliamentary support consisted overwhelmingly of privileged MPs such as Letwin, Hugo Swire and Osborne himself. Swire, who kept the books which recorded the names of MPs backing Cameron, occasionally had to massage the figures for the sake of the team's morale. Andrew Robathan took over the duty as the summer sweltered on.

Despite all this, Osborne was eminently relaxed and largely absented himself from the campaign office in Greycoat Place. He viewed the summer as a phoney war and expected serious combat to begin no earlier than the party conference in October. He had also studied Davis and concluded that a long contest would eventually expose what he regarded as his lack of imagination and his limits as a communicator. 'He saw Davis's flaws', according to Ian Birrell, a journalist and friend of Cameron's who often found Osborne more confident of eventual victory than the candidate himself.[93] This insight into other people, and their weaknesses above all, would inform Osborne's approach to taking on Brown, but it was another of his assets – his facility with parliamentary numbers – that really calmed his nerve. For a supposedly near-certain winner, Davis had few avowed supporters: twenty-one by mid-August, and fifty-five by the time of his official launch in September. Most Tory MPs had doubts about his ability to compete with Blair as a political performer, and many disliked his allegedly abrasive allies. Osborne was reminded of the suicidal overconfidence of Portillo's allies in 2001.

Osborne and Cameron were determined to avoid another of Portillo's fatal mistakes. He refused to compromise with the right and seemed to actively enjoy discomfiting them with liberal provocations. Cameron, by contrast, strove to reassure the right while heading towards the centre ground. A myth has emerged of a bravely, unabashedly modernising campaign, but it is exposed by a quick tour of some of Cameron's public statements that summer: a pledge to withdraw Conservative MEPs from the main centre-right caucus in the European Parliament, a reiteration of his support for the Iraq war, a critique of multiculturalism as a threat to 'shared national culture', repeated eulogies to the family. Cameron's campaign was modernising in its tone and direction but mildly conservative in its specifics. This was not intellectual confusion – although Cameron would sometimes be guilty of that in later years – it was subtle, sinuous politics. Osborne's hand in it all was obvious.

There is another, less charitable take on Osborne's insouciance that summer. Some on the campaign suspected that he was half-expecting to lose and discretely positioning himself to thrive in a Davis-led Tory party. They were right to see political motives in his conspicuous flirtation with the idea of a flat income tax. He never seriously considered adopting the policy but knew that feigning an interest would win friends on the right for Cameron's campaign – and also for himself. 'It was almost entirely political positioning,' according to one of Osborne's closest allies. His critics would accuse him of doing something similar two summers later, when he renounced 'über-modernisers' amid speculation of a looming election that had the potential to end Cameron's career.

This perception of Osborne as a Vicar of Bray, always willing to recalibrate his views and loyalties to get on, was exaggerated. But it was encouraged when he, along with Swire, attended a dinner at the Nottinghamshire home of Andrew Mitchell, Davis's campaign manager. Mitchell tried delicately to persuade his guests that Cameron's time would come later, but Osborne was unmoved. Both he and his host received anxious text messages during the evening from their respective candidates; Davis was as paranoid as Cameron that the dinner would conclude with the defection of his campaign manager. Osborne is now teased by friends about his 'night in Transylvania', but Cameron and his supporters were not so relaxed about his motives at the time.

Whether or not Osborne 'went wobbly', as some allege, he was justified in focusing on his job as shadow Chancellor. Brown had the Treasury's monolithic might behind him; Osborne had to make do with a tiny, windowless office above the Commons chamber which contained two chairs, a bookcase and his desk. Before Hancock arrived from his gardening leave – imposed by the Bank of England's Governor Mervyn King, who feared his institution's independence being compromised – Osborne's team consisted of a parliamentary researcher, a diary secretary and Ed Staite, who was based in Victoria Street. When a journalist from the *Financial Times* turned up to interview Osborne for a profile, Staite had to lie on the floor at an angle to be able to fit in the room. Osborne's ability to build a serious operation was constrained by the uncertainty over his own future. Many saw him as a caretaker shadow Chancellor, with Willetts expected to take the role under a Davis leadership.

As the party conference approached, the first beads of sweat surfaced on Osborne's brow. With the election rules increasingly unlikely to change, he worried that Cameron would lose out to Clarke or Fox for the right to go before the grassroots with Davis. (The candidacy of Malcolm Rifkind, the former Foreign Secretary, was not taken seriously.) In a meeting at Cameron's home in mid-September, Osborne told him, rather firmly, that he had to dispel the suspicion he was only running to position himself for a future race. Spectacular gestures were required to convey hunger and urgency. A powerful conference speech was the bare minimum; the official launch of the campaign before that was just as important. To this day, many on the campaign, including Greg Barker, identify the launch and not Cameron's Blackpool oration a week later as the real 'turning point'.[94]

The Royal United Services Institute on Whitehall was booked for 29 September, just hours after Davis's own launch at the nearby Institute of Civil Engineers. Mitchell asked Osborne to change the date but was rebuffed. Osborne knew that such a direct competition with Davis on the day would encourage the media to view the pair as the only serious candidates. Steve Hilton set about curating the event with a budget of £20,000, a fifth of the maximum permitted cost of the campaign, which he spent on lighting, refreshments (including smoothies that dangerously evoked the modish fare served at Portillo's campaign launch four years earlier) and a stylish stage.

The impressive setting, and Cameron's fluent notes-free speech, stunned journalists who had just arrived from Davis's rather milquetoast affair around the corner.

Cameron dominated the following day's press coverage but did not rush to capitalise on his momentum by touring the Commons tea room or ploughing through media appearances. Instead, he retired to his London home with Hilton and began preparing for his Blackpool speech. His narrow focus, and conservation of energy, would prove devastatingly well-judged.

The conference was one of the few in recent decades that changed the trajectory of politics, but Osborne's role in it was nugatory. (The same would not be true of another transformative conference two autumns later.) It was Maude, knowing Davis's limitations as an orator, who crafted the event as a beauty contest in which each candidate would have a set-piece speech to make their pitch. It was Frank Luntz, an American political consultant, whose (hardly rigorous) focus group for the BBC's *Newsnight* electrified the media by showing Cameron to be the most popular candidate with ordinary voters. It was Hilton who controlled the look and feel of the campaign's presence in Blackpool. It was Cameron's decision to avoid the fringe circuit in favour of preparing for his turn on stage. Most of all, it was Davis whose dismal speech on the Wednesday made Cameron's winning effort the day before look superhuman.

Again speaking without notes, Cameron toured myriad policy areas, oscillated from solemnity to lightness and argued for 'fundamental change' to the Conservatives' 'culture and attitudes and identity'. More importantly, his technical execution of the speech was superb. This, more than his substantive message, drove the extraordinary surge in his poll ratings among party members and wider voters in the aftermath of the conference. 'It was hardly the Gettysburg Address,' argues an MP who backed Davis, but talent, not content, is the first test of a plausible Prime Minister. Duncan Smith ultimately failed to hang on to the Tory leadership because he was not quite up to it, not because of doctrinal differences with his colleagues. Davis, though plainly upper-Cabinet material, failed to win the leadership for exactly the same reason.

MPs cascaded towards Cameron upon their return to

Westminster after the conference season. Rifkind pulled out of the contest on 11 October. In the first ballot a week later, Cameron was supported by fifty-six MPs, only six short of Davis and fully fourteen ahead of Fox. He was likely to inherit many of the thirty-eight who backed Clarke, who was eliminated. In the second round two days later, Cameron crushed Davis by ninety votes to fifty-seven. Fox was eliminated with a respectable fifty-one. Polls suggested that Cameron would win the member-ship ballot handily, the result of which was to be announced on 6 December.

There were rumples along the way, though. Cameron was dogged by rumours that he had taken illegal drugs in his younger days, perhaps at university or during his tenure at Carlton. He neither denied nor confirmed them, preferring to insist that he was not obliged to disclose details of his private life that predated his time as a frontline politician. As a line of defence, it was working – but then, on 16 October, the allegations spread to his running mate. The *News of the World* splashed with 'Top Tory, coke and the hooker', showing an old photo of Osborne with his arm around Natalie Rowe, a prostitute he and his friends had encountered soon after leaving university. On a table in the foreground was what looked like cocaine. Rowe was quoted alleging that Osborne had snorted the drug, though not that he had engaged in sexual activities with her.[95]

The same piece included a strenuous denial by Osborne, who explained that he had met Rowe via a friend of his (later revealed to be William Sinclair) with whom she was in a relationship. It became clear that he was abusing drugs and, at the instigation of Osborne and others, he eventually sought treatment. 'That is and always has been the sum total of my connection with this woman,' insisted the shadow Chancellor, who implored people to leave his friend and his young child alone.[96]

In the end, the story did little lasting damage to Osborne. It boiled down to one woman's word against his and, by 2005, drugs (even serious class A ones) had lost their power to shock voters. However, the way the story was handled by the tabloid gave rise to further insinuations. Some allege that Andy Coulson, its editor at the time, presented the revelations in the least damaging way possible (an odd thing to read into the headline 'Parties with a cocaine snorting dominatrix') and was later rewarded with the job of director of communications for the Conservative Party. Others speculate that more damning photos of Osborne were held back and continue to lurk in a dusty file somewhere. Although Osborne worried about the story's impact on his young family, his private reaction was largely stoic. 'How on earth do you cope with it?' asked one of his closest friends, only to hear Osborne coolly observe that such sensational intrusions were a part of British public life. 'George is remarkably unemotional about these things,' says one of those who know him best. Of all the local difficulties he has endured – his controversial visit to a Russian billionaire's yacht in 2008, criticisms of his performance as shadow Chancellor, the scornful reaction to his 2012 Budget – the tabloid sting bothered him least.

The fact that Cameron was strolling to victory certainly helped his mood. Before the official result came in December, Osborne, eager for an economic message with which to define himself, announced a new fiscal principle. It nudged the party away from free-market dogma but dated badly. Instead of matching or besting Davis's vision for £35 billion of tax cuts the shadow Chancellor promised to 'share the proceeds of growth' – that is, revenue – between public spending and tax cuts. It was classic triangulation: the state would shrink over time as a share of the economy, but taxes would only be cut if there was money in the Treasury. Osborne was repudiating his party's electorally

ruinous habit of promising to scythe taxes under any circumstances. The courage for this modernising gesture came from
his assumption that Cameron would become leader, but he was
also increasingly confident that he would be retained as shadow
Chancellor whoever won. Davis, he calculated, would need
someone from the left of the party as his number two. Willetts, a
Davis supporter, had been the favourite until a botched flirtation
with the Cameron campaign.

There was, however, a problem with Osborne's new policy. It
rather took growth for granted, and at a time when the economy
was already expanding at a diminishing rate. What would he do
in the event of zero or negative growth? How would he ensure
that growth continued? In a *Daily Mail* column titled 'We want
a Tory, not a new Tony' on 22 October, Simon Heffer, modernisation's great tormentor, was scathingly prescient: 'Before Mr
Cameron can share these mythical "proceeds" he will have to
secure them, and he won't do so without far-reaching, structural
reforms of our economy.'[97] It was only a small dose of the disdain
that Osborne's policy would attract a few years later.

There were other indications around this time that Osborne
was not entertaining any prospect of a downturn or recession.
In Westminster's Quirinale restaurant, two free-market journalists of almost monastic conviction, Fraser Nelson and Allister
Heath – both of whom have gone on to shine as editors – strove
to persuade Osborne that Brown's concoction of borrowing,
spending and labour market regulation would bring down the
economy before long. He was dismissive.

Osborne's confidence in endless growth was misplaced, as
time would prove. It was grounded in personal experience and
encouraged by the prevailing national mood. The economy had
grown continuously since his time as an undergraduate and,
if he complacently assumed that it would continue to do so,

then he was in some formidable company, including that of the Chancellor of the Exchequer. Like Britain's entry into the ERM, the notion that 'boom and bust' had been tamed provokes much more scorn now than it did (and should have done) at the time. Given, too, that moderniscrs had urged the party to soften its tone and embrace optimism, it would have been perverse for Osborne to stand almost alone against Britain's sunny, money-making zeitgeist. It was his private lack of curiosity about the sustainability of the boom that was less forgivable.

On the weekend before the result was announced, Osborne gave a speech to Jeremy Hunt's constituency association. As the new MP for South West Surrey drove Osborne there from London, he told him that he had learned from his time in busi-ness that 'leadership is lonely'. 'David's success depends on your partnership with him, so you must be shadow Chancellor,' said Hunt. 'Don't worry,' Osborne replied, 'I will be'. A few days later, at the Royal Academy of the Arts in Piccadilly, it was announced that Cameron had beaten Davis by two-to-one among Tory members. He was now burdened with leading Her Majesty's Opposition, and Osborne was liberated to begin his shadow chancellorship in earnest. Although the outcome had not been in any doubt since October, Osborne took a long time to absorb what had happened. 'I can't believe how easily we have taken over the party,' he would tell friends, months after the result.

The more time passes, the odder and more esoteric Cameron's opening moves as Tory leader seem. His embrace of environ-mental issues, which were peripheral to voters even before the crash, has aged badly. His visit to a melting glacier, his ostenta-tious cycling, his attempted installation of a wind turbine on his home, his exhortation to 'vote blue, go green' – all this came to betray, for some, the soft-headed priorities of those who have never had to scrape a living or fret about the quality of their local state school. Confounding this view was the identity of the strategist behind it all: Steve Hilton, the least privileged person in Cameron's political clique. Like Andrew Cooper, he knew that Tory policies would not command support until voters trusted the party's motives and character. Unlike Cooper, his favoured approach was not to dwell doggedly on kitchen table concerns but to embrace high-minded issues that carried a symbolic message beyond their practical relevance to most people. Foreign aid was in the running to be the big soft theme that defined Cameron, but the Tory leader (along with Osborne) concluded that it was already 'owned' by Brown. Hilton argued for greenery and won.

Osborne went along with this happily. His own take on modernisation had a more populist edge, and his enthusiasm for green policies has dimmed since the crash, but he saw Hilton's logic. He also thought environmental gestures would seem congruent coming from politicians who lived fairly green lifestyles themselves. Worries about authenticity and plausibility did for another theme advocated by a senior Cameroon (as the new leader's supporters were coming to be known in the press). Michael Gove, who had left journalism for Parliament, was among those who suggested that Cameron's mission should be to improve the life chances of people from poor backgrounds. Confronting the issue of social mobility directly would neutralise Cameron's poshness, and resonate with voters far more than aid or greenery. But Cameron and Osborne have always doubted their ability, as men of extraordinary privilege, to espouse this cause convincingly. It was a rather important issue to abdicate. Their decision created the sense that modern Conservatism stood for *noblesse oblige* rather than aspiration. It was an impression they would never quite dispel.

Although Osborne did not resist Hilton's environmental gestures, he did show signs of resentment at his privileged access to Cameron, and perhaps not without cause. During the early months of the new dispensation, Hilton would spend Sunday evenings at Cameron's house agreeing events and announcements for the coming weeks, before instructing Tim Chatwin to plan their execution. At various times, both Osborne and Patrick McLoughlin, the Chief Whip, complained about this exclusive informality, arguing that it should give way to open meetings and proper protocol – to no avail, at least initially.

Access is not the same as influence, however, and Osborne enjoyed plenty of the latter. Indeed, looking back, the most enduring pronouncements made by the Conservatives in January 2006 – a month planned, as they still are by Tory strategists, on a 'grid' with different themes marked out in different colours – were those partly or wholly crafted by Osborne. He insisted that Cameron give a speech professing his ardour for the NHS, which came on 6 January at the King's Fund. Talk of vouchers and private provision was toned down; the message was diehard commitment to an institution that, as Nigel Lawson once remarked, had long since made the transition from health service to national religion. Osborne would tell colleagues that the Tories' position on the NHS should be no more sophisticated than 'We love the NHS. No, we promise you, we really, really love the NHS.' He was only half-joking. Later in the year, Cameron uttered one of his better slogans: 'Tony Blair once explained his priority in three words: education, education, education. I can do it in three letters. NHS.' It was Osborne's line.

Then, on 23 January, came the announcement that would ground Osborne's economic policy thereafter. In front of an audience at the Cass Business School in London, he pledged, in words conjured by Oliver Letwin, 'stability before tax cuts'. 'If the public finances are in a mess, then sorting them out will have to take priority over promises of tax cuts.' The right objected, invoking the American economist Art Laffer to argue that tax cuts could actually fix the public finances by stimulating growth and therefore extra revenue. But Osborne doubted that voters would ever believe this.

More to the point, although he was open to the basic principle pictorialised by the Laffer Curve, which showed revenue falling once taxation hit a certain level, he knew that nobody could say with any certainty where Britain currently was on the curve. Was there frustrated economic activity that a tax cut would release? If so, which tax cuts would achieve this? How much would they raise? How long would it take for the revenue to flow to the Treasury? No credible fiscal policy could be built on such shaky footings. Osborne and his team briefed journalists that his speech was a turning point in Conservative economic thinking. The shadow Chancellor was identifying himself with traditional fiscal conservatives rather than supply-side tax-cutters. When the next day's *Financial Times* led with the speech ('Stability before tax cuts, says Osborne') he held it up in front of Hancock and declared: 'THAT was a media operation!' Hancock, now an MP, still keeps a copy of the newspaper in a desk drawer in his constituency home.

Osborne would deepen his fiscal conservatism at the party conference but, before that, he had to build a team. Eager to avoid the poisonous enmity that festered between Blair and Brown, he and Cameron moved to a shared suite of offices in Norman Shaw South, an eastern adjunct of the parliamentary estate. The new space had to be filled with staff and Cameron already had most of his, including Ed Llewellyn, a former adviser to Chris Patten in Hong Kong, who was his chief of staff, and Kate Fall, Osborne's old colleague from CRD, who served as Llewellyn's deputy. Osborne only really had Hancock, however.

Raised in the guild, Osborne took the process of finding

back-room reinforcements extremely seriously. Cameron likes
to surround himself with old friends; he had known Llewellyn
and Fall since his time at Central Office and would later bring
in a university friend, Andrew Feldman, to run the party's headquarters. Osborne, however, prefers to recruit strictly on merit.
Like Blair, who assembled the mightiest kitchen Cabinet of any
post-war party leader – Peter Mandelson, Alastair Campbell,
Jonathan Powell, Philip Gould – through systematic headhunt-
ing, almost nobody in Osborne's team was known to him before
his thirtieth birthday. (Greg Hands, the Treasury whip who
dabbled in Fulham's local politics with Osborne in the 1990s, is
an exception.)

In the spring of 2006, Hancock was joined by Rohan Silva,
a 25-year-old Treasury civil servant whose left-leaning assumptions had been disrupted by a Master's course at the London
School of Economics, where the work of Karl Popper and John
Gray left him with a vision of an open and happily chaotic
society of entrepreneurs and activists. 'Iconoclastic' remains his
favourite adjective. Word of his energy and flair had reached
Osborne via Alan Duncan. 'I'm not an economist, you know,'
he told the shadow Chancellor during his job interview. 'Don't
worry, neither am I,' came the reply. Over time, however, Silva's
intellectual interests would draw him closer to Osborne's rival
for Cameron's ear, Steve Hilton, who shared the young man's
wariness of the bureaucratic state.

Then, in the summer, came Rupert Harrison from the unim-
peachably pukka Institute for Fiscal Studies. Having shone at
Oxford, the 26-year-old was approaching the end of a PhD
at UCL examining the impact of new technologies on wages
and skills in emerging economies. He was among the outstanding micro-economists of his generation. He had campaigned
against the euro at university but avoided party politics and,

like Silva, found Howard's election campaign the previous year distasteful.

The Osborne team would swell with other recruits over time – including Seth Cumming, Eleanor Shawcross and Claire Perry, who has gone on to a parliamentary career – but the trio of Hancock, Harrison and Silva were its unchanging core. The division of responsibilities saw Hancock as chief of staff, a role as political as it was economic; Harrison as the purest technical economist; and Silva as a free-ranging source of ideas and speeches on other policy areas. That each came from a citadel of economic authority was not lost on Osborne. In a world of limited time and information, he knows that any association with venerable third-party institutions will impress a layperson, which is why he continues to covet the approval of the likes of CBI and the IMF for his policies. He would show guests around his office and introduce 'Matt from the Bank of England, Rupert from the IFS and Rohan from the Treasury.'

Their first mission was to seal Osborne's reputation as a budgetary conservative by preparing a provocative announcement for the party conference in Bournemouth. Osborne wanted to take his commitment to stability even further by explicitly ruling out promises of 'unfunded' tax cuts at the next election. Any proposed tax cut would have to be paid for by a corresponding reduction in spending or an increase in taxation elsewhere. Nebulous 'efficiency savings' would not count. Osborne was desperate to avoid another experience like the James Review. The problem was that he had already commissioned Lord Michael Forsyth, a Thatcherite grandee, to produce a report on tax policy without instructing him that its recommendations had to be 'fiscally neutral'.

As Bournemouth approached, intense focus was given to the nuance and wording of the speech. Osborne wanted to pick a fight with the right to persuade journalists and swing voters that he was committed to the centre ground, but he was also anxious to avoid a hostile reaction in the hall. The first objective required no effort: Thatcherites such as Lord Tebbit, Edward Leigh and John Redwood had already publicly deplored his aversion to unfunded tax cuts, as had commentators like Irwin Stelzer. The second aim was harder to fulfil. The solution lay in a quote from Thatcher herself that Osborne excavated from an anthology of her speeches: 'I am not prepared to go on with tax reductions if it meant unsound finance.' Osborne had only met her once before ('It wasn't much of a two-way conversation,' he quipped to *The Independent* that autumn) but he knew that linking sound money to her name would win over his audience.[98] It helped that, away from the commentariat and parliamentary ideologues, 'there is not actually a big majority in the party for deficit-funded tax cuts', according to one of his advisers.

In the speech, Osborne said that he could not make tax promises in 2006 for an election in 2009 as there was no way of knowing what the public finances would be like by then. It seemed a reasonable enough argument at the time. In retrospect, it was rather more than that. Had Osborne gone into the recession with a pledge to cut overall taxation, the collapse of the public finances in 2008–09 would have killed the policy – and his party's credibility, and perhaps his career – stone dead. It is a political reality that has seldom been acknowledged by his critics on the right. Fiscal conservatism is not by itself a full and satisfying economic policy, but it served usefully as Osborne's *idée fixe*, a kind of Archimedean point on which the rest of his policies could be assembled. Osborne still regards the speech as his most technically impressive, and the most stimulating to write. It might have also been the best strategic judgement he made during his entire shadow chancellorship.

There was, however, still the nuisance of the Forsyth report. Osborne had failed to persuade the peer to avoid recommending an overall tax cut. Things deteriorated when a staffer at Victoria Street mistakenly put the document online twenty-four hours before its official release date in October. Ed Balls, the Economic Secretary to the Treasury and Brown's closest ally, brandished the report as proof of Tory plans for £21 billion of spending cuts. As panic broke out in Norman Shaw South, so did comedic farce. The now deceased American actor Ron Silver, a friend of Finkelstein's who was visiting Parliament, switched into his spin-doctor character from the *West Wing* and took charge of the situation: 'Alright guys, this is what we're gonna do!' The light relief was very much transient as Osborne's claims to fiscal discipline (and basic competence) suffered badly that afternoon. Until then, he had been taken with the Brownite gambit of commissioning 'independent' reports to produce proposals conveniently in line with government policy, but the Forsyth experience put him off. 'If you get the wrong person and the wrong terms of reference,' says one of his aides, 'they can come back and bite you.'

Osborne bound himself to other, less shrewd commitments in 2006. In a summer speech to Oxfam, Cameron, with his shadow Chancellor's approval, announced that the Conservatives would not only match the government's target to spend 0.7 per cent of GDP on foreign aid by 2013, but might go even further. Such unquestioning fealty to an arbitrary spending goal set by the United Nations in 1970, the year before Osborne was born, was the kind of munificence that defined booming, absent-minded, pre-crash Britain. It now stands out as perhaps the oddest item in the government's fiscal plans. The party had women and high-minded professionals in mind when crafting the policy but there were surely cheaper and more rigorous ways of appealing to them. 'It was a marginal call at the time and it still is,' admits a professed über-moderniser. 'In retrospect, maybe we should not have done it.'

Then, in the autumn, a ride on the famed *Shinkansen* during a visit to Japan helped to persuade Osborne that Britain needed high-speed rail capacity that extended beyond the existing link from London to Paris. He felt genuine enthusiasm for the policy but he was also happy to be able offer something eye-catching. Getting noticed is, after all, the first hurdle of opposition politics. 'Your basic economic speech,' says an aide, explaining the high-speed rail announcement 'is fiscal policy, monetary policy and then supply side reform, which consists of things like regulation, skills and infrastructure. The problem is that the third part of the speech is really boring because it is just a list. Making it fly is the challenge.' That the proposed high-speed extension served areas of northern England which felt neglected by the Conservatives did not evade Osborne's electoral eye either. Still, the policy remains an expensive way of shortening rail journeys by not very much.

History records Osborne's most notorious error during this period as an act of omission not commission. Since the Big Bang of financial deregulation twenty years earlier, the City of London had romped its way to global primacy as a banking hub. While Wall Street served mainly the continental North American economy, the Square Mile served the world. As well as hosting the global or European headquarters of most major investment banks, it attracted private equity outfits and hedge funds, utterly dominated foreign exchange and sustained an expansive ecosystem of law firms, management consultancies and business services companies. Its gargantuan boom found tangible expression in the shimmering towers of Canary Wharf, an outpost of the City that languished as derelict docks until the turn of the 1990s, in the impossibly multinational hordes scurrying from

Bank or Moorgate or Tower Hill stations each morning, and in salaries and bonuses so vast that, were they excluded from official statistics, Britain's income distribution would resemble that of a typical Western European social democracy.

Osborne did not worry about an impending financial crash in private. Nor did he evince any fear of one in public, even as a perfunctory gesture to cover his back. This was despite intimations, for those willing to look, of fearsome leveraging on the part of not only banks but the households and businesses that make up the wider economy. Compounding the sheer scale of leveraging was the mystifying complexity of some of it – financial innovation, powered by advanced computer modelling, had spawned products so densely constituted of bits and pieces of other debt that some institutions did not fully understand what they were trading. The financial bubble was not merely capacious but also opaque. Osborne did not, except in passing, fret that the British economy was precariously over-reliant on financial services either. 'We did not, unfortunately, claim that there was anything fundamentally wrong with the economy apart from some household debt,' admits one of Osborne's closest advisers.

Again, though, Osborne's best excuse is that almost the entirety of elite opinion was equally complacent. It is almost impossible to overstate the breadth of relaxed consent, if not evangelical support, for the City and its doings at the zenith of the boom. The ruling left had few complaints about a sector that sent tax revenues cascading into the Treasury. This was true not only of Gordon Brown but the avowedly socialist mayor of London, 'Red' Ken Livingstone, whose willingness to treat with the City might now be remembered for its Molotov-Ribbentrop incongruity but, at the time, was vaunted as a model of municipal pragmatism.

The consequences of this complacency about the banking

sector would come later. In the meantime, Osborne was establishing himself as the first shadow Chancellor to trouble Brown. By the end of 2006, the Conservatives were as trusted as Labour to run the economy, according to YouGov polls. Eighteen months earlier, they had trailed by 13 percentage points. In the intervening period, growth had continued and inflation remained low but, crucially, the public finances soured. As a result, Osborne's commitment to fiscal rectitude was not only exorcising the spirit of dogma from the Conservative soul but narrowing the party's credibility gap with Labour much faster than he had expected.

But there was more to Osborne's success than policy. His predecessors had never evolved a way of dealing with Brown's personal force. He bludgeoned them in the Commons with rhetoric and a raw presence that sometimes radiated actual physical menace. When even Michael Howard confesses to being cowed, a heavyweight is at work. Osborne avoided their fate by deploying his ability to analyse other personalities and identify their vulnerabilities. He worked out that Brown found weakness provocative, angered easily and lacked courage beneath all that surface pugnacity. Osborne's approach was to evince absolutely no sign of fear, even when he felt it, and then match Brown's aggression. After all, the worst the Chancellor could do was scream and scowl – this was Westminster in 2006, not the duelling age – and every so often he would forfeit his composure and dignity.

On one occasion, Brown was so irked by Osborne that he hurled his order paper at him across the despatch box. Osborne, noticing that it was covered in Brown's handwritten notes, passed it on to Staite, who then showed it to the press. Enterprising reporters hired a graphologist to study Brown's scrawl and published the verdict, which Osborne gleefully quoted at the Chancellor at future engagements in the Commons. The note's author apparently suffered from 'unreliable and poor judgement', lacked 'control of their emotions' and was liable to be 'evasive'. Even aside from the jokey gambits, Osborne was the Chancellor's parliamentary equal – or at least he was on set-piece occasions, such as the Budget. 'He would deliver a big performance in big events,' says a former aide, 'and you wouldn't really know where it came from.' Matching Brown in the chamber was a small victory next to the revival of Conservative economic credibility but neither Lilley nor Maude nor Letwin nor Portillo nor Howard had managed to do it.

It helped that Osborne genuinely despised Brown. Ministers and their opposite numbers often enjoy convivial relations, or at least regular direct contact, away from the camp biliousness of the Commons or the television studio. Nothing like that was true of this pair. The proximate cause of the enmity is often thought to be a telephone conversation about voting arrangements in which the Chancellor ranted at Osborne before abruptly hanging up, but Osborne had rather weightier grievances than that. Brown was trailed by a gang of acolytes whose dark facility with plots and anonymous briefings only later became public knowledge. In the early years of Osborne's shadow chancellorship, some of them allegedly spread unfounded rumours about him and his past. Some of the scurrilous stories that found their way to Osborne's ear – usually via Silva, who received tip-offs from lobby journalists – would provoke the fury of even the meekest and most uncomplaining soul.

While it was rooted in real and ugly experience, the sheer vigour of Osborne's contempt for Brown shocked some who observed it at close quarters. In the office, he occasionally referred to the Chancellor as a 'bastard' and delighted in impersonating him as a lurching monster. He bristled at any praise he encountered for Brown – and there was plenty of that in the years leading up to the crash – insisting that he was a phoney who cloaked brutal machine politics and moral cowardice in pious Presbyterian bromides. This private scorn slipped into public sight during an interview with the journalist Mary Ann Sieghart on the fringe circuit of the 2006 conference. When she suggested that Osborne's adolescent fixation with historical facts and events was 'faintly autistic', he replied, to the slightly confected outrage of many: 'We're not getting on to Gordon Brown yet.' Like his references to the 'guild', it was a typical Osborne quip: ostensibly comedic but true to his underlying thoughts.

As Osborne flourished against Brown, his clout within the Tory firmament grew. Cameron was already relaxed about delegating political duties to his shadow Chancellor so he could concentrate on fronting the party, but this division of labour became ever more pronounced. Osborne emerged as a kind of line manager for the shadow Cabinet, issuing instructions and monitoring performance. Cameron's indifference to print media, and eagerness to spend his evenings with severely disabled son Ivan and the rest of his family, meant that Osborne also became the party's emissary to the world of editors and proprietors, a role he relished. When daring political gambits were attempted, Osborne again did the planning and execution.

An example which now seems like history getting ahead of itself was the covert effort to secure the defection of David Laws, the crisp, intelligent, market-friendly Liberal Democrat who would later, and very briefly, serve as Osborne's Chief Secretary to the Treasury. The two had enjoyed amiable conversations since entering Parliament together. 'I detected a certain dryness on economics,' says Laws of Osborne, 'and he was also an incredibly shrewd analyst of the politics of other parties.'[99] Towards the end of 2006, Osborne arrived at Laws's spartan office at 1 Parliament Street, where he still works, and told him that he had Cameron's express approval to invite him to join the Tory frontbench. Laws graciously declined. He explained that his Orange Book liberalism was not quite the same thing as Osborne's modernising Conservatism; he was, for example, more concerned with social mobility than the Tories seemed to be. Osborne was baffled that such a small difference in philosophy could justify spurning a chance at real power, but their relationship remained cordial. The conversation seems to capture two categories of political animal – the purist and the realist – but both men have a little of the other in their make-up.

The Tories had made more progress in 2006, the first full year of Cameron's leadership, than they had expected – but there were intimations of trouble to come. The big-ticket items of modernisation, namely the embrace of the NHS and Osborne's fiscal rectitude, were well conceived and executed adroitly, but the fiddlier gestures were neither. Some of the party's efforts at rebranding seemed nebulous (a scolding, backed by no policy at all, for retailers who locate sweets near checkouts), badly judged (criticism of American foreign policy on the fifth anniversary of 9/11) or hopelessly removed from public opinion, such as Cameron's plea for more 'love' and less 'blame' for young, anti-social delinquents. Tories in the media and in Parliament subjected Cameron to the first serious bout of criticism in his leadership, effectively ending his honeymoon.

Most of these missteps were driven by two, apparently contradictory Cameroon impulses. The first was a preoccupation with the views of liberal metropolitans over those of ordinary swing voters in swing constituencies, who are not only much more numerous but also far more open to actually supporting the Tories. This was not entirely without a rationale: *bien pensant* types are tiny in number but disproportionately likely to wield influence as members of the media. But it is a rather circuitous way of winning an election. A direct pitch to the striving classes in places like Bolton West and Birmingham Edgbaston was in order. The political logic behind Cameron's indulgence of youthful miscreants, immortalised by a newspaper sub-editor as the 'hug a hoodie' speech, continues to defy analysis. Of course the Tories had to stop dwelling on issues (such as crime) where it was already favoured, but to actively soften the party's line on it was eccentric politics.

The other impulse was a kind of soft Anglican paternalism that has never been far from Cameron's soul. The Tory leader is ultimately a mild cultural conservative who happens to have thoroughly modern attitudes to race and sexuality. Anxiety about the behaviour of some businesses and the families in which criminals are raised is as likely to felt by traditionalists as by liberals. These instincts were drawn out of Cameron by Danny Krueger, a man of faith who wrote his speeches during this period. It would not be the last time the modernisers made common cause with Christian conservatives: the mod-God coalition shaped welfare reform and the high-minded voluntarism of the Big Society.

Osborne – who weighed in, though not especially demonstratively, against these gestures – shares neither of these two instincts. He is a rigorous and classical liberal. He believes that individuals must be left to live as they choose unless they infringe upon others, at which point the state must punish them. He is less likely than Cameron to impute any 'duty' to business beyond making a profit and obeying the law. (He is also averse to dinner-party sneering at American foreign policy.) Much more than all this, he has an awareness, and even healthy fear, of public opinion forged by years of serving a party that had been on the wrong side of it. On crime, especially, he knows where voters stand. Of all the modernisers, he is the most likely to wonder how a policy will play 'on a poster in Wolverhampton'.

His favourite book on New Labour – and he has read them all – is Philip Gould's *Unfinished Revolution*, which opens with a eulogy to the striving classes and their hard-headed views. Unlike Gould, he did not grow up among them, but, with the sole exception of Gove, no other Tory moderniser understands them better. 'One of the things that struck me about George was his instinctive grasp of public opinion,' says someone who worked alongside him under William Hague, 'as you wouldn't expect it from such a privileged person.' Michael Gove agrees that 'George has a greater identification with those who strive than you might assume from his background.'[100] Apparently unknown to his many critics on the right, he argues for a more conservative line on crime, welfare and enterprise in the back-room meetings which hammer out the current government's business. Two of the coalition's most vivid retail policies, the cap on immigration and on household benefits, were designed by Osborne.

The right-wing press struggled to understand Cameron's cultivation of fashionable opinion, and the hoodie speech in particular, but they knew they didn't like it. Their reaction confirmed Osborne's existing doubts about the party's media management. George Eustice was only temporarily serving as Cameron's press secretary and he tended to concentrate his efforts on the lobby. In early 2007, Osborne suggested to Cameron that their joint operation needed someone who could venture beyond daily briefings and range across the full spectrum of strategic communications, including the fostering of relationships with editors. Cameron agreed and the search began. The BBC's Guto Harri interested them but their pursuit came to nothing, although he went on to work for Boris Johnson as Mayor of London.

Then a rather daring option occurred to Osborne. His embarrassment two years earlier at the hands of the *News of the World*, which published old photographs of him in the company of a paid dominatrix and what looked suspiciously like cocaine, had acquainted him with its editor, Andy Coulson. The pair met again at editorial lunches hosted by the tabloid. Far from resenting Coulson, he warmed to his practical competence and easy manner. Osborne, who fancies his ability to gauge a person's politics without asking them directly, also sensed that he was not only a Tory but the kind of Tory who was entirely absent from the party's top table. Coulson was a self-made success from Billericay who shared the mystification of the masses at some of Cameron's more soft-headed gestures. Osborne suggested to the Tory leader that they had their man, and he agreed.

Coulson's other advantage was his availability, but he was not a free agent for any benign reason. In January, he had resigned from the *News of the World* after the newspaper's royal reporter Clive Goodman and a private investigator called Glenn Mulcaire were jailed for intercepting mobile phone voicemails left with aides to Prince William. The convictions and his resignation seemed to mark the end of the phone-hacking scandal, and Coulson's own culpability for it. So, that spring, Osborne met Coulson for a drink in a London hotel and asked him whether he would be interested in working for the Conservatives. Osborne assumed that he had already received other offers and braced himself for a gracious rejection.

Instead, Coulson playfully observed that whereas the Tories had taken several weeks to get in touch, Blair and Brown phoned him with commiserations on the day of his departure – so he could see Osborne needed to improve his media operation. Although he was looking forward to an extended walking holiday abroad, he was interested and agreed to come in for more formal discussions. As Osborne revealed to the inquiry into media ethics by Lord Justice Leveson five years later, he asked Coulson 'in a general sense, as you might do in a social encounter, whether there was more in the phone-hacking story that was going to come out, that was not already public, that we needed to know about – and he said no'. On his way back from the hotel, Osborne phoned Cameron to tell him that Coulson was open to a formal offer of employment.

In a brief and perfunctory way, he also asked the then editor of *The Sun*, Rebekah Brooks, about Coulson.

Exactly what was asked about Coulson's past in subsequent meetings and conversations remains opaque. Insiders say that Coulson claimed not to be aware of any illegal activity under his editorship, as he continues to. But it is unclear if either Cameron or Osborne specifically asked him whether he had known of any instances of phone-hacking. His hiring would come to be seen as perhaps their single greatest misjudgement when the resurgence of the hacking scandal provoked his resignation from Downing Street in January 2011, and the closure of the *News of the World* seven months later. The ongoing Leveson inquiry into media ethics has prolonged and intensified the scrutiny of the whole affair. Cameron has told Parliament that with hindsight he would not have employed the former tabloid man – who, it must be said, turned out to be sublimely able and one of the best-liked individuals at the top of the Conservative Party.

The Tories' decision to recruit Coulson represented a *volte face* in their approach to the media that has rarely been acknowledged. In the first year of Cameron's leadership, he and many of those close to him, especially Hilton, remained aloof from the world of editors and press barons. After his seven-year immersion in the television industry, Cameron had come to regard the power of the printed press to be naively overrated. The fact that he had won the Tory leadership in the face of dismissive doubt from newspapers only encouraged this view. The medium that mattered to them was broadcast: the pursuit of Harri, the recruitment of the BBC's Craig Oliver years later and even Osborne's hiring of the more junior David Hass from the *Today* programme confirmed as much. Cameron's team even discussed the idea of breaking up the established system of parliamentary journalism by refusing to give privileged, off-the-record briefings to the lobby. This remained a possibility even after the recruitment of Coulson, who was open to the idea.

What changed in 2007 was straightforward if not particularly edifying: the Tories panicked. The right-wing newspapers, including *The Sun*, the *Mail* and the *Telegraph*, were oscillating from incomprehension to outright scorn in their treatment of Cameron and his creed. The left-wing *Guardian*, which some around Cameron thought could be at least neutralised, remained hostile. Osborne, always more attentive to Fleet Street than Cameron ('George gives the best briefings, by some margin,' says one prominent journalist, and not one enamoured of the Chancellor), was anxious to improve the party's standing among the press. He was, as ever, haunted by his experiences as a young Tory adviser, when each day brought a fresh wave of newspaper bile for the party.

The mistake is to assume that he set about wooing News International's outlets specifically. Coulson was identified as someone who could liaise with editors and proprietors generally, not just Rupert Murdoch and his people. After all, Murdoch's *Times* was and remains the only paper that could even loosely be described as Cameroon; the *Mail* and the *Telegraph* were much bigger headaches for the Tories. Indeed, if Cameron and Osborne have ever had a mission to cultivate a particular part of the media, it was the national broadcaster. 'There was always a BBC strategy,' admits a member of Osborne's team. To this day, Oliver is prized by the government despite being less of a newspaper man than Coulson, and not as much of an all-round political operator. The reason? He knows how to influence 'the six' and 'the ten' – Downing Street shorthand for the BBC's *Six O'Clock News* and *Ten O'Clock News*.

Any hesitation Cameron and Osborne felt before appointing Coulson vaporised when they suffered the first genuine crisis of their time in charge of the party. In May, David Willetts, their education spokesman, gave a radio interview and then a speech ruling out any expansion of grammar schools under a future Tory government. This was merely a reiteration of existing policy but something in the vehemence of his argument enraged the right. Graham Brady quit as a frontbencher, and Michael Howard had to be talked out of publicly criticising the party's policy, before Willetts was nudged by the leadership into moderating his line.

For both traditionalists and modernisers, the row crystallised Cameron's flaws. The first bunch said the grammar schools policy was an intellectual capitulation to the left and exposed the Etonian's indifference to aspiration. The latter saw in Cameron's refusal to stand behind Willetts a wavering commitment to modernisation. Hilton, in particular, urged him to face down the right. Osborne was more sensitive to the right's anger. He was also far from distraught at the plight of Willetts, a man who had always wanted to be shadow Chancellor but now staggered on as a diminished figure and was quickly demoted in favour of Gove. More seriously, Osborne also knew the Tories' need for an effective media man was now urgent. Coulson was appointed director of communications at the end of May.

The newcomer's inheritance was the grimmest period of Cameron's leadership. The political summer of 2007 has attained a surreal quality in the memory, but it was strange enough at the time. Westminster and Whitehall was virtually suspended in anticipation of Tony Blair's departure as Prime Minister, which came on 27 June. After his final statement in the Commons, MPs broke convention by standing and applauding him on his way out. Cameron waved to his backbenchers to join in but Osborne did not need the invitation. His political career had taken place almost entirely under Blair's dominating shadow. By 2007, lots of Tories admired Blair – Gove had 'come out' in a *Times* column in 2003, Cameron was his self-described 'heir' in 2005 – but Osborne's ardour was older and deeper. He referred to him in private as 'the master' and even, during Duncan Smith's stewardship of the party, 'our real leader'.

Less clear is whether Osborne admired him for the right reasons. Blair did not achieve electoral mastery of the centre ground through calculated triangulation – he actually was, by conviction, a centrist. On crime, economics and foreign policy, he believed Old Labour was wrong and that the public were right. As *The Times* noted that summer in a magisterial full-page editorial which merited its portentous title of 'Man and Time': 'Because Mr Blair is a man of the middle of the spectrum and a pragmatist, many contend, falsely, that his is an outlook without a coherent philosophy, or basic convictions, lying behind it. This is to underestimate man and mission.'[101] Some around Osborne worried whenever he marvelled at Blair's habit of locating himself in an electoral sweet spot somewhere to right of Brown and to the left of the Tories, as though the lesson of the thrice-elected Prime Minister's career was essentially tactical.

Even his forgivable awe at Blair's brilliance as a performer sometimes missed the point. The enduring insight of his memoirs, titled *A Journey* and published in 2010, was to dispute the popular distinction between conviction politicians and presentational geniuses. Only by believing his argument, Blair argued, can a leader persuade others of it. The irony of all this is that Osborne's underlying convictions *are* truly Blairite. The former Prime Minister had given rise to what his old speechwriter Philip Collins has described as a new orthodoxy of moderate economics, cultural liberalism, public service reform and hawkishness on home affairs. Osborne's views fit effortlessly into that space and yet, compared to someone like Gove, he is still more likely to savour Blair's political craft than the 'irreducible core' beneath it.

Osborne's take on Blair's coronated successor requires less elaboration. He did not merely despise Gordon Brown – he also, albeit *sotto voce*, questioned his vaunted political prowess. But this appraisal was confounded by the new Prime Minister's first few months in power. He immediately distinguished himself from both Blair and Cameron through a combination of unglamorous stolidity and competent crisis-handling. These traits were also exuded, more authentically, by his new Chancellor, Alistair Darling. The school motto Brown invoked outside No. 10, 'I will do my utmost', was a masterwork of grounded normality next to Floreat Etona. Few political poster campaigns were as deft as the one Labour launched that summer depicting Brown as 'not flash, just Gordon'. In the press, the Prime Minister was admired as a post-partisan 'father of the nation', hosting Margaret Thatcher at Downing Street while keeping floods, rural pestilence and terrorist attacks at bay.

Meanwhile, Cameron offended many by honouring a commitment to visit Rwanda while the floods were forcing Britons out of their homes – a decision that Osborne came to regard as a mistake. The result of all this was a surge in the opinion polls for Labour; the government enjoyed a double-digit lead for much of July and August. Although the parliamentary term had another three years to run, Brown now faced an enormous temptation to call a snap general election. It would allow him to cash in on popularity that was uncertain to last. Victory would give him a personal mandate that he lacked and, if it came with an extension of Labour's 66-seat majority over the Conservatives, it would also probably mean Cameron's defenestration as leader. Even toying with the idea would torment his opponents. When the Prime Minister's aides swaggered into *The Spectator*'s summer party that year, the symbolism of Brownite dominion over cowed, effete, privileged Conservatism was not lost on the other guests.

The ensuing tragicomedy now seems a footling event next to the global financial crash that came after it. But it was probably the sharpest and most decisive turning point in British politics since the Falklands war a quarter of a century earlier.

From the middle of July to the end of September, the Tory modernisers (and their project) were at the mercy of an imperious Prime Minister. There were 'endless meetings', according to insiders, to hastily design posters, themes and indeed policies for an imminent election. 'Day after day, week after week, we wondered whether Brown would call an election.' Cameron gamely feigned enthusiasm for a snap poll – even imploring Brown to go to the country – but his party were nothing like ready. Michael Spencer, the treasurer, told the leadership that money could be found to fight a campaign, but he knew it would be a serious stretch. During this period of prolonged trepidation, only Hilton was certain that Brown would not go ahead with the election, so much so that he simply refused to attend many of the planning meetings. Cameron's disposition was one of private concern but almost indecent outward composure, leaving Spencer to observe that he had never seen anyone in all his time in business cope with pressure so well.

Osborne suspected that Brown's personal foibles – ultra-caution, indecision, a suppressed fear of his own narrow national appeal – made a snap election unlikely. But he also knew the situation was finely poised, and that many of Brown's most aggressive aides were urging him to finish Cameron off while he had the chance.

If Osborne's analysis was equivocal, his actions were coldly decisive. He made two manoeuvres – one for himself, and one for his party. At the end of September, he shored up his own political position with a *Spectator* interview in which he renounced the

> über-modernising view that some have had, that you can't talk about crime or immigration or lower taxes. It is just that you can't do so to the exclusion of the NHS, the environment and economic stability. I have always argued for a more balanced message, and that is what I hope you would see at this party conference.[102]

Osborne's intervention was interpreted as a selfish ploy to extricate himself from impending electoral calamity by flattering the right, who would likely run the party if Cameron fell. This cynical view ignores Osborne's record: he had always argued that modern Conservatism must be tough in areas where the public were tough, principally crime. He was not to blame for the frothiness of modernisation at its worst. Still, the suspicions about his motives were not wholly misplaced. Osborne's appearances in the media are meticulously planned (he will have ruminated over the phrase 'über-modernising' before deploying it) and he was asserting his conservative credentials in more substantial ways too. Perhaps because journalists were still mapping the ideological topography of recent intakes of Tory MPs, it seemed to escape them that Osborne's handpicked shadow ministerial team were all from the moderate right of the party: David Gauke and Mark Hoban, both of whom had backed Davis for the leadership, and Justine Greening, who gave her vote to Liam Fox. Greg Hands, who would join later, was another case in point. 'He is happy to be seen as a bit to the right of the other modernisers,' according to an ally.

If Osborne's minor response to the snap election saga was to protect himself against the worst, his major response was to ensure that the worst did not happen. From the earliest weeks of his shadow chancellorship, he had received representations from Tory MPs to ease the burden of inheritance tax. Levied on estates worth over £250,000, it was beginning to ensnare households that did not regard themselves as well-off. 'It was surprising how many MPs, even from not very rich seats, told us that their constituents wanted something done about it,' remembers an Osborne aide. But the idea seemed to fail the party's self-imposed test for all new policies – that they should be judged by their impact on the poor. The likes of Gove and Letwin were particularly hostile to a policy that would appear to entrench privilege.

Osborne broadly agreed with them until the summer of 2007, when evidence of the unpopularity of the tax became irresistible. In a focus group that Hancock observed from behind a glass wall, nine of the ten participants objected to inheritance tax as it was levied on assets that had already been purchased by taxed income. The other member of the group held out in confusion at what inheritance tax was. When it was explained, she too raged at its apparent injustice. Around the same time, journalists from the *Express*, that tribune of the strivers, came in to the shadow Chancellor's office to show him a petition of their readers demanding a change to inheritance tax. 'If something's a big issue, then it's a big issue,' Osborne began to say to colleagues. He was searching for a policy spectacular enough to change the political weather. He had thought about proposing a subsidy for working parents to buy childcare but Brown's spending on Sure Start and other early-years programmes gave him credibility in this area. A radical reform of inheritance tax seemed more distinctively Tory, and likelier to electrify the press. The remaining questions were profound, however: how to pay for it and how to prevent it being portrayed as a sop to the rich.

The solution occurred to him while he was lying in a hammock on holiday in Corfu. 'I've got it,' he said to Hancock upon his return to Westminster. 'We'll get the money from even richer people.' His plan was to raise the threshold of inheritance tax to a big round number, probably £1 million, and pay for it by raising money from wealthy individuals who lived in Britain but were not domiciled there for tax purposes. These 'non-doms' had become tabloid villains and Harrison had already done some research into ways of bringing them within the tax system.

By now, opponents of the policy accepted that Osborne was set on it, and switched their energies to moderating its scale. When the subject was discussed in a meeting in Cameron's office, the likes of Letwin and Gove favoured a lower threshold of perhaps £500,000. Osborne insisted that this was not vivid enough to cut through to voters. 'No, it has to be a million,' he insisted. A colleague recalls that: 'He was very clear that we needed something that would change the terms of political debate.' To pay for this, along with a parallel policy to abolish stamp duty for many first time buyers, Osborne needed to find just over £3 billion.

Harrison was set to work. He concluded that an annual levy of £25,000 on non-doms would be enough. This was optimistic, but available data about non-doms was so sketchy that nobody would be able to prove the Tory calculation conclusively wrong. 'The government would try,' says an insider, 'but we could bog them down in a row about it.' The formation of the policy was Harrison's blooding as a political adviser. Osborne, who had always teased him for his Corinthian scholarship, was gratified by his conversion to the ruthless expediency of politics. 'Ah, Dr Harrison,' he would jibe. 'Where's your PhD now?'

When the Conservatives gathered in Blackpool that October, a confluence of events suddenly gave them the political momentum that Brown had hogged since June. A nakedly political visit to Iraq during the conference made the Prime Minister look, for the first time, anything but statesmanlike – as Liam Fox, the Tories' irate defence spokesman, argued from the podium. In an elegantly lethal intervention, John Major condemned Brown for 'the nods, the winks, the hints, the cynicism, the belief that every decision is being taken because it is marching to the drumbeat of an election rather than to the drumbeat of solid, proper government'. Another sparkling, notes-free speech from Cameron made Brown's limp effort at his own conference the previous week look all the worse.

But the single most important event was Osborne's announcement of his inheritance tax reform, complete with its raid on non-doms. The rapturous reaction in the hall shocked Osborne himself; the delirious coverage in the following day's press was exactly what he had bargained for. The Tories surged in the polls and suddenly the snap election that Brown had toyed with since July became a foolhardy gamble. Had he gone to the polls when the idea first occurred, he would have won. Had he ruled it out from the start, he could have got on with governing. By doing neither, by taunting his opponents with a Damoclean threat without ever even privately deciding whether to use it, he had allowed the speculation to get out of control. He now faced a choice between holding an election that he would, at best, win with a diminished majority, or backing down ignominiously. When he discovered that a survey of marginal constituencies about to be published in the *News of the World* gave the Conservatives a small lead, his mind was made up.

He summoned Andrew Marr of the BBC to Downing Street and told the nation that there would not be an election after all. At a press conference soon after, he denied, with laughable implausibility, that his decision was motivated by the souring polls. Then, during the subsequent pre-Budget report, the Chancellor Alistair Darling announced a version of the Tories' inheritance tax policy while Brown grinned demonically, bizarrely delighting in his own intellectual capitulation and tactical game-playing. Taken together, the snap election fiasco was a clarifying event. Tentatively whispered criticisms of Brown – his inability to take a decision, his obsession with political tactics, his bouts of pusillanimity – immediately became received opinion. It is almost impossible to overstate the pace and depth of his fall. From the moment of the Marr interview, it became hard to imagine Brown winning a general election – whenever it was called.

Osborne remains convinced that it was his intervention, more than anything else, that did for Brown. He is right. But the inheritance tax announcement was a clarifying event for him, too. Just as it showcased his political prowess, it also exhibited some of his weaknesses. The policy was itself as tactical as anything in Brown's repertoire. Exquisitely calibrated for the moment, it was to look embarrassingly inappropriate in the dire economic conditions to come. Three years later, Osborne would neither mention his inheritance tax policy during the general election campaign nor fight for it in the subsequent coalition negotiations with the Liberal Democrats.

It may have also inflicted strategic damage by undermining the party's claims to social justice. The average British house, at just £170,000, was never in any danger of incurring inheritance tax. Even if there was a case for lifting the threshold somewhat, raising it to what was effectively £2 million (by allowing the £1 million threshold to be transferred to a spouse) was an extraordinary leap. As Labour recovered its pluck and poise in the run-up to the election, they were able to mock the policy as perhaps the only tax change whose beneficiaries were all known personally to its author.

Today, in the view of a growing group of thoughtful Conservatives, including the blogger and columnist Tim Mongtomerie, the Tories' gravest political danger is being seen as defenders of entrenched wealth rather than earned income. The solution, they say, is to gradually shift the burden of taxation from wages to assets. Cutting inheritance tax does the opposite. In 2007, Osborne's policy was an ingenious gambit that genuinely changed political history. But it was very much of its time, and nobody who was asked about the policy's future for this book believes that it will ever be implemented.

Amid the euphoric din surrounding Osborne's policy, another announcement was lost. He confirmed that the Tories would match Labour's spending plans, which would take overall expenditure from £615 billion in 2008/09 to £674 billion in 2010/11 – although he left the final year's total open to later review. The political justification for the commitment was Osborne's homespun baseline theory: any deviation from a Labour government's macro-economic fiscal policy would be mercilessly portrayed as an assault on public services. By hugging the Labour line, he would neutralise tax and spend as an electoral issue in the way Brown had done a decade earlier. There was also an economic case: the Labour plan was slightly more cautious than previous spending rounds. It envisaged spending growing more slowly than the economy, which gave the Tories scope to honour their pledge to use some of the proceeds of growth to cut taxes. Nevertheless, there were grumblings among the right. Within a year, they would almost drown Osborne out.

An extraordinary turnaround had been wrought. The

Conservatives had gone into their conference braced for a fourth consecutive election defeat. They left it as favourites to form the next government. Brown was diminished and Cameron enhanced, but Osborne was the only individual who could claim to have actively engineered the change in fortunes. It would turn out to be the high watermark of his own shadow chancellorship, and a turning point in the modernisation of the Conservative Party. That project had always taken economic prosperity as a given. Its tolerance of munificent spending, its subjugation of GDP to 'general well-being', its preening verbosity on environmental matters – all this assumed that the central issue in politics, the economy, was no longer very central.

That assumption was falling apart even as Osborne collected his personal glory that autumn. Financial institutions were increasingly nervous about their exposure to the American sub-prime mortgage market, where returns were undershooting expectations. The rate of interest at which British banks were borrowing from each other rose steeply in September, forcing Northern Rock, a mortgage-lender based in Newcastle, to seek emergency finance from the Bank of England. As soon as this news broke, Northern Rock branches were deluged by customers demanding to withdraw their deposits. Alistair Darling soothed the panic by guaranteeing all Northern Rock deposits but its share price continued to collapse. Worse, anxiety infected other institutions, and lending began to freeze up. After two decades of cheap and plentiful finance, the phrase 'credit crunch' became ubiquitous. Within a year, it would soon give way to 'crash'.

IO.

The Big Bang

'George realised that where this was all
going to go eventually was public debt.'

In the aftermath of 9/11, George Will, the American
Pulitzer Prize winner, pronounced the end of his country's 'holiday from history'. The decade leading up to the
attacks was frivolous and indulgent, he argued. Seemingly
invincible peace and prosperity had enervated a great nation
of its seriousness and sober vigilance. Looking back, Britain's
own holiday from history did not end until the autumn of 2007.
The previous decade and a half had seen an unprecedented
economic expansion built on hard work, competitive tax rates
and flexible labour laws – but also cheap credit, government
largesse and a rigged housing market that created hordes of
accidental millionaires. The demise of Northern Rock was the
beginning of the end of this culture of easy money.

It was also Osborne's opportunity to turn his moment of
strength into lasting ascendancy. After all, the government had
not only presided over the first run on a bank in over a century,
it was floundering in its search for a private buyer for Northern
Rock and dithering over whether to take it into public ownership. More fundamentally, the institutional architecture it had
put in place to regulate the financial system – a 'tripartite' model

comprising the Bank of England, the Treasury and the Financial Services Authority (FSA) – had palpably failed. But the decisive blow was never dealt. Instead, Osborne himself drew the severest criticism of his time as shadow Chancellor so far. That autumn, as it became increasingly obvious that nationalisation was the least bad option for the stricken mortgage lender, Osborne opposed it. Meanwhile, Vince Cable showed decisive alacrity in urging public ownership. The Liberal Democrat Treasury spokesman, a generation older than Osborne and a former chief economist for Shell, became the early star of the credit crunch. Those close to Osborne now confess they found him an 'irritant' who was 'completely brash in claiming credit for predicting the crash'.

By February, the government had accepted the inevitable and made arrangements for Northern Rock's nationalisation. Cable, whose facility with both economics and one-liners had made him the 'real shadow Chancellor' in many minds, claimed vindication. The Tories continued to flounder. When Osborne and Cameron held a joint press conference to announce the death of New Labour, their own reputation suffered more than the government's. True, Osborne had by now evolved an internally coherent alternative to public ownership: a 'Bank of England-led reconstruction' in which Threadneedle Street would preside over a winding down and revival of Northern Rock. But the legal power to do this did not exist (it does now, thanks to new legislation) and his team knew they were defending a weak position: 'We were saying the government should do this and castigating the government for not having introduced the powers to do it. You can't make both points at the same time.'

Why was Osborne so averse to public ownership? Many accused him of right-wing dogma but he is an unlikely ideologue. A simple lack of imagination was closer to the truth. Throughout his adult life, nationalisation was synonymous with an unelectable Labour Party. In the particular case of Northern Rock in 2007/08, it was the purest common sense. His intellectual frame of reference failed to adapt to dramatically different circumstances. But the main reason for his position was political. 'George had learned from years in opposition that if you agree with the government, you become totally irrelevant,' says a senior Tory. 'Our principal reason for opposing it was tactical.'

Osborne was generally only willing to support a government policy if it was so in line with centre-right ideals that the Conservatives would be mad to oppose it, or if there was a chance of driving a wedge between the Prime Minister and his backbenchers. His support for Tony Blair's city academies was a case in point. The ugliness of this approach lay in its cynicism and tactical focus. The sunnier interpretation is that, were Osborne in power, he would most likely have nationalised Northern Rock, or at least not resisted it on principle.

That was not the only mitigating aspect of Osborne's reaction to the bank's woes. He was also increasingly conscious of the government's fiscal position. Although Britain was heading into a likely recession with a Budget deficit – itself astonishing after fifteen years of uninterrupted economic growth – Osborne was earlier than most senior politicians in wondering exactly how much banking intervention a stretched public purse could afford. 'George realised that where this was all going to go eventually was public debt,' says Hancock.[103]

That winter, Osborne and Cameron were joined at the top table of British politics by another youthful, expensively educated centrist and professional politician. By an excruciatingly fine margin, the Liberal Democrats had chosen Nick Clegg over the more left-wing Chris Huhne to replace their outgoing leader, Menzies Campbell. Clegg, like Laws, was a free-market liberal on the 'Orange' wing of his party. He was also cosmopolitan and socially liberal. But for their divergent views on foreign policy – Clegg was a Europhile, and more dovish on the use of force – he was rather like Osborne. Yet the shadow Chancellor was dismissive of Clegg. This was partly pique brought on by the new leader's refusal of a dinner invitation from Osborne and Cameron, but there was more to it than that.

Osborne had pondered the Lib Dems' strategic dilemma since his time as their tormentor in the Conservatives' Political Section. The party was the product of the old Liberals and the defunct Social Democrats who broke away from Labour in the '8os. He believed that their electoral interests lay in honouring the latter tradition and taking votes from Labour. (Finkelstein agreed and wrote columns throughout Clegg's time as an opposition leader deriding the political wisdom of his classical liberal platform.) Osborne's self-interest was obvious – a left-leaning third party would split the anti-Tory vote – but he genuinely believed that Clegg was politically clueless. He would have to revise this view during the next general election campaign.

Neither Osborne's confusion over Northern Rock nor his increasingly unsustainable commitment to match Labour's spending plans was hindering the Tories' progress in the polls. What had been a modest lead over Labour for much of the two years of Cameron's leadership suddenly widened in the spring of 2008. The excitable Brownites who had counselled a snap election were right about one thing: the economy, which showed signs of weakness throughout 2007, was never likely to be better the following year. In private, Osborne struggled to disguise his eager anticipation of a quarter of negative growth that would finally blemish Brown's immaculate record. It finally came in the third quarter of 2008. The implications of the news were fearful: tax revenues would dry up and unemployment benefits soar.

Harrison received intimations from Stewart Wood, an adviser

to Brown who had taught him at Oxford, that the public finances were experiencing a sheer drop.

Indeed, the Tories were doing so well that Cameron felt able to cope without his strategist Steve Hilton, who departed for a year in California, where his wife Rachel Whetstone worked for the technology giant Google. Of all the individuals at the very top of the party, Hilton was the most unusual, compelling – and misunderstood. Although he had made his name as an advertising man, and choreographed Cameron's symbolic visit to a melting glacier in 2006, he was much more animated by a desire to shake up Britain's hulking, centralised and haughtily opaque state. He advocated radical reforms to the public services and a spectacular devolution of power not only to local government (which he thought should take the form of elected mayors rather than faceless councils) but to individuals, communities and voluntary groups. He was the ultimate 'punk Tory', both in his worldview and in the ornery, incendiary way he pushed it.

Hilton's exit risked disrupting the political balance at the top of the party. Cameron had always gone to Hilton for vision and to Osborne for political calculation. As political courts go, this one was exquisitely balanced. 'It helps David's thought process to have different views around him,' says one of those closest to him. 'He triangulated between Steve and George.'[104] With the radical gone, and with the influence of the no-nonsense Coulson burgeoning, Cameron now had a surfeit of hard-headedness but nobody in his inner circle with a clear and synoptic view of what a modern Conservative government would actually do. The impulse to modernise – to be restless in finding ways of showing that these were not the 'same old Tories' – might also flag. To avert all this, Hilton was to remain in constant touch with Cameron and other senior Conservatives during his time in California.

There were more tangible gains for the Tories that summer than mere poll leads. In May, the death of the veteran Labour MP Gwyneth Dunwoody created a by-election in her Crewe & Nantwich seat, not far from Tatton. The Conservative candidate was Edward Timpson, a scion of the shoe repair fortune who was born in Osborne's constituency. Labour fought a nakedly class-based campaign against him. When he prevailed regardless, it was not only interpreted as a revival of the Tories' popularity in the north but also as confirmation of the death of class war. Both conclusions were sanguine, especially the second. Timpson's parents were rich but exceptionally big-hearted, fostering eighty-seven children over a period of thirty years. Labour's crude tactics, which included trailing him with an apparatchik dressed in a top hat and tails, were never likely to impress voters. None of this meant that a subtler critique of the Tories as a party of privilege could not work, especially against a less sympathetic candidate.

In June, the Tories won another by-election but in the oddest circumstances conceivable. Brown had passed legislation allowing terror suspects to be detained without charge for up to forty-two days. The Tories, led by David Davis, who melded a hawkish line on crime with a rather doctrinaire civil libertarianism, had fought the legislation. This was despite the advice of Gove, who sympathised with the government's argument, and Osborne, who also worried about the political danger of seeming soft on terrorism. In perhaps the most eccentric resignation in postwar political history, Davis then left the shadow Cabinet, and Parliament, so that he could stand in the subsequent by-election on a single-issue libertarian platform. He won, predictably and utterly pointlessly. Osborne could scarcely believe he had thrown away his frontbench career (for neither he nor Cameron were minded to bring back a character they regarded as erratic) so cheaply. One colleague recalls it as the only occasion he had ever seen Osborne truly lose his temper, cursing Davis as flaky and self-indulgent. But Osborne's anger was, in itself, a kind of compliment. Davis – intelligent, forceful and thoroughly self-made – was an asset, and the Tories would never adequately replace him as shadow Home Secretary.

Such disruptions were as nothing next to Labour's deafening implosion. In August, the two great curses of Brown's premiership – economic failure and the government's own fissiparousness – collided when Darling gave an interview to *The Observer*. With what now reads like magisterial understatement, the Chancellor told his inquisitor that the recession would be the worst for sixty years. This contradicted more soothing but less realistic noises put out by the Prime Minister and his allies, who then unleashed what Darling would call 'the forces of hell' upon the Chancellor. Days of vicious briefing left the Treasury feeling less like Whitehall's mightiest ministry than a besieged fort. Osborne's delight at the government's self-mutilation was tempered by the knowledge that Darling was right. Nobody at the top of the party expected anything other than a deep and prolonged recession. Letwin was 'always the most gloomy', according to one insider, but Hancock also put the chances of a 'cataclysmic meltdown' at one in four.

Letwin is among the most curious specimens of Tory anthropology. He inherited scholarly gifts from his mother, the philosopher Shirley Letwin, and taught at Princeton University before making his way in the cerebral corners of the City. None of this suggests a worldly ken and at times he seems almost uniquely unsuited to practical politics. Yet his cunning and judgement are underrated. In the summer of 2008, when the Tories were as high as 50 per cent in the polls, he privately insisted that the next general election would result in a hung Parliament. He foresaw

a resurgence for Brown and grasped the mathematical reality
that fewer and fewer voters were supporting the major parties.
Nobody in the upper reaches of the Conservative Party was
anything like as bearish.

Letwin, who served as a kind of policy overlord, was struck
by Osborne's ability to 'combine robust and meticulous attention to detail with a capacity to abstract from it and see the big
picture historically, politically and economically'.[105] The shadow
Chancellor called upon this faculty as the global financial system
suffered sickening paroxysms that summer. He knew that he had
to respond to the upheaval with a strategic, overarching vision
rather than the tactical gestures with which he met Northern
Rock's downfall. That vision would turn out to be the fiscal
conservatism he had first adumbrated in 2006, and which defines
his chancellorship today.

His instinctive fear earlier in 2008 – that public debt was
about to become a crippling affliction for Britain – hardened as
figures showed the government had borrowed £38 billion in the
first six months of the financial year, the highest amount since
records began in 1946. Economists close to the Osborne team
were warning them to expect a Budget deficit of at least £100
billion to be announced the following year – a bracing estimate
which actually turned out to be too sanguine. 'In the long term,
all anyone is going to be talking about is debt,' Osborne told
colleagues that summer.

Contemplating the chaos from his office in Westminster,
Osborne, in a moment of clarity chronicled by Finkelstein in
The Times:

> … took out a piece of paper and started drawing boxes on it. He
> drew quite a number. 'VAT cuts', read one little box, 'spending',
> read another, 'the top rate', read a third. Then his pencil hovered

over the paper. 'Only one of these boxes can be a fixed point,' he explained. 'My strategy for opposing Alistair Darling and fixing the economy depends on selecting that fixed point. The other boxes move around it.' And then George Osborne brought his pencil down. 'And this is my fixed point,' he said, stabbing the box that read 'lower borrowing'.[106]

Restoring Britain to fiscal health was to be his mission. Austerity, though he would almost never use the word, would be his strategy. The next eighteen months would be spent giving it substance. On 5 September, he appeared as the guest on BBC Radio 4's *Great Lives*, a programme which allows a public figure to choose a hero from history. Osborne plumped for Henry VII. 'He's not, probably, a very likeable man, but he's the man who sorts out the finances of the Crown,' he explained, with an eerie prescience that he could not possibly have grasped.[107]

His first idea was the least contentious. One reason Brown had been able to get away with his profligacy was the absence of any independent fiscal authority to reckon with. The Treasury itself made forecasts for growth and borrowing, and could tweak these according to political expediency. If borrowing was expanding alarmingly, Brown could nudge up the growth forecasts to make the projected deficit look more bearable. When he seemed to be flunking his own 'golden rule' of balancing the Budget over the economic cycle, he could simply extend the definition of that cycle. So, in the run-up to the Conservative Party conference in Birmingham, Harrison drew up a proposal for an independent Office for Budget Responsibility (OBR). It would handle forecasting and pronounce upon whether the government was meeting its own rules and targets. It lacked the formal power to sanction the Chancellor, leading some to worry that it was just a statutory version of the IFS, but he would be politically constrained in a way that he currently was not.

Osborne's second move was to extricate himself, ignominiously but unavoidably, from his commitment to match Labour's spending plans. Throughout the summer, senior Tories had discussed whether and how to do this. The most hawkish included Letwin, Coulson and Hilton, who had worried about the commitment from the beginning. Michael Spencer, the party treasurer, made the same case more tentatively. Osborne, like Cameron, had resisted their pressure for fear that Brown, yet again, would bludgeon the Tories with talk of 'investment versus cuts'. But the politics of clinging to an incredible policy were now even worse than the politics of departing from the safety of the baseline.

When, in early September, Osborne finally indicated that he would not match Labour's spending total for 2010/11, he honoured the letter of his original commitment. He had always left that final year, when he expected to be in government, open to revision – 'so we never actually U-turned', says a member of his team. Regardless, just as Osborne's refusal to countenance unfunded tax cuts in 2006 was vindicated by the crash, so too was the right's opposition to his spending pledge. Worse than this humiliation at the hands of his own side, he would never be able to accuse Labour of feckless spending without being reminded of his own tacit indulgence of it.

Osborne's commitment to match Labour's plans illustrated the extent to which he was haunted by the recent past. He had seen his party offer the electorate slightly slower spending growth than Labour in 2001 and 2005, and lose heavily on both occasions. Although he had never shown outward fear of Brown, he was enduringly scarred by his brutal dominance of the fiscal and economic discourse of the latter boom years. His brief time as shadow Chief Secretary had left him with a particularly deep mark – and a determination to never again let Brown deploy his lethal mantra of 'investment versus cuts'. One observer of Tory politics believes that Osborne's time as an opposition apparatchik during Brown's all-conquering chancellorship left him 'mentally trapped' by the man he professes to hate. 'He fights old wars and is always a zeitgeist behind. If his job were done by someone who had come from outside Westminster, the Tories would never have adopted [Labour's spending plans].'

Even an adviser close to Osborne likens him to an 'abused puppy' that flinches at anything even vaguely evocative of its old tormentor. His traumatic experiences had taught him the folly of failing to match the government's spending totals. Indeed, a shadow Chancellor who chose to deviate from Labour's fiscal plans for a third successive election would have risked meeting Einstein's definition of insanity. The irony of all this is that Osborne would go on to do exactly that.

As the conference season approached, the global financial system entered its first truly existential crisis since the 1930s. Even a bank as venerable as Lehman Brothers was struggling to raise enough money on the markets to continue operating. Over a weekend in New York, the federal government brought the heads of all the major American banks together to find a private-sector solution but refused to contemplate a bailout. On 15 September, these efforts failed and Lehman filed for the biggest bankruptcy in American history. Osborne and his team were surprised by the willingness of Hank Paulson, the US Treasury Secretary, to let Lehman go under. After all, he had saved Bear Stearns, a less important bank, earlier in the year and extended a credit line to the insurer AIG the day after Lehman's collapse. Banks suddenly realised that they could no longer count on the implicit guarantee of government support if the worst came to the worst. Predictably, they tightened lending even further and markets almost completely froze up.

Closer to home, the Prime Minister was resurgent. Brown had faced veiled leadership threats from David Miliband over the summer but the Foreign Secretary's prevarication, and Brown's own poise in the face of the financial crisis, had put paid to all that. His speech to his party conference in Manchester showed exactly the clarity of vision that eluded him a year before. True, he had the ultimate advantage over his opponents – the formal power to act during the crisis – but he used it deftly, bringing another ailing mortgage-lender, Bradford & Bingley, into public ownership at the end of September. Harrison drew up two options for a Conservative response to this latest nationalisation. They could honour the precedent they set when Northern Rock failed by opposing the nationalisation, and justify it on the 'Bagehot principle' that only large, systemic banks should get a public rescue. Alternatively, they could support it on the basis that what began as a contained credit crunch in 2007 had become a mortal menace to the global economy. Osborne and Cameron, both of whom felt trapped by their opposition to Northern Rock's nationalisation, chose the latter course without much enthusiasm.

Brown's impressive grip on the crisis was eroding the Conservatives' poll lead. He had another opportunity to take charge when, on 29 September, the first day of the Tory conference in Birmingham, the US Congress voted down Paulson's Temporary Asset Relief Programme (TARP), effectively a bailout of American banks. Markets convulsed. If Lehman exposed the American government's lack of will to stem the crisis, TARP's rejection revealed something far more terrifying – its outright inability to do so. For all the outward grandeur of the presidency, the separation of powers ensures that an American government has less power within its own country than any British administration with a comfortable majority.

Osborne, who gave an unremarkable speech earlier in the day whose main item was a voter-friendly freeze in council tax, watched the news on the television in Cameron's hotel suite, with a dazed Hilton lying flat on the floor. At a late-night party – where, as throughout the conference, MPs and advisers were instructed by the leadership not to be seen drinking champagne – Harrison was asked by a layman about the implications of Lehman's collapse and the rejection of TARP. 'Worst-case scenario is that the global financial system just stops,' answered one of the least excitable personalities in politics.

The Tories' plans for a conventional conference – with Cameron doing no more than a *tour d'horizon* in his keynote speech – were now shot. The leader, desperate to avoid being seen as partisan, gave an emergency mini-speech on 30 September pledging statesmanlike support for the government in its efforts to deal with the crisis. He would not allow technical objections, such as the Tories' preference for the Bank of England over the Financial Services Authority as the lead body in dealing with troubled banks, to get in the way of a solution. It was a purely symbolic gesture, of course, as Labour's parliamentary majority freed it from any need for Tory support, but it was well-judged regardless.

Afterwards, Osborne and Harrison headed to London for a courtesy briefing on the crisis from Darling, during which the shadow Chancellor offered his support for the government's proposed banking Bill. Osborne also met Hector Sants, the head of the FSA, and spoke to Mervyn King on the telephone. Meanwhile, Cameron's team reworked his main speech for the last day of the conference. This was a chance to expound a measured but distinctively Conservative approach to the financial crisis as a whole. Instead, it dwelt on Cameron himself. The Tories were right that a leader's character is a surer guide to his performance in a crisis than any particular plan or policy, but this kind of personal exposition demands stronger material than they managed. 'I've studied economics at a great university,' is not a line that has improved with time.

Whatever travails he has known since – the failure to win a general election, the economy's double-dip recession – October 2008 remains the most personally trying month of Osborne's career. Cable continued to radiate a clout and sardonic sagacity that captivated journalists, so much so that they spared him the scrutiny to which Osborne was subjected. Brown, too, was enjoying the bounce in the polls predicted by Letwin a few months earlier and sought to press his advantage with a stupefyingly improbable Cabinet appointment. In the cold war between Blair and Brown that began when the former claimed the Labour leadership in 1994, no individual drew as much ire as Peter Mandelson. Brown, in a classic case of psychological displacement, blamed him for somehow engineering Blair's coup. It was a Brownite journalist, Paul Routledge, whose biography of Mandelson in 1998 revealed the controversial mortgage arrangements that forced Mandelson out of the Cabinet. He would return the following year only to resign over another scandal and seek his fortune in Brussels as the EU's trade commissioner.

But Brown never lost his regard for Mandelson's political skills. He was more than the oleaginous spinner of caricature, he also possessed executive competence and a Blairite feel for public opinion. So, during a visit to London, Mandelson was summoned to Downing Street by his nemesis and offered a peerage, the substantive job of Business Secretary and the honorific title of 'First Secretary of State' – just to underline the broader political influence he would wield within government. Osborne was even more astonished than the rest of Westminster. He had encountered Mandelson on his summer holiday in Corfu, where both were guests of the financier (and Osborne's student friend) Nat Rothschild, and gleaned no sign that his relationship with Brown was healing. Indeed, as Osborne mischievously mentioned to journalists during the Tory conference, Mandelson actually 'dripped pure poison' in his ear about Brown. The quote was published and attributed to Osborne in the *Daily Mail* and the *Daily Telegraph* on 6 October.

If Osborne thought he was being cunning, the initial evidence proved him right. The media examined whether Oleg Deripaska, a Russian aluminium tycoon who was also among Rothschild's guests, had benefited from decisions taken by Mandelson as Trade Commissioner. But the scrutiny soon turned to Osborne himself. His gossip inaugurated a sequence of events that almost ended his career. First, Mandelson indicated to journalists that he could reveal equally embarrassing remarks that Osborne had made about the Conservatives during their time together in Corfu. Then, on 21 October, a letter from Rothschild appeared in *The Times* that deplored the newspaper's focus on Mandelson and immediately embroiled Osborne in serious scandal:

Not once in the acres of coverage did you mention that George Osborne, who also accepted my hospitality, found the opportunity of meeting with Mr Deripaska so good that he invited the Conservatives' fundraiser Andrew Feldman, who was staying nearby, to accompany him on to Mr Deripaska's boat to solicit a donation.

Since Mr Deripaska is not a British citizen, it was suggested by Mr Feldman, in a subsequent conversation at which Mr Deripaska was not present, that the donation was 'channelled' through one of Mr Deripaska's British companies. Mr Deripaska declined to make any donation.

Donations from foreign nationals to British political parties are not permitted by law. Fighting for Osborne's career, Conservative Campaign Headquarters (CCHQ) issued a statement denying that either he or Feldman had solicited any money from Deripaska or suggested any mechanism by which a donation could be channelled legally. He then had to face the media himself. With Hilton and Coulson, he drafted a statement in Cameron's office repeating his denial of Rothschild's allegations before setting off to CCHQ to deliver it in front of journalists and cameramen. The staff rose and applauded him on his way out.

The statement was strong enough to buy him time and highlighted the fact that no donation had actually been given. 'Journalists say "follow the money" but in this case there is no money to follow,' quipped Osborne, who also had to sit down with one of his aides, Seth Cumming, and draw up a chronology recounting his movements and conversations during his time in Corfu. When Brown demanded an investigation into the matter the following day, it actually served to shore up Osborne's position as the authority in question, the Electoral Commission, confirmed that, even if he had asked Deripaska for a donation, solicitation itself was not an offence.

Exactly how close Osborne came to losing his job divides opinion among senior Tories. Cameron showed no outward sign that he was contemplating his friend's dismissal, even in front of his very closest aides. Ian Katz of *The Guardian* called his friend Hilton to say that he thought Osborne would go, only for Hilton to vehemently trash the idea. But neither Osborne himself nor his own team were anything like as confident. He knew that even if his behaviour in Corfu did not by itself merit a resignation, the timing of its revelation to coincide with unconvincing performances as shadow Chancellor could do for him. Osborne had been planning to announce his idea of a National Insurance 'holiday' for employers but he was forced to delay it. 'We can't do this one because if it goes wrong, I'm finished,' he said to his aides, 'so coolly it was as if he was talking about someone else.' 'That was a very, very bad forty-eight hours for George,' agrees another member of his team. 'He genuinely thought he could go.' Many other leaders would have ditched him. The episode captured the strangeness of the relationship between the Tories' ruling duo: Osborne alternated between effectively managing Cameron to only holding onto his own job because of Cameron's indulgence.

Osborne and his family had been taking holidays in Corfu in the years leading up to 2008. As they were approaching the end of their stay that summer, Rothschild, according to Osborne, asked him to extend his holiday by a week and stay at his hillside villa, where he was to host Elizabeth Murdoch's fortieth birthday party. Before the soirée, Osborne and his wife were invited by Deripaska, whom the shadow Chancellor had met in Davos that year, to board his yacht, the *Queen K*. Ironically, Osborne thought that this would be politically uncontroversial precisely because Mandelson, a European Commissioner no less, was already staying on the boat. Osborne was impressed by Deripaska, who is an intellectual as well as an industrialist, and the pair discussed Russian history and politics. They met again on three occasions during the holiday – once more aboard *Queen K* – but Osborne insists that neither he nor Feldman (who had dropped by from his own nearby holiday) ever discussed donations with the Russian.

Although Osborne survived his brush with political mortality, it put him out of commission during a momentous period for the world economy. Brown was planning a massive bailout for Britain's banks, including the Royal Bank of Scotland, Lloyds TSB and HBOS, and a discretionary fiscal stimulus comprising a temporary cut in VAT to boost demand, but the Tories' main economic spokesman could not respond. 'There was a two- or three-week period when George couldn't get his economic message across,' admits a member of his team, who says that this was doubly problematic because that message was complicated: yes to a bailout but no to a stimulus. One of Osborne's critics in the media suggests, counter-intuitively, that the scandal actually helped the shadow Chancellor by giving the impression that his biggest failing was one of ethical judgement rather than basic economic competence.

'Yachtgate' exhibited Osborne's personal foibles. His attraction to glamour and power, his addiction to the 'game' of political intrigue, his occasionally sybaritic lifestyle – all these dangerous and, ironically, Mandelsonian quirks had long been known to insiders, but were now unmistakable to a wider audience too. If he joined the Bullingdon Club out of a restless desire to belong to the loftiest social circles, perhaps he boarded Deripaska's yacht for much the same reason. Although Cameron was another Buller man, it was hard to imagine him craving glitzy company in quite the same way. In the aftermath of Yachtgate, Coulson told a colleague that the difference between Osborne and Cameron could be captured by one thing: 'Dave would never have got on that boat.'

For all this, the scandal did leave one constructive legacy for Osborne's career. It made it petrifyingly clear to him how few friends he had among Conservative MPs. During the worst of the crisis, Liam Fox was almost the only prominent Tory to take to the airwaves in his defence. Many others were (anonymously) contemptuous of him, and at best indifferent as to whether he survived. Ever since, he has toiled as hard to win friends in Parliament as he always has to cultivate allies in the media and in business. He spends time in the Commons tea

room and invites backbenchers to dinners and seminars at No.
11. This strategic sociability is often interpreted as the ground-
work for a future leadership run but Osborne's first motive
is defensive: he knows the vulnerability that comes without a
parliamentary base.

Two weeks after the worst of the scandal had died down,
Osborne received a friendly text message from Rothschild.
He did not respond. Nowadays, Osborne prefers to holiday
in Majorca.

Osborne's political position had stabilised in time for Darling's
pre-Budget report (PBR) of 24 November. The Chancellor
confirmed that VAT would fall from 17.5 per cent to 15 per cent
for just over a year. The cut, introduced in time for the Christmas
shopping period, would cost £12.5 billion and, along with other
measures, send borrowing up to £118 billion the following year.
It was an 'exceptional' measure, Darling said, to mitigate what
he had correctly predicted would be the deepest recession since
the war.

Osborne's opposition to the tax cut remains the single
most contentious decision he made in his five years as shadow
Chancellor. But it was virtually assured from the moment, earlier
in 2008, that he alighted upon government indebtedness rather
than the immediate collapse of growth as the gravest economic
threat menacing Britain. A discretionary stimulus would, he
argued, raise interest rates in the long term and sully Britain's
credibility in international financial markets. This was fully
eighteen months before sovereign debt did indeed become the
central problem in the world economy – a lag that rendered
Osborne's judgement either prescient or premature.

The Tories thought it was for the Bank of England to fight the
immediate battle of the recession. In a speech on 31 October,
Osborne invoked Nigel Lawson's Mais Lecture of 1984 – an

intellectual influence on him, and on Harrison – to argue that fiscal policy should be set for the long term while monetary policy adapts to control short-term demand. It remains the essence of his economic strategy, and a point of difference with Ed Balls, his more Keynesian opponent on the Labour benches. Osborne also doubted the effectiveness of the tax cut on its own terms. Not only was a minor easing of the sales tax an expensive way of making not very much difference to economic pandemonium, it might actually dampen demand and increase saving. This was because of 'Ricardian equivalence', the theory that consumers are canny enough to know that any tax cut will be offset eventually by a tax rise, and to prepare their finances accordingly. Indeed, Darling's statement included plans for future hikes in income tax and National Insurance.

In short, Osborne opposed the stimulus because he genuinely believed it was a mistake. His purely tactical aversion to agreeing with the government was nothing like as pronounced as it had been over Northern Rock. The emergence of an elite consensus in favour of Keynesian intervention, including among fiscally conservative publications such as *The Economist*, made the short-term politics of opposing the government actually rather grim. The Tories were isolated from respectable opinion, and even from some of their own backbenchers, who never met a tax cut they didn't like. In the final weeks of 2008, Cameron felt vulnerable to Brown's bludgeoning depiction of the Conservatives as a 'do nothing' party, as emails he exchanged with his closest colleagues reveal. On the evening of Sunday 7 December, Cameron insisted that:

> Our main reason for being against the fiscal stimulus in the UK is that we cannot afford it – we would take a different view and support tax reduction now if we had a surplus as some other

countries do. (The US is different, reserve currency, much lower imports as share of GDP, etc. I don't think we should get into a row about this. We are arguing the right thing for the UK.)

The whole point about the PBR is that it showed the government can't afford it – as they had to announce future tax rises etc. – this is where the economic narrative ('We can't afford it') meets the political narrative ('They screwed up and are trying to bluff their way out of it').

Cameron's anxiety about America being invoked by Labour as vindication of their own policy was shared by Hilton, who wrote the day before that:

we really need to nail the US point. On a superficial level, people hear all this talk of hundreds of billions being spent in America – the read-across is that they're doing a fiscal stimulus – so why not us? We really need to explain the argument and cite academic sources etc. etc. and address the great depression thing too.

Osborne, for his part, was less worried about the 'do-nothing' charge, as was Hancock. (Harrison and Silva were more nervous.) Osborne wrote in an email on 7 December that the Tories' real priority was to:

respond to Brown/Mandelson's idea of the 'smart strategic state' which the commentators have been salivating about for the last three days ... Attack it as a return to failed corporatism, dressed up in new language. Where is the evidence that a Labour government will be smarter at picking winners in 2007 than it was in 1977?

He also wanted to stress the long-termism of his position.

A key theme ... could be the inter-generational fairness one –
i.e. you shouldn't be doing things now (as they did in 60s/70s)
which make things so much more difficult down the track for the
next generation. It's a strong theme that underpins the national
debt/tax bombshell arguments. It's got a good Conservative
pedigree etc.

What the Conservatives really needed were tangible signs that
the tax cut was not working, and these arrived in the new year.
Not only were retail figures disappointing but a survey by the
British Chambers of Commerce showed that three-quarters of
businesses found the VAT cut of no use, while 16 per cent actually said it was more of a burden than a boon. Meanwhile, the
public finances plummeted.

None of this, of course, was categorical proof that Darling's
policy had failed. Despite the mystifying certainty of both left and
right during and since the crash, economics is not a pure science.
It does not generate absolute metaphysical truths grounded on
incontestable evidence in the way mathematics or the natural
sciences do – something Harrison, who initially studied Physics
at university before switching to Politics, Philosophy and
Economics, understands better than most. Even the most basic
of its assumptions – that prices go up in response to demand, for
example – don't always hold in real life. Instead, it is a discipline
of arguments and counter-arguments, with each side able to
quote greater or lesser amounts of evidence in their support. It
will never be 'known' whether Osborne was right to oppose the
stimulus (or to favour monetary activism, or to embark upon the
spending cuts that define the current government). But the early
months of 2009 bolstered his case. His position suddenly seemed
less lonely.

Consumer inactivity was not the only drag on Brown's

resurgence as a financially convulsive 2008 became an economically dismal 2009. The Conservatives were sharpening their economic message too. They launched a pugnacious poster campaign in the new year carrying Osborne's warning of the generational iniquities of debt: 'Dad's nose, mum's eyes, Gordon Brown's debt', read the slogan, over an image of an infant. Then, on 23 January, came official confirmation of Britain's first recession since 1991, when Osborne was an undergraduate. The economy, which had contracted by 0.6 per cent in the third quarter of 2008, had shrunk by another 1.6 per cent in the fourth – the worst quarter since 1980. Britain would go on to lose a total of around 6 per cent of its GDP during the recession. The depth of the contraction was, in part, caused by the magnitude of the prior expansion.

A provocateur might argue that, in retrospect, Britain and much of the West would have done well to undergo a recession when America did, briefly, in the early 2000s. That would have been in line with the economic cycle since the 1970s and mitigated the severity of the eventual crash. But cheap, plentiful credit – a policy that commanded the support of major governments as well as the Bank of England and the Federal Reserve – kept the economy artificially buoyant. It remains a wonder how policymakers have avoided the blame for the crash, which has been largely borne by bankers. Two of the pathologies that afflicted the rich world (and particularly Britain) during the boom, loose monetary policy and Budget deficits, were examples of government failure, not market failure.

For some observers, the ultimate culprit was Mervyn King. As Governor of the Bank of England, he was accused of a narrow, almost academic, focus on the monthly ritual of setting interest rates. More practical matters, namely the real-world financial system, commanded less of his attention. In a faintly autocratic process chronicled by Chris Giles of the *Financial Times*, he also instilled this approach throughout Threadneedle Street, sidelining those who worried about skittish markets and over-leveraged banks.[108] The consequences were dire: the Bank failed to see the credit crunch coming – even holding a conference on 'the sources of macroeconomic stability' as Northern Rock was going under – and delayed injecting capital into the financial system.

There were even doubts as to whether King deserved to be reconfirmed as Governor; the government hesitated before renewing his five-year term in January 2008. Osborne accused Brown of stoking uncertainty, and called for King to be kept in his job. Both Osborne and King seemed to favour a fiscally conservative but monetarily active approach to the unfolding crisis, and even used similar language. Their amity was such that, in the autumn, Darling wondered whether the shadow Chancellor's relationship with the politically neutral Bank was entirely proper. 'There was a deliberate strategy to stay close to Mervyn,' admits someone close to Osborne, before stressing that the two men had reached similar views independently – the shadow Chancellor was certainly not taking his intellectual cue from the Governor.

Suspicion lingers that Osborne, a politician driven to secure the endorsements of third-party organisations, cultivated King because he was the ultimate third-party.

But he was not alone in admiring King's handling of the crisis after his initial tardiness and complacency. The Governor introduced a special liquidity scheme in the spring of 2008, sensed the vulnerabilities of Britain's largest banks and made plans for the vast recapitalisation that took place towards the end of the year. Nor was it unreasonable of the shadow Chancellor to argue that the tripartite regulatory system had to give way to a leading role for the Bank. The question is whether Osborne has lurched to the opposite extreme by giving Threadneedle Street too much power – over the banks, insurance companies and the overall financial system – in addition to its existing monetary role. Other than his first Budget in 2010, Osborne will probably never make a more important decision than his choice of successor to King, whose term expires in 2013.

Even as he was suspected of sub-contracting his macro-economic thinking to the Bank, Osborne was attracting praise for his intellectual effervescence in other areas. The most creative of the young brains in Norman Shaw South was Rohan Silva, who restlessly scoured emerging fields such as behavioural economics and the nexus between government and technology. Osborne seized upon his ideas, including a commitment to transparency that would see the next Tory government publish unprecedented amounts of data online. He served as Osborne's emissary to Silicon Valley and the avant-garde of American academics, and helped to write Cameron's speech to the TED conference, a kind of hipster Davos, in early 2010. Osborne cherished Silva's work, which was cheer-led by Hilton, for making him more than a pounds-and-pence shadow Chancellor, and for giving some substance to his party's portrayal of Brown as 'an analogue politician in a digital age'. Despite having worked at McKinsey and studied at Harvard, Claire Perry regarded her time in Osborne's office as 'the most intellectually stimulating two years of my life'.[109]

As much as Osborne encouraged intellectual fizz among his staff, he never allowed his focus to waver from politics. At the turn of 2009, the Tories matched Mandelson's revival with the restoration of Ken Clarke as a front-rank politician. Osborne, again busying himself with wider political duties, had been 'indirectly sounding me out', says the former Chancellor, about a return to the shadow Cabinet.[110] He hosted him for dinner in January and finally asked him directly whether he would accept the role of business spokesman. Clarke agreed and Osborne cleared the appointment with Cameron. Hilton, still a prolific source of counsel from California, argued against Clarke's return, not least because it would undermine Osborne's own primacy in the eyes of the media, but he has changed his mind since.

If Yachtgate advertised the shadow Chancellor's shallowest traits, Clarke's appointment brought out his most generous and noble. His ultimate virtue is self-knowledge. He does not allow pride or insecurity to cloud his analysis of his own strengths and weaknesses. He understood perfectly that he was regarded by many as callow and remote, and that the Tories' economic message would never truly carry until it had another, more grizzled messenger. If that meant some transient humiliation for himself, then he was happy to bear it for the sake of his party. 'A less secure and strategic politician would not have done it,' argues Rick Nye.[111] 'He is the most self-aware person I have ever met,' says a Tory who is often critical of Osborne.

Earlier and more vociferously than any prominent Tory, Osborne had despised Brown and his acolytes. While others were braver in challenging his profligacy during the boom years, nobody was more alert to the way in which he (or at least elements of his following) did politics. Osborne's devoted study of the internal workings of the Labour Party had acquainted him with their facility with hostile briefings and paranoid plotting. He never fell for the easy myth that Brownites and Blairites were equally culpable for the hostilities between them. He sneered at the fragrant profiles of Brown as a Church of Scotland innocent determined to do the right thing, and wondered aloud when a whiff of the noxious culture around him would reach the public. In April, it finally did.

On the evening of the 9th, thousands of Westminster villagers were intrigued by an entry posted on the popular Guido Fawkes website, run by the libertarian entrepreneur and investigative blogger Paul Staines. It showed a photo of Damian McBride, perhaps Brown's most tenacious aide, with a cross-hair target super-imposed on his face under the headline 'He who lives by the smear…' Staines was about to break a story that would claim McBride's career and wound Brown's moral authority. He had acquired emails sent three months earlier by McBride (or 'McPoison', as Mandelson knew him) to Derek Draper, a former Labour apparatchik, suggesting scurrilous stories to publish about senior Tories on a new blog that was to be called Red Rag. They included innuendo about Cameron's sexual past, tittle-tattle about Osborne's behaviour as a young man and insinuations about his wife.

Osborne's anger was tempered by his utter lack of surprise. He had, after all, been the target of smears allegedly emanating from Brownites since becoming shadow Chancellor. Cameron, who was less worldly about these things, raged incandescently. 'I'm proud there isn't a McBride in here,' he would say in front of his team of advisers for months afterwards. McBride resigned and, though there was no suggestion that Brown himself knew of the skulduggery, the Prime Minister eventually offered contrition after a week of mealy-mouthed equivocation. He even sent Osborne a handwritten letter, which the Tory has kept. It addresses him as 'Geoge'. As the note contains an apology from perhaps the least apologetic politician of his era, Osborne's friends say he regards it as 'an extraordinary artefact'.

Osborne and Cameron declared the end of New Labour upon the nationalisation of Northern Rock. They were fourteen months early. It was actually Darling's Budget in April 2009, with its projection of a £178 billion deficit and its new 50p top rate of income tax, that finally did for the government's claims to economic moderation. The second measure carried particular symbolism as Blair and Brown had always renounced income tax rises as disincentives to strive. Its ultimate purpose was to trap the Conservatives, as Osborne realised. He could deplore the unwelcoming signal it sent to globally mobile high-earners but he could not commit to scrapping the tax without compounding the Tories' image as a party of the rich, for the rich. Instead, he promised to reverse the rise in National Insurance that was announced in the pre-Budget report. It would turn out to be the deferral, not the evasion, of the 50p trap.

If anything stemmed Brown's bleeding that spring, it was, perversely, a shaming series of revelations in which he was among the first to be targeted. For years the Commons had fought efforts by freedom of information campaigners to publish the details of taxpayer-funded expenses and allowances claimed by MPs. When the resistance ultimately proved futile, they gathered the data in preparation for its eventual release. The *Daily Telegraph* acquired a copy of it and, on 8 May, began a sustained exposition of its worst contents. Brown's claim for the cost of a cleaner in his Westminster flat featured in the first batch of stories, more for his prominence than the gravity of the sin. Other Cabinet members, backbenchers and senior Tories followed. Osborne was shown to have claimed £400 for a chauffeured journey from Cheshire to London, while Cameron charged even more to the taxpayer for work done to his constituency home. The real popular rage, however, was provoked by MPs who gamed the system by 'flipping' the designation of their main residence between London and their constituency – and by offensively eccentric expenses, including video porn, tennis court drainage and a duckhouse.

Although the Lib Dems were marginally less guilty, especially of flipping, than the other two parties, Cameron is still thought to have summoned the most impressive response to the crisis. To pre-empt revelations in the press, he commissioned Oliver Dowden and Douglas Smith, two of his political aides, to commandeer an office in Norman Shaw South and painstakingly study the claims made by Tory MPs. He instructed offenders to pay back money, including shadow Cabinet members who insisted (often rightly) that their claims were strictly within the rules. He apologised effusively on behalf his party.

Despite his alacrity, however, the Tories barely benefited. The expenses scandal tainted MPs as a community, stoking the nihil-istically anti-politics mood that is as central to the British zeitgeist as economic despair. In doing so, it might have actually left Brown as the relative winner, as the Conservatives could not campaign convincingly as high-minded agents of change. Cameronism was always designed to ease the country's hatred of his party. It has never managed to defuse the country's hatred of his profession. There was also damage to the Tory leadership's already poor relations with backbenchers, many of whom resented what they saw as punitive and arbitrary treatment by a gilded clique who had never had to worry about money.

The expenses scandal was born of two pathologies that curse British public life: a preference for muddling through over rational design, and a reluctance to abandon a failing system until it falls apart in a crisis. As MPs' earnings fell over time behind those of other professions, they could have explored, openly and from first principles, the issue of their pay and expenses. But rather than risk a candid debate, they improvised a solution by treating expenses as a way of augmenting their income. Then, instead of ceasing this experiment when its flaws came to light – mini-sleaze stories had abounded in recent years – they equivocated until this torrent of revelations forced their hand.

The last summer before the general election began propitiously for the Tories when James Purnell, the Blairite Work and Pensions Secretary, resigned from the Cabinet in protest at Brown's leadership. The news came as polls closed for the local elections on 4 June, which the Conservatives won handily, and for a few hours at least the Prime Minister was at the mercy of his own Cabinet. Had Purnell been followed by David Miliband, Brown would have fallen. Again, however, the Foreign Secretary demurred, leaving Brown weakened but almost certain to lead his party into the next election – the best of both worlds, from Osborne's perspective. His relish at Labour's agonies was transient, though, as he was immediately immersed in the most agonising conundrum of his time as shadow Chancellor.

The great arc of Osborne's fiscal conservatism began with 'stability over tax cuts' in January 2006 and continued with his renunciation of unfunded giveaways that autumn. It dipped with his commitment to match Labour's spending plans the following year but returned to its prior trajectory by the end of 2008, when he extricated himself from that pledge. Now Osborne wanted it to soar onwards, and that meant two things. First, he had to acknowledge for the first time that the next government, regardless of its political colour, would have to cut spending. Only by doing this could he prepare public opinion for the pain he would have to inflict as Chancellor. It would also put pressure on Brown to concede that his trusty mantra of 'investment versus cuts' was misleading – his own Budget contained implicit plans for austerity. Second, for the sake of candidness and credibility, Osborne then wanted to go even further by elucidating at least some of the specific cuts he would make.

It is impossible to understand the political magnitude of these decisions without a grasp of the recent Conservative past. 'It seems obvious now that spending would have to be cut but at that time it was shocking,' remembers Seth Cumming, then an

Osborne aide.[112] Again and again, the party had suffered at the hands of Brown, and the electorate, for proffering policies as tentatively Tory as increasing spending at a slightly slower rate than one of the most munificent governments in British history. The mark those defeats had left on Osborne was so deep that he had evolved his own politico-fiscal doctrine that foreswore any deviation from the 'baseline' spending plans of the government. He remembered the searing Labour posters in 2001 that condemned 'Tory cuts', with the 'y' represented by a pair of scissors. He shuddered at the recollection of all that Sisyphean toil he had done defending the James Review in 2005. Now he was setting himself the goal of not only selling outright cuts to the public but also forcing Labour to acknowledge that they would do the same.

Despite the ambition of this task, Osborne's rationale was grounded in realism. He really would have to cut spending if he became Chancellor, and that would only be feasible if he had warned the public beforehand. In short, he needed a mandate for austerity. He was stirred into action by an accident. During a radio interview on the morning of 10 June, Andrew Lansley, the Tory health spokesman, said that the party was contemplating cuts of 10 per cent in departmental budgets, excluding his own and that of international development. He failed to stress that cuts of this order of magnitude were in the government's own plans, and Labour brandished his slip in the way they did Letwin's remarks to the *Financial Times* in 2001 – proof that the Tories craved cuts but lacked the courage candidly to argue for them.

Cameron and Osborne fumed at Lansley's slip. They prized their claims to honesty and moral authority over an obscurantist Prime Minister, and feared forfeiting these in a single morning. With PMQs just hours away, they huddled to craft their response.

There was an obvious temptation to renounce Lansley's words, but Osborne insisted that they go on the offensive. They would accept that there would be cuts, and challenge Labour to admit the same. Cameron used all six of his questions to force this concession out of Brown and was similarly mono-maniacal in the following few weeks. 'We used PMQs as a battering ram,' says Hancock.[113]

They were helped by the forensic journalism of Fraser Nelson, the political editor of *The Spectator* who had confronted the Prime Minister about his implied plan for cuts at a recent press conference, and by Labour's own Mandelson and Darling, who privately pressed Brown to give up his incredible message of investment versus cuts. Five days later, on 11 June, Osborne wrote a column in *The Times* stating baldly that 'real spending will have to be cut, whoever is elected'.[114] Harrison had drafted a version which stopped just short of saying that, but Osborne sent it back to him with a revised paragraph containing the explicit acknowledgement of cuts.

All this relentless pressure yielded a concession at the Trades Union Congress in September, when Brown finally conceded Osborne's point. A fortnight later, Osborne fulfilled the second half of his mission by setting out some of the specific cuts he was planning to make. Although he had made dramatic speeches to his party conference before, the risk had always been moderate. Ruling out unfunded tax cuts could have provoked anger in the hall but was never going to bring him down. Had his inheritance tax policy failed to excite voters the following year, the result would have been a snap election defeat that was on the cards anyway. This time, however, the potential downside was terrifying. Eight months before a general election, Osborne was going to tell voters exactly what they stood to lose from a Tory government. He agonised over this speech more than any he has given before or since, commissioning huge quantities of polling to study the likely reaction to his message. The findings were perturbing but he ultimately felt the fear and proceeded.

'This is it then,' he said to Hancock before boarding the stage in Manchester on 6 October. There, he announced that he would freeze the pay of public sector workers who earned more than £18,000 in 2010/11, and withdraw tax credits from households with an income above £50,000. He kept the rhetoric calm, presenting the cuts as a concession to reality rather than an ideological choice, but he knew he was taking a risk with his party's poll rating. When he returned to his team backstage, he was anything but elated. 'Now let's see if I've cost us the election,' he said.

The next evening, Osborne was applauded by diners – mainly Tory activists – as he took his table at the Yang Sing restaurant in Princess Street with Daniel Finkelstein and Michael Gove. He was also receiving the most favourable press coverage of his career. 'That's more like it', declared the cover of *The Economist*, over an image of the shadow Chancellor. Even those who disagreed with the economics of his speech, such as *The Guardian's* Martin Kettle, found it 'really quite brave'. The speech was his matriculation as a truly serious and substantial figure. Perhaps no other prominent Western politician was being so explicit so early about the inescapability of austerity. It was also the culmination of a journey to fiscal conservatism that began with his speech to the Cass Business School in January 2006.

However, Osborne's political fears were founded. For all the calumnies aimed at the general election campaign fought by the Conservatives in the spring of 2010, the party's opinion poll lead actually began to dissipate from the autumn of 2009. Three years on, he is philosophical. He knows that the embrace of austerity probably sapped the Tories' popularity (though he is not entirely certain, given that it took a few weeks for the polls to shift after the conference). But he is even more convinced that there was no better option available to him. His team agree – one of his Treasury ministers estimates that the speech cost the party at least twenty seats at the election but made it easier to govern.

It is difficult to gainsay that verdict. The coalition's time in office has produced glimpses of the political horror that Osborne avoided by being honest before the election. Towards the end of 2010, the Liberal Democrats provoked overwhelming anger by supporting an increase in university tuition fees despite having promised to abolish them entirely before the election. No single thing has done more to diminish Nick Clegg's personal standing. It was not the new policy that wounded him as much as the apparent betrayal. After all, the Tories have barely sustained a scratch from the rise in tuition fees. If a failure to prepare the ground in an area as marginal as university funding can have such calamitous consequences, then consider, if the stomach allows it, the backlash that would have met an unexpected freeze in public sector pay and the removal of tax credits. The main business of this government – its deficit-reduction programme – would have proved virtually impossible to execute had it not been adumbrated by Osborne in 2009.

The speech also marked his personal metamorphosis. If Osborne's career has a hinge, a moment in which he had to decide what kind of politician he wanted to be, this was it. Until then, he had almost delighted in being the most political of politicians: more operator than ideologue, more calculator than crusader; pragmatic to a fault, a fervent believer in not much more than the necessity of victory. At school, he was bewitched by the prospect of power but less interested in what he would do if he ever acquired it. As a young apparatchik, he was early in recognising that the Tories had to change to win, but rarely asked himself what he wanted to win for. In Parliament, he evinced a worldview – on foreign policy and cultural issues, especially – but only teasingly and unsatisfyingly. Even in his first three years as shadow Chancellor, his fiscal conservatism was conveniently aligned with electoral common sense.

2009 was different. For the first time as shadow Chancellor, the expedient course of action clashed with what he believed was the right thing to do. Political logic demanded strict adherence to Labour's spending plans, but the country's own interests were served by austerity, which could only be implemented if it was telegraphed in advance. Anyone who had studied Osborne's rise would have expected him to choose politics over economics. In fact, he did the opposite. Getting elected was pointless if he could not be an iron Chancellor.

None of the Above

'There was nobody in charge.'

For all their enmity, George Osborne and Gordon Brown were deceptively similar politicians. Both combined a facility for the high politics of economic strategy and international summitry with an almost childlike ardour for the sheer sport of electoral campaigning. Brown, the organisational force behind Labour's victories in 1997, 2001 and 2005, pioneered the modern model of the political Chancellor, stooping to oversee election posters, media management and get-out-the-vote drives in a way that would have been unimaginable of rarefied predecessors such as Nigel Lawson and Denis Healey. Osborne is in his image. Since May 2005, the month in which he became shadow Chancellor and David Cameron's campaign manager, his endeavours have been as much political as economic. The wisdom of this double burden was only fitfully questioned – until 2010.

Although the campaign for a British general election only officially commences a few weeks before polling day, it effectively begins with the new year. In January, the Conservatives made a calamitous start from which they never really recovered. On the 4th, the party launched a poster campaign showing a tieless, open-collared, unusually glossy Cameron next to the message:

'We can't go on like this. I'll cut the deficit, not the NHS.'
Osborne, who had begun chairing a daily election meeting at
8.30 a.m. at CCHQ, arranged for it to adorn a thousand billboard sites across the country. Within days, however, the poster
became a liability. Rumours emerged that a computer airbrush
was responsible for rendering Cameron's face eerily smooth and
defined so that he resembled nobody so much as Lieutenant
Commander Data of *Star Trek: The Next Generation*. Amid newspaper mockery and left-wing spoof posters that proliferated on
the internet, the message was lost.

A botched poster campaign should be a nuisance rather than
a disaster, but this one seriously wounded Cameron by crystal-
lising concerns that already abounded about the authenticity of
this former PR man. The most damaging political mistakes are
those which confirm what voters already suspect. To this day,
Steve Hilton believes the poster did more than anything else
to cost the Conservatives the election. He points to the party's
poll ratings, which fell steeply throughout January, and to the
precedent of the 1992 election. In January of that year, a Tory
poster warning of Labour's 'tax bombshell' summoned to the
surface suppressed fears of Neil Kinnock's economic policies.
John Major's eventual victory, Hilton thinks, was secured within
a week of the poster's unveiling.

The making of the Cameron poster also captured in microcosm the troubles that would dog the wider campaign. Instead
of a single creative source, it was 'designed by committee', says
an insider. Cameron insisted that his own image dominate the
billboard, Hilton argued for the emphasis on change ('We can't
go on like this' was accompanied by 'Year for Change' in the
corner of the poster) and Osborne pressed for the inclusion of
the party's commitment to cutting the deficit while sparing the
NHS. Everyone was given something, but at the cost of overall

coherence. Part of the problem was the Tories' lack of advertising expertise. In 2007, Hilton had tried to hire his former employers M&C Saatchi as he believed only they truly grasped the unique demands of electoral politics. However, Transport for London was among their biggest clients and Ken Livingstone, then mayor of the capital, threatened to withdraw TfL's custom if Saatchi helped the Conservatives. Hilton signed with Euro RSCG instead, an outfit less steeped in political advertising. In the end, senior Tories were forced to design the poster themselves.

January's other misstep took place in Davos, where Cameron was attending the annual World Economic Forum. During one session, he indicated that any cuts a Conservative government made in 2010 would not be very 'extensive'. The phrase was innocuous and accurate – Cameron would ultimately oversee 'in year' cuts of £6 billion – but Harrison told the Tory leader afterwards that it would be interpreted as proof of the Tories panicking in the face of souring opinion polls. He was right. Most senior Tories insist that Cameron's remark was unplanned but it was followed a few days later by his ruling out of any 'swingeing' cuts within the year. One of the MPs closest to Osborne believes that Cameron was indeed deliberately reassuring voters alarmed by the prospect of austerity – and that he only succeeded in making the Tories look weak. 'It confused me, and I was a Treasury spokesman. We seemed unsure of ourselves.'

By now, Osborne was less puckish than usual. He had to cauterise the Tories' self-inflicted wounds while rearranging his private office. During Cameron's visit to Davos, Hancock was selected as the Conservative candidate in the safe seat of Suffolk East. Harrison, who had combined the trip to Switzerland with a skiing holiday, heard the news while on a slope with his wife. He was immediately appointed as Hancock's replacement. This apparently arcane reshuffle of unheard-of back-room boys was actually rather significant. Senior politicians depend much more on their advisers than is usually understood. This is especially true of shadow (or actual) Chancellors, most of whom are not trained economists. Subtle differences in temperament and ideology between one chief of staff and another can have tangible consequences for Treasury policy.

Hancock and Harrison have similarly powerful minds but quite distinct personalities. In many ways, Hancock resembles Osborne at the same age. He has a pitiless focus on the political bottom line and a pugnacious approach to his Labour opponents. His Threadneedle erudition vies with a more martial spirit, and does not always win. Harrison, for all that he has been politicised by years of Osborne's tutelage, remains an economist who does politics rather than a political operator who also knows economics. His ambition is cloaked by a magisterial personal style. Both men have capacious hinterlands: Harrison's friends are drawn from the arts as well as politics, and Hancock is a sportsman who played a game of cricket at the North Pole and won a charity horse race at Newmarket. Hancock is bolder ideologically – though neither is, even compared to Osborne, very doctrinaire – while Harrison is more forensic. As *consigliere* to the Chancellor, Hancock might have buttressed Osborne's natural ways. Harrison offsets them.

In February, it became obvious that the Tories' decline in the polls was no transient glitch. Regular meetings of Cameron's innermost circle – Osborne, Hilton and Coulson, often with Llewellyn and Fall also present – took place in his London and Oxfordshire homes. But they yielded nothing more decisive than lists of things to do. Any hope of a clear and strategic message was faltering, as was their collective sense of composure. 'We had a real crisis on confidence in January and February,' confesses one of those who attended these exclusive meetings. On their way to one summit at Cameron's rural house during a snowbound evening, Coulson crashed his car and

Hilton, whose own country retreat was nearby, narrowly avoided a cycling accident. The metaphor of a party losing its way was exquisite. Osborne, the great stickler for simplicity, found himself announcing as many as 'eight benchmarks' by which his economic policies should be judged in a speech at the British Museum. Many of these were sensible – retaining Britain's triple A credit rating was the first item – but, as a member of his team now confesses: 'The trouble with all that is that you end up with a list and a list is not a message.'

It was apparent by now that Osborne was campaign manager in name only. The reality was that Cameron preferred to have an oligopoly of strategic voices around him. There was Osborne, Hilton and Coulson, but at a lower level also Stephen Gilbert, who ran the party's ground campaigns; Andrew Feldman, who oversaw Millbank; and Lord Ashcroft, who managed his own target-seat operation. Disagreements multiplied but the central fault line divided those, led by Osborne and Coulson, who espoused a hard-edged message telling voters that the party was 'on their side' on issues such as crime and the economy, from others, represented by Hilton, who wanted a more high-minded campaign about change. Osborne regarded Hilton's vision as nebulous, while Hilton found Osborne's approach grim and uninspiring. Neither ultimately prevailed, leaving the Tory message bereft of definition. 'There was nobody in charge,' laments one member of the campaign.

Osborne saw off Hilton's suggestion that the campaign slogan should be 'Rethink Everything' but they continued to grapple. Cameron never really decided who was to wield the ultimate authority. He was used to going to Osborne for political nous and to Hilton for the vision thing, and saw no reason to choose between them. This was a fine way to craft a programme for government but an electoral campaign requires clarity and a chain of command that ends with a single person. 'George was not the dominating campaign manager that Lynton [Crosby] might have been,' according to a senior Tory. But he was never licensed to be. Hilton, for his part, now accepts that his own reluctance to defer to Osborne was part of the problem. 'George was never the campaign manager, in the sense that what he says goes,' says another insider.

By March, a YouGov poll showed the Conservatives leading Labour by just 37 per cent to 35 per cent. With the vagaries of the electoral system, this meant that Labour was on course to remain at least the biggest party in Parliament. Cameron's closest advisers, who had borne the stress of the snap election speculation in 2007 with fortitude and equanimity, began to row among themselves. 'Arguments are healthy as long as they don't get in the way of the campaign, but they did,' says one insider. Hilton and Coulson, who had wildly divergent ideas of how the Conservatives should campaign, were even moved into a shared office at CCHQ in the hope of establishing some coherence between them. At best, it half-worked.

A deeper excavation of the polls revealed where the party was going wrong. Voters were ravenous for change but unsure what kind of change the Tories represented. This ruinous ambiguity was partly the fault of the campaign message, or the absence of one, but it had in truth characterised much of Cameron's leadership. In focus groups conducted by Andrew Cooper in the years leading up to the election, the word people most often used to describe the Tories was 'confused' (the adjective for Labour was 'tired'). The shift from soft, cultural themes to hard, economic ones after the crash was wholly unavoidable, but it also served to muddy the party's message. Cooper told the leadership to define themselves instead of attacking Labour. 'It's not them, it's us,' was his mantra.

By the spring of 2010, however, the Tories were mono-mani-acal in their crusade against a battered Prime Minister. With Saatchi finally on board, they released a poster campaign in March showing a grinning Brown next to slogans such as: 'I let 80,000 criminals out early. Vote for me.' It was searing stuff but did nothing to elucidate the Conservative alternative. Osborne's disdain for Brown might have clouded his judgement. 'A boot stamping on Gordon Brown's face forever' is how one insider described Osborne's vision for the campaign. Lord Ashcroft's post-mortem on the election curses 'the sheer pointlessness of attacking Gordon Brown'.[115]

When Osborne gave an opaque interview about Conservative economic policy to the *Today* programme on 25 March, commentators were scathing. Coulson phoned one of them, a right-wing scribe, not so much to remonstrate as to concede the point and wearily plead for clemency for his bungling colleagues. Senior Tories were eminently capable of throwing away the election, he explained, and remorseless scrutiny from usually friendly media might result in another five years of Gordon Brown as Prime Minister.

By the end of March came a preview of the most cruelly pillo-ried aspect of the Conservative campaign. In a venue on Coin Street in London's South Bank, David Cameron, backed by a series of shadow Cabinet warm-up acts, unveiled his vision of the Big Society. From the start of his leadership, he had insisted, against Thatcher's endlessly misinterpreted aside, that there was 'such a thing as society' – but it was not the same thing as the state. This formulation neatly distinguished him from both her and Labour. Although Hilton was the animating force behind this focus on the communities, charities and families that make up civil society, it was congruent with Cameron's own instincts.

It was also substantiated with policy. Largely unnoticed by the press, the Conservatives had spent much of Cameron's leadership drawing up plans for a great give-away of power from the centre of government. Schools would be funded by the state but run by charities and parent groups. Directly elected commissioners would oversee the police, the least reformed of all the public services. Local government would be given more fiscal power, welfare-to-work contracted out to a range of non-state providers, and giant quantities of government data published online. Hilton, Rohan Silva and James O'Shaughnessy, Cameron's main policy adviser, travelled the world – and especially America – to study how other countries were empowering citizens at the expense of the state. Until Coin Street, all these devolutionary brainwaves lacked – appropriately enough – a central, unifying slogan. 'The Big Society' was it. Within a month, the slogan would become a manifesto.

On the morning of 6 April, Gordon Brown visited the Queen and received her agreement to dissolve Parliament. The election campaign had formally begun. Outside Downing Street minutes later, with his Cabinet behind him, he declared himself the product of 'an ordinary middle-class family'. On the same spot almost three years earlier, he had recited the modest motto of his state school. His most cherished point of difference with the Tory leader – that, for all his dark unknowability, he was of the people – had not changed from the first day of his premiership to the last. On the other side of Westminster Bridge, Cameron launched his own campaign with a soapbox speech to a small outdoor gathering, as John Major might have done. He then boarded his campaign bus, which included a private booth for him at its rear, and began touring the nation.

Cameron and Osborne were put up in suites at the Park Plaza hotel across the river from Parliament, although the shadow Chancellor would spend occasional nights at home in west

London. He would arrive at the party's Millbank headquarters in time to chair a 6 a.m. meeting of principal staff, where discussion would dwell on the overnight news, the coming day's announcements and Cameron's itinerary. He would then direct the campaign from a desk in the open-plan main office. (Cameron had a separate office but was generally out in the country campaigning.) Every other day, Osborne would board a helicopter at 10 a.m. to visit a marginal seat somewhere in the south east before returning in the afternoon. At 4 p.m., he would speak to a gathering of all the staff to stoke their morale and motivation. Assisting Osborne was Tim Chatwin, a former CRD staffer. He managed the 'grid' on which each day of the campaign was planned. He had also compiled a 'war book' of practical contingencies for every aspect of the campaign, from printing the manifesto to stocking the Millbank fridge. This was designed to keep Osborne from having to worry about petty details. He would return to his hotel at 10 p.m. and dine with Cameron before retiring for the day.

Some who worked alongside Osborne claim that he was obsessed with 'winning the day'. In meetings, he was 'magpie-like' in spotting opportunities and made 'better tactical observations than anyone', but the bigger picture was usually painted by others around the table, especially Gove. Each afternoon, Osborne presented a t-shirt bearing the accolade 'Tory of the Day' to whichever underling had conjured the most winning idea. The first winner was a junior hand who suggested positioning a 'vote for change' sign outside Buckingham Palace as Brown arrived there to see the Queen. The daily ritual of prize-giving raised spirits, but also encouraged staff to focus on gambits and gimmicks. But this tactical fixation was a pragmatic recourse in the absence of an overarching message for which he was only partly to blame. As long as the campaign lacked a lucid strategy, it made sense for Osborne to at least get the day-by-day thrusts and parries right.

He was also responsible for the few clear and resonant aspects of the campaign. His policy to reverse Labour's rise in National Insurance turned into a crusade against the 'jobs tax', a phrase that voters began using unprompted on the doorstep. He also promised to avert Labour's 'death tax' when the Health Secretary, Andy Burnham, proposed raising the inheritance duty to pay for a national care service. Osborne curses the Tories' failure to develop such clear and punchy messages across a wider range of issues. For all the big thinking the party had done on welfare reform, there was no single, concrete proposal that could fit on a poster. Some have emerged since, most vividly the cap on the sum of benefits a household can claim in a year, but largely at Osborne's own instigation.

The cupboard was even barer in other policy areas. When the grid's 'NHS day' arrived, he was dismayed to discover that the ideas prepared by Lansley were too feeble to trouble the day's news bulletins, let alone dominate them. With less than a month before polling day, the party's lack of definition was an incurable blight. 'At least in 2005, we offered reasons to vote Tory,' says a veteran of both campaigns. When George Bridges lamented the paucity of doorstep policies, Osborne agreed, visibly irked by the party's failure to craft them in time. When another senior figure asked him how he was enjoying the campaign, the response was quietly seething. 'I'm hating every minute of it.'

Osborne's frustration with his shadow Cabinet peers cannot be understood without a glimpse of the time and toil that he himself commits to developing simple, saleable policies. The jobs tax campaign, for example, was a year in the making. He deputed Feldman, Fall and Eleanor Shawcross, another of his aides, to begin soliciting support from leading businessmen for the Tory position. He invested his own time in persuading the CBI and the chief executives of major companies to write letters to newspapers in support of his policy. He road-tested several slogans before settling on the cuttingly resonant 'jobs tax'. Nothing was left to chance. He wondered aloud why other frontbenchers were less diligent in 'weaponising' policy, but the answer, as ever, lay in his own uniquely wounding experience of politics. Unlike Lansley, or indeed Cameron, he had never been on the winning side of an election. His formative memories were of defeat and futile exertions to attract at least the attention, if not the affection, of voters and the media. The trauma left him with an unabashedly retail approach to politics – and a scathing view of more Corinthian colleagues. Tellingly, one of the few frontbenchers who shared Osborne's taste for clarity was Gove, with his insider's grasp of the media.

The bravest moment of the Conservative campaign was also, in retrospect, the most misguided. Manifestos are neither widely read nor formally binding, but they are a more comprehensive statement of a party's plans for government than any speech, billboard or political broadcast. They are usually presented as an accessibly banal and copiously illustrated magazine. The Tories' effort, which was put together by Hilton, did not observe any of these rules. He delivered a hardback book of 130 pages. Instead of a winning picture of Cameron on the cover, there was an impersonal 'Invitation to join the government of Britain'. The manifesto's overarching theme was the dispersal of power from central government to the Big Society, rather than anything so worldly as the economic troubles of the day. The initial response to the manifesto, which was launched on 13 April at a skilfully choreographed event in Battersea, was one of polite curiosity. That morning, at a gathering of the most senior lobby journalists, Osborne was able to show them the manifesto on an iPad that

Silva had acquired before the product's official launch in Britain. 'Osborne 1 Mandelson 0', pronounced the *Evening Standard*.

Before the day was out, however, curiosity gave way to bafflement and mockery. In a package for *Newsnight*, the BBC's Michael Crick asked members of the public what they made of the Tories' invitation to run the country. The few who could make sense of the offer found it eminently resistible. For Conservative candidates fighting for votes in marginal seats, the manifesto proved impossible to communicate on the doorstep; many of those who ended up winning simply ditched the Big Society theme and crafted their own pitch focused on tax, crime and public services. All these problems were foreseeable if only the Big Society had been tested on focus groups and opinion polls before its deployment. This never happened. 'Steve is really not interested in polls,' says one of the most senior figures in the campaign. 'He will do something if he thinks it is right.'

When news of this basic dereliction reached the ears of Bill Knapp, an American political consultant who was seconded to CCHQ, he was apparently 'speechless'. It is the kind of sloppiness that Osborne, with his ardour for Washington-style professional politics, might have cursed too. Yet he never fought for influence over the manifesto, which was made Hilton's fiefdom as part of Cameron's eagerness to keep all his main advisers happy instead of privileging any one of them. Once the shadow Chancellor's team were satisfied that the document had 'all the economic bits in it', they took the view that the manifesto was 'just a day in the campaign'. 'The manifesto was basically Steve's thing,' says one of them. 'We had a veto on anything that was in it but the concept was Steve's.' Indeed, Osborne was attracted to the theme of giving power away as he worried about the Conservatives being defined by economic miserliness alone. Coulson, who struggled to disguise his disdain for

Hilton's epic visions, was more worried about the manifesto. Again, though, none of the principal strategists had the authority to overrule another. The Conservative campaign was itself a Big Society.

Hilton's manifesto was bizarrely oblique for any general election, especially one taking place in the immediate aftermath of a recession, and the failure to trial it on voters was careless. However, an incredible notion has taken hold, especially among the right, that the Big Society was a major factor in the Conservatives' failure to win the election. This near-consensus is blind to two realities. First, the Big Society was not the theme of the whole campaign. In fact, it took up a single day in the grid. The real fault of the campaign is that it did not have a dominating theme at all. More fundamentally, the party's poll rating did not begin falling when the manifesto was launched, or when Cameron heralded the Big Society at Coin Street. The decline set in after the party conference the previous autumn. It was the cold promise of austerity, not the fluffy talk of community, that really repelled swing voters.

If the actual election campaign itself was lost in a single day, it was not 13 April but 15 April: the night of the first televised debate between the main candidates to be Prime Minister. Exactly why the Conservatives agreed to such a hazardous engagement when they were favourites to win the election has been the subject of speculation and insinuation. Frontrunners had always found an excuse to avoid TV debates, including Tony Blair in 1997. The conspiracy theory that has Coulson, operating as a loyal Murdoch man, bouncing reluctant colleagues into the debates to please Sky News has almost nothing to support it, however. Leaving aside the fact that the BBC and ITN would also each broadcast a debate, the other Tories did not need to be strong-armed into it. They took the decision in principle in the summer of 2009 and then deputed Coulson to lead the negotiations with the broadcasters. The final deal was done in December.

The Tories agreed to the debates, the first of which was to take place in Manchester, for two reasons. They felt bound by statements they had made about the idea in the past. 'David had been on the record as being in favour of debates for years,' says one of those who involved in the decision. 'It would have been a big betrayal of trust [to renege] and the media would have really screamed about us running scared.' More than this, they were sure that Cameron would win handily. The one thing that united the heterogeneous band of modernisers – Osborne, Hilton, Gove, Llewellyn, Fall – was an admiration of Cameron that sometimes verged on awe. He had shimmered at the centre of their social and political circle since the 1990s, and some of them owed their eminence to his patronage. They were certain that he would outperform the Prime Minister on TV and never even entertained the threat represented by Nick Clegg. 'Our enemy was Brown, we did not have the Lib Dems in our sights at all,' says a senior Tory.

The moment they woke up to their own fatal complacency came a fortnight before the first debate, when rehearsals were held in CCHQ. During their stay in Davos that year, Osborne and Cameron were advised to prepare rigorously for the debates by the American political strategist Mark Penn. On the recommendation of another American, Mayor Michael Bloomberg of New York, they hired Bill Knapp and Anita Dunn, two of Washington's most respected consultants, who helped to set up a mock version of a TV studio and coach Cameron. Osborne was too busy to reprise his old function as political mimic, so the part of Brown was played by Damian Green. Osborne personally selected Jeremy Hunt to play Clegg.

The shadow Culture Secretary's performance was eerily

good. So thorough was his research that he quoted an obscure programme for young offenders in Clegg's Sheffield constituency that the Lib Dem leader ended up mentioning in the real debates. With each answer, he effortlessly branded Cameron (and Green-as-Brown) as creatures of the establishment. For those looking on, it was suddenly, painfully obvious that Clegg's position as the third man of the debate would allow him to define himself as the fresh alternative. 'We realised two weeks before the first debate, when we had begun prepping, that Clegg had all the best lines,' says one of those present. 'Well, I'm voting for that guy,' said Dunn, pointing to Hunt at the end of the first prep session. The only other sound in the room was horrified silence.

Sure enough, Clegg triumphed in Manchester. Not only did he paint Brown and Cameron as a pair of establishment clichés, he also had 'these two' bidding for his goodwill even as he goaded them, a bizarre spectacle that gave rise to the national catchphrase 'I agree with Nick'. His structural position in the debate conferred a huge advantage, of course, but he exploited it with a performance that was stunningly accomplished. When it came to the most elementary of techniques – looking into the camera to connect with viewers at home, addressing questioners by name to win over the live audience – he was he an utter natural. His voice was raspier than Cameron's, his body language less forced. 'You were the future once', he must have been tempted to say to the Tory leader.

Of all the Conservatives watching the debate in the green room in Manchester, Osborne was the most intensely engrossed. A young press officer tried to engage him in conversation but he was 'in his own world', almost joining in the debate as a football spectator might mime the striking of a ball. When it was over, he walked out into 'spin alley', a congested corner of the media hall where senior members of each party strove to persuade journalists that their man had won. He did his best but, compared to the likes of Gove, Mandelson and the jubilant Lib Dems, he was subdued. His own political instincts told him what the opinion polls taken in the minutes after the debate confirmed: there had only been one winner.

Over the next few days, the Lib Dems surged in the opinion polls, briefly threatening to push Labour into third position, and Clegg enjoyed a more rapturous moment of popularity than any British politician since Blair in 1997. The boost faded in the following weeks as right-leaning newspapers, fed with stories by CCHQ, trashed Clegg with embarrassing stories and scrutiny of his party's liberal line on crime and immigration. His performance in the second and third debates, in Bristol and Birmingham respectively, did not match his first. But a transformation had been wrought nevertheless. A party that had expected to poll significantly less than it did five years earlier, when it profited from hostility to the Iraq war, ended up scoring almost exactly the same amount – taking many votes from the Conservatives in the process.

Neither Osborne nor Cameron laments their decision to agree to the debates. Osborne believes the clamour was too intense to defy, unless the Tories wished to be portrayed as cowards in the run-up to the election. Cameron goes even further. He privately posits that the debates actually helped the Tories by sucking the life out of the rest of the campaign, which Labour would have spent grinding them down on fiscal policy as they had done in 2001 and 2005. In the end, Brown only managed to do this in the final week of the campaign, deluging voters with leaflets warning of Tory plans to cut tax credits and vital services. But he had struggled furiously to sell the same message throughout the campaign – holding endless press conferences on 'Tory cuts' – only to encounter a media that was preoccupied with the debates. For all that it seems like self-exculpation, Cameron's theory is plausible, and proof that his political mind is as supple as Osborne's – even if he is less showy with it.

On 20 April, two days before the second debate, Osborne dined at Cameron's London home. Fed up with debate preparation, the pair had a wider-ranging conversation. They talked about the prospect of a hung Parliament for the first time during the campaign. Unprompted, Cameron said he would react to that eventuality by trying to form a coalition with the Lib Dems instead of governing as a minority Prime Minister. Osborne had never heard his friend mention the c-word before. After witnessing a grim presentation a few days later from Stephen Gilbert, who dispelled lingering hopes of an overall majority, Osborne told Cameron that they had to make detailed plans for an indecisive election result. Cameron agreed but insisted that he could not campaign for a victory while arranging contingencies for a hung Parliament. As ever, the work was delegated to Osborne, who was now shadow Chancellor, election strategist and coalition project manager.

On the penultimate weekend before the election, Osborne gathered Hague, Letwin and Llewellyn at his home. Their first collective decision was to not contact the Lib Dems at all during the campaign; any leaks would embarrass both parties and jeopardise an eventual agreement. Hague, wielding the authority of a former leader, gave his approval to the idea of a coalition. Llewellyn, an aide to Paddy Ashdown during his time in Bosnia, was asked to examine previous statements the Lib Dems had made about their likely response to a hung Parliament. Letwin, who had brought a copy of the Lib Dem manifesto with him, was instructed to study it for policies that united the two parties. He drew up a paper setting out what a Conservative–Liberal agenda for government might be. 'That is basically the coalition agreement,' says a senior Tory. 'It did not change a huge amount from that original document.'

It was easy to misread the campaign as polling day approached. Brown was outwardly foundering and seemed to commit an unrecoverable blunder on 28 April, when a microphone caught him disparaging an elderly, Labour-sympathising grandmother he had just met as a 'bigoted woman' for the sin of grumbling about immigration. The Prime Minister endured unwatchable ignominy when cameras filmed his slumped, head-in-hands desolation as the offending clip was played back to him in a radio interview hours later. But the tragicomedy 'had absolutely no discernible impact on voting intention polls … because people had long since formed a judgement on Gordon Brown', according to Lord Ashcroft.[116] More than this, street by street, house by house, away from the media's gaze, Labour were actually fulfilling Osborne's worst fears. With union resources and a laser-beam focus, the party warned voters of the benefits and services they stood to lose under Tory austerity. It was working; even candidates canvassing large homes in prosperous areas encountered fears of withdrawn tax credits. Brown's expansion of the welfare state had ensnared middle-class voters, as it was meant to.

On the eve of the election, Cameron, on Dunn's suggestion, embarked on a sleepless round-the-clock campaign blitz via bus and helicopter, while Osborne oversaw the final formalities of the operation in London. On 6 May, polling day itself, Osborne went to Hilton's house in Oxfordshire, where he was joined by Coulson, Llewellyn and Fall. They knew they would find more peace there than at Cameron's house, surrounded as it was by journalists and cameramen. Their first political act of the day was to allocate jobs in a putative Conservative Cabinet. Had Tony Blair been peering through the window, he might have smiled wryly. The Tories had always scolded him for running a 'sofa government'; here were five of them, only one of whom (Osborne) had ever been elected to anything, drawing up Her Majesty's Cabinet in a cosy living room. Decisions were made to appoint Theresa May as Britain's first female Conservative Home Secretary, and to revive Iain Duncan Smith as Work and Pensions Secretary.

The friends then held a sweepstake on the number of seats the party would win. Although they had just appointed an exclusively Conservative Cabinet, none of them forecast an overall majority for their party. The predictions ranged from 295 to 315 seats. Osborne forecast 310, but Fall came closest to the 306 that were ultimately won.

After dinner, Osborne was transported by helicopter to Cheshire. From there, he was driven to the home of his constituency secretary, where Harrison and two other aides, Ramesh Chhabra and Poppy Mitchell-Rose, were waiting for him with his wife Frances. He chose this venue as his own constituency home was too high up in the hills to command reliable mobile phone reception. At 9.55 p.m., he took part in a conference call with other senior Tories in which he learned that the BBC's exit poll, due in five minutes, would predict a hung Parliament, with the Conservatives as the largest party and the Lib Dems, for all the Cleggmania of previous weeks, actually down a few seats.

Osborne's reaction was not disappointment – weeks had passed since he seriously entertained the prospect of winning outright – but pleasure that Labour had definitely lost, and puzzlement at the Lib Dems' apparent underachievement. This equanimity faded, however, when he saw Mandelson and May being asked to interpret the exit poll on TV. The Labour man spun it as a failure for the Conservatives and May struggled to gainsay him. The Tories needed someone of Mandelson's wiles to go before the media.

During another conference call at 10.20 p.m., it was agreed that Osborne, who would ordinarily have arrived at his constituency count at 1 a.m., would go immediately. He arrived at 10.45 p.m. and gave a series of television interviews insisting that the Tories had won the election. Then, in one of the endearing indignities to which Britain subjects even its grandest politicians, he whiled away the small hours of the morning in the humble café of this Macclesfield leisure centre, following the results on a tiny television. The Tatton result was announced at 4 a.m.; he was returned as its MP for the third time, with an increased majority of 14,487. 'The country has voted for change,' he said in his acceptance speech. 'It is clear that a Prime Minister never elected in the first place has lost his mandate to govern.' Brown had the constitutional right to try to form a government first, but Osborne pointedly insisted that 'David Cameron and the Conservatives will do what needs to be done to give Britain the new and decisive government it needs.'

Osborne took a helicopter from Manchester airport to an airfield near RAF Northolt, and then a car to CCHQ, where he arrived at around 6.30 a.m. Cameron was there with his closest advisers watching the last few results come in. The exit poll was largely right: the Conservatives had won 306 seats, twenty short of a majority, to Labour's 258. He told his team, Osborne included, to get some sleep and reconvene in his suite at the Park Plaza hotel at 10 a.m. At that bleary-eyed gathering, he declared that his mind was made up: he would offer the Lib Dems a coalition.

Osborne telephoned William Hague, Ken Clarke, Liam Fox and the Chief Whip Patrick McLoughlin to confirm their support, while Hilton wrote a draft of the speech that Cameron would give imminently at the St Stephen's Club, a Tory redoubt in Westminster. Osborne read it and replaced the explicit proposal of a 'coalition' with a 'big, open and comprehensive offer' in order to give the Tories some room for manoeuvre. Hilton printed out the final version and handed it to Cameron as he rushed out of the hotel. The Tory leader only read this historic speech for the first time on his way to the Club.

His 'offer' electrified the audience of fatigued journalists, who were expecting a more tentative statement. A minority Tory government, with the Lib Dems providing support in parliamentary confidence motions and finance bills, had always seemed likelier than a coalition. But the Conservatives knew that a 'confidence and supply' arrangement would break down before long. A second election might then be lost in the autumn or the new year to an invigorated Labour Party, perhaps led by David Miliband. In the meantime, the government would be too precariously poised to do very much, even in the way of urgent deficit-reduction. This would jeopardise Britain's credibility in already anxious financial markets. The background noise was riotous turmoil in Greece, whose government was announcing austerity measures in return for a bailout from the EU and the IMF.

On Friday afternoon, Cameron had a phone conversation with Clegg, who was honouring his long-standing pledge to give the biggest party in the Commons the first chance to negotiate with the Lib Dems. Osborne told Cameron to press for talks as soon as possible. Momentum mattered, and so did location. Gus O'Donnell, the Cabinet secretary, Britain's uppermost civil servant, offered the use of the Cabinet Office, a room in Parliament or an anonymous government building in south London. Osborne chose the first for its symbolic position at the heart of government. O'Donnell made the arrangements, and told Osborne that the country needed a government as soon as possible.

Exploratory talks began between the two parties that evening. The Conservative delegation comprised Hague, an elder statesman before his fiftieth birthday; Osborne, who wielded the vital Treasury brief and the broadest political expertise; Letwin, the master of policy; and Llewellyn, who brought a grasp of protocol and an affinity the Lib Dems, whose team consisted of Danny Alexander, who served as Clegg's chief of staff, David Laws, Chris Huhne, their home affairs spokesman, and Andrew Stunell, an MP steeped in the party's ways and thoughts.

Relations between the two sides were immediately convivial (Osborne and Alexander discovered that they had mutual friends during their time at university) but more surprising was the alacrity with which they agreed on the pressing matter of fiscal policy. The Conservatives had campaigned on a plan to eliminate almost all of the structural Budget deficit within the parliament, starting with cuts in 2010. The Lib Dems proposed to delay cutting until the recovery was secure, which they envisaged to be 2011. Their rapid migration to the Tory position has been portrayed as a sordid concession for the sake of power, and it is true that in-year cuts were 'never negotiable' for Osborne and his team. But there was no capitulation, as one of the Lib Dem negotiators explains:

The differences on deficit reduction had been hyped up by all the parties to differentiate their product at the general election. We had actually decided by early 2010 that any coalition government would need to be seen to going more quickly on deficit reduction because of the febrile state of the financial markets … Even leaving aside what was happening in Greece we didn't think there would be a lot of confidence in a coalition government in the UK. Part of our pre-election planning was to make sure we avoided being blamed for financial instability if coalition talks took place … We assumed George would want to do something tough on the deficit and we were open to in-year cuts and a deeper overall strategy.

Sure enough, before the election, Clegg had used an interview with the *Financial Times* to stress that his party would demand action on the deficit in any coalition talks that took place. Of course, there were also outside pressures for a rapid and radical fiscal consolidation: not just the chaos in Greece but the widely known view of the Treasury and the Bank of England that in-year cuts were necessary to keep the markets at bay. But the Lib Dems were barely exposed to these as they shuttled from the talks to debriefing sessions with Clegg and the occasional scrap of rest. Vince Cable, the most Labour-leaning of the major Lib Dems, was 'completely in touch' with the talks, according to one of the party's delegation, and approved of the hawkish line on the deficit. For all his obvious discomfort at holding power with the Tories, he has yet to waver on austerity.

Although Hague was the Tory delegation's nominal leader, the Lib Dems found Osborne the most active negotiator. He understood the detail of many policy areas, and grasped the politics of absolutely all of them. He told them that his party would not wear proportional representation – the Lib Dems' eternal project – but said they were open to a referendum on the alternative vote (AV) system. Indeed, he then set about persuading Cameron, Clarke and Hague behind closed doors that such an offer would be necessary to clinch a deal with the Lib Dems. He was also happy to give up policies of his own that he had come to regard as liabilities. His famous pledge to lift the threshold of inheritance tax was downgraded as a priority, giving way to the Lib Dem idea of raising the threshold of income tax to £10,000. 'G certainly didn't seem to be the slightest bit worried about dumping it in the negotiations,' says one of the Lib Dems. 'He seemed to be relishing the opportunity.'

This was Osborne in his element: haggling and deal-making in exclusive chambers of power, unencumbered by the public's searching gaze or his own party's ideological clamour. His efforts to strike a deal went beyond politics and policy. He became something like a motivational coach to the negotiators. Whenever the talks sagged, he would coax both sides of the table to intensify their efforts, often walking to a window that offered a tantalising view of No. 10. 'Look, Brown is in there clinging on,' he said, eager to unseat the Prime Minister he hated. 'We're so close to getting him out.'

By Monday morning, agreement was more or less in place on deficit reduction, and Clegg and Cameron had spoken again. But there was no deal on electoral reform, leaving Osborne glum about the chances of a coalition at a time when other Tories were confident. At 5 p.m., Brown shook the negotiations with a double announcement: his party was about to enter negotiations with the Lib Dems, and he would remove an obstacle to those talks by quitting as Prime Minister once a replacement had been elected in the autumn. Many Tories panicked and despaired, fearing that Labour would offer whatever was necessary on electoral reform to get a deal done. In response, Cameron, with the permission of his parliamentary party, offered the Lib Dems a referendum on AV.

Osborne was almost unique among senior Tories in being unruffled by Brown's intervention. As he told his wife that evening, the party had done whatever it could in the negotiations. Following his first law of politics – that one must be able to count – he concluded that a Lib-Lab pact, which would have to rally minority parties such as the SNP and the SDLP to cobble together a majority, would quickly collapse. 'And then we will kill them in an election,' he told friends.

The following day, Llewellyn received a text message from Alexander urging the Tories not to give up. Osborne took this to mean that the talks with Labour were not proceeding well. He was right. Labour's delegation was split on the rather elementary question of whether a coalition with the Lib Dems was really feasible. On one occasion, while Lord Adonis expounded on options for electoral reform, Ed Balls, his fellow Labour negotiator, cut across him to say that the party's whips did not think the parliamentary rank and file would vote for an AV referendum. The Lib Dems knew that a politician as shrewd as Balls would not say that aloud if he really wanted the talks to go on. Cabinet members went public with their scepticism, including Burnham, who said that Labour had to 'respect the results of the general election'. It was when grandees such as John Reid and David Blunkett dismissed the idea of a Lib-Lab coalition that Osborne knew he would end up in government in some form.

The Lib Dem team went to brief Clegg on their talks with Labour, only to find that he had already been visited by his predecessors – Paddy Ashdown, Charles Kennedy and Ming Campbell – all of whom had lobbied him to reach an agreement with Labour. Contrary to the suspicion that remains popular in Labour, he was open to their pleas. It was the testimony of his negotiators, who told him that Labour were not serious about a deal, that made the difference, not any personal eagerness to govern with the Conservatives. 'The impressive thing about Nick before the election right through the coalition talks was how pragmatic and non-ideological he was [about which party to enter government with],' says Laws. 'He always had the view that his options would be defined by the public.'[117]

At 7.30 p.m. on 11 May, Brown's extraordinary career came to an end as he tendered his resignation to the Queen. Last-minute phone conversations with Clegg had failed to revive any prospect of an agreement. While the final sticking points between the Conservatives and the Lib Dems were resolved in a diplomatic frenzy, he gathered his family and staff into a Downing Street office for some valedictory photographs, the last visual records of a premiership he had hankered after since his precociously academic teenage years. 'As I leave the second most important job I could ever hold,' he told the country outside No. 10, 'I cherish even more the first – as a husband and father.'

Just over an hour later, another husband and father arrived at the same spot as the youngest Prime Minister since Lord Liverpool some two hundred years earlier. Cameron's speech, stilted with exhaustion, promised 'strong' and 'decisive' government, a reassurance aimed as much at trading floors as ordinary voters. Eighteen years earlier, and a few hundred yards away, he stood behind Norman Lamont as the Chancellor, his own boss, announced Britain's humiliating exit from the ERM. So began the long Conservative purgatory in which Osborne had made his career. Cameron knew better than most, better even than Osborne himself, that the markets brook no defiance, even from a sovereign government that once ruled the world.

As Cameron and his wife Samantha entered the door of No. 10, Osborne watched with uncontainable joy on a television in a Cabinet Office anteroom. His mobile phone still contains the photos he took of the moment. Like Brown, he had coveted high office as a youth and forged a political partnership in order to get there. Indeed, a Lib Dem in the same room sensed that Osborne was happier for Cameron, his friend and frequently his protector, than he was for himself.

However generous and outward-looking his satisfaction, it was not entirely warranted. Against an opponent that he himself disdained as abysmal, in the immediate aftermath of the worst recession since the war, and after five years of Conservative modernisation, Osborne's party had failed to win a general election. The first rule of politics, he had always said, was that one must be able to count. In this case, the arithmetic was simple and unflattering: at 36 per cent, the Tories' vote share was less than 4 percentage points higher than the result he lamented in 2005. This was despite Labour's second lowest score since 1918, just 29 per cent.

Some reasons for the Tories' underachievement were unavoidable: Osborne's embrace of austerity was unpopular but brave and far-sighted, and the electoral system favoured their opponents. But they themselves were also culpable, for running a nebulous campaign, for modernising in an unsatisfying and often esoteric manner, for underestimating Clegg, and for believing the wishful consensus circa 2006 that their extraordinary and conspicuous privilege would not stop them bonding with striving voters in swing constituencies. 8 October 1959 is a date that should have loomed larger in the modernisers' minds than it did: it was and remains the last time a privately educated Conservative won a general election.

Osborne, perhaps more than most, deserved some clemency. He had always argued for a grounded and tangible Conservatism, and performed manfully as a campaign director who was actually no such thing. Just after 9 p.m. he walked into Downing Street via the corridor that connects it to the Cabinet Office. He sat down with Cameron in the same room where Brown, Balls, Douglas Alexander, Peter Mandelson and Alastair Campbell had lounged and bantered just hours earlier. There with the two Tories were Jeremy Heywood, the top civil servant in Downing Street, James Bowler, the Principal Private Secretary to the Prime Minister (old and new) and O'Donnell.

Cameron and Osborne went to the Cabinet room to make a few more ministerial appointments: Clarke was given the Justice portfolio, as Clegg had earmarked Cable for Business. Their gifted friend, Michael Gove, would take his mission for education into government. As David Laws would work with Osborne as Chief Secretary to the Treasury, Philip Hammond, the man who held that brief for the Tories, headed off to Transport. The last few appointments finalised, Osborne went home for the night. When he returned the following morning, it was through the famous black door of No. 10. As he and Cameron discussed the government's plans for its first few weeks in power, Osborne suddenly realised that one formality had been overlooked amid all the tumult and upheaval:

'You know, at some point you actually have to ask me if I want to be Chancellor of the Exchequer.'

'Oh yeah. George, would you like to be Chancellor of the Exchequer?'

'Yes.'

12.

Paying for the Past

'This is what austerity looks like. What
did you think was going to happen?'

'I feel like a poker player who has been dealt a two and a three.' Confiding in friends, George Osborne excavated his family's gambling tradition for a metaphor for his economic inheritance from the outgoing government. But before he could get to grips with this burden, he had to observe the quainter formalities of assuming high office. On Wednesday 12 May, Osborne was among twenty ministers-to-be in an ante-room of Buckingham Palace waiting for the Queen. She would induct him into the Privy Council, something Gordon Brown had hitherto blocked him from entering. When she eventually summoned him, he kissed her hand and took possession of the seals of office before heading to the Treasury.

To avoid any tinge of vainglory in the midst of a fiscal crisis, Osborne insisted on a low-key arrival at Whitehall's mightiest ministry. He welcomed David Laws on the doorsteps of the building, before speaking to a gathering of Treasury staff in the ground-floor conference room. 'I like people who speak their minds to me,' he told them, knowing that Gordon Brown, his predecessor but one, had been less collegial to many of those he was addressing. 'And you can call me George.'

Rupert Harrison asked Dan Rosenfield, the Principal Private Secretary to the Chancellor, to arrange for Osborne to begin serious work as soon as possible. Mandarins pressed him to make an immediate decision on Capital Gains Tax (CGT), which he had pledged to increase, as any delay might incentivise businesses and investors to distort the market by bringing forward asset sales. Osborne resisted, asking instead for a briefing on the true state of the public finances. This was the Treasury's 'internal forecast', and it was intimidatingly bleak. After perusing the numbers, Osborne and Harrison concluded that they would have to save £40 billion more over the parliament than Alistair Darling had planned in order to eliminate the structural deficit. However, as with the narrow matter of CGT, no immediate judgement was made.

Osborne's first major decision as Chancellor was to implement cuts of £6.2 billion in 2010 – enough, he thought, to convince markets of the new government's seriousness. 'We were very supportive of it,' says a Treasury mandarin. 'We saw it as a down payment on the future. There was also a view that, given the sums of money out there, £6 billion should not be too hard to find.' Both the overall figure and its composition were easy to agree with the Lib Dems, who managed to extract the concession that £500 million should be reinvested in education and social housing. The Department for Business, Innovation and Skills (BIS) would have to cut its budget by £800 million, quangos would lose half a billion pounds and a hiring freeze would be imposed across the civil service.

Osborne's mind then turned to the question that would define the government and the era: how deeply and quickly should he cut the deficit? He was eager for an 'emergency' Budget but undecided about its precise content. 'The Treasury saw this as an historic opportunity to turn the public finances around,' confesses a civil servant, and the department presented the Chancellor and his Chief Secretary with a menu of options for deficit-reduction. It included a ferocious, 'off the radar screen' proposal for an extra £60 billion of tightening over the parliament, which the Treasury did not expect the new government to entertain. In drawing up the options, Nicholas McPherson, the languidly brilliant Permanent Secretary, wanted to avoid a repeat of 1979, when the Treasury underestimated the radicalism of the new government. His extreme option was designed to be seen as extreme even by Osborne.

At the opposite end of the menu stood a much softer strategy (not very different from the Darling plan) which was presented as slow for the markets' liking. 'Right from the summer of 2007 we had been very, very close to the markets, following them in a way we had not done during my time here,' says another Treasury high-flyer of twenty years' standing. Then, in the middle, was a fiscal consolidation only slightly more aggressive than the one Osborne ended up embarking on. In other words, far from imposing an extreme and ideological will, the Chancellor went with the grain of mainstream Treasury thinking. Where he departed from his mandarins was over the exact schedule of the austerity plan. Although Osborne aspired to eliminate the bulk of the structural deficit by 2014/15, he sought room for manoeuvre by setting himself the formal target – or 'fiscal mandate' – of doing so by 2015/16. The Treasury said that this might be too far in the future to satisfy the markets but Harrison insisted on giving his boss this leeway. He would end up needing it.

The emergency Budget came together over a series of dinners between Osborne, Cameron, Heywood, Harrison and, for a while, Laws. The effortless collaboration between Nos. 10 and 11 discombobulated Treasury officials, hardened by more than a decade of feuding between Blair and Brown, and then Brown and Darling. They also regarded his junior ministers, especially Gauke, as 'truly first rate' and 'constantly in touch with George', whereas some of Brown's had been out of their depth (especially, say civil servants, Dawn Primarolo) and sometimes went months without a proper conversation with him. There were other, more quotidian changes. Brown's office had been a Spartan affair; Osborne's, which overlooked St James's Park, soon filled with coveted items of modern art that he personally selected from government collections, including Grayson Perry's subversive *Print for a Politician*, a favourite of Andy Burnham's.

Some vestiges of the Labour years did survive, though. Osborne and Harrison behaved as near-equals in each other's company, as Brown and Balls had done. 'It quickly became clear that Rupert had a very healthy relationship with George, and could actually contradict him directly in meetings and could have mini-rows with him,' says one intimate observer. Civil servants were also struck by the ease with which Osborne took to the job, commenting on his 'clarity and confidence' and placing his approach somewhere between Ken Clarke's magisterial overview and Nigel Lawson's forensic attention to detail. His lack of formal economic training, endlessly invoked by Osborne's doubters, never worried them. Chancellors tend not to be economists: Darling, Geoffrey Howe and Clarke (who notes that academic economics teaches technical modelling, not macro-economic policy-making) were lawyers; Healey a classicist; Brown, like Osborne, a history prodigy. Civil servants and special advisers furnish technical expertise. The Chancellor is there to decide.

Laws, on the other hand, was steeped in the subject. Punctiliousness incarnate, the Chief Secretary sometimes seemed genetically engineered for the job of pruning the public finances Budget by Budget, line by line, item by item. Labour foes who cursed his exposure of the valedictory note left for him by his predecessor Liam Byrne ('there's no money left', it cheerily conceded) nevertheless observed his command in the Commons with something approaching awe. However, his partnership with Osborne failed to survive its first month. Allegations surfaced that he had broken parliamentary rules by using taxpayers' money to pay rent to a man who was also his partner. On 29 May, he resigned, leaving behind the 'vital work which I feel my entire life has been leading up to'. Danny Alexander, who had served Clegg as chief of staff and then coalition negotiator, was invited by the Prime Minister to take 'the worst job in British politics'. At the most trying time in its recent history, the Treasury's two Cabinet members now had a combined age of seventy-seven.

On 16 June, Osborne turned his focus from fiscal policy to perhaps the next biggest challenge of his chancellorship: the regulation of a financial system whose breakdown and subsequent bailout had devastated the public finances. His broader reforms would come with the Financial Services Bill in 2012, which concentrates the power of oversight in the Bank of England, but his immediate task was to fix Britain's hulking banks. He set up the Independent Commission on Banking under the chairmanship of Sir John Vickers, a former director of the Office of Fair Trading. His mission was to reduce the systemic risk posed by banks to wider economy by considering a separation of their retail and investment operations. The Treasury, which worried that Britain might regulate the City out of global competitiveness in a pique of banker-bashing, regarded a lengthy commission as a 'good way of calming the debate down a bit'.

A week later, in his emergency Budget, Osborne set the parameters within which British politics still takes place. Flanked by Clegg and Alexander, he read out the astonishing numbers. He would embark on a fiscal retrenchment of 6.3 per cent of GDP, or roughly £113 billion, over the parliament, more than three-quarters of which would come from spending cuts. The remainder would take the form of tax rises scheduled for the early years of the parliament, including an increase in VAT from 17.5 per cent to 20 per cent and in capital gains tax from 18 per cent to 28 per cent. Departmental budgets, other than those of Health and International Development, could be cut by an average of up to a quarter, though settlements would not be decided until the autumn's spending review. The public sector pay freeze would last for two years. The increase in the state pension age to sixty-six would be accelerated. Households earning more than £40,000 per year would see their tax credits diminish. A new tax would be levied on banks.

The only relief came in the form of a steady fall in corporation tax (largely offset by the abolition of various allowances) and a rise in the income tax threshold to £10,000. But if Osborne's fiscal plans were overwhelmingly bleak, his growth forecasts – or, more accurately, the OBR's – seemed rather sanguine. The economy was projected to expand by 1.2 per cent in 2010, 2.3 per cent in 2011 then 2.8 per cent, 2.9 per cent and 2.7 per cent in the following years. Having initially resented the creation of the OBR, the Treasury quickly came to cherish it for assuming the thankless burden of making forecasts. But its sunny assumptions about manufacturing exports and business investment were as faulty, if not as ignoble, as some of Brown's jiggery-pokery as Chancellor. Labour warned as much, as did commentators as distinguished as Martin Wolf of the *Financial Times*, who lamented Osborne's 'pre-Keynesian' approach and 'the Treasury view', which historically underestimated fiscal policy's impact on the real economy.[118]

The coalition's boldness reached beyond economic policy. As well as shrinking the state, the government wanted to make it more open and more local. The coalition agreement struck between the two parties, formalised in the Queen's Speech, contained plans to overhaul almost every limb of the Leviathan. The plans envisaged free schools and many more academies, the commissioning of healthcare falling to family doctors, elected commissioners to oversee the police, referenda for the introduction of twelve new mayoralties, the overhaul of the welfare system and a plebiscite on AV. Tony Blair had made his name as a reformer by attempting tentative adumbrations of these policies. With a much weaker mandate, and in far less propitious circumstances, the coalition was trying to do it all. That summer, *The Economist* devoted a worldwide cover to 'Radical Britain – The West's Most Daring Government', with an image of Cameron sporting a punk rock, Union Jack-coloured mohican. He still has a blown-up version framed and displayed in his Downing Street flat.

Osborne saw the innate value of most of these ideas but also the practical obstacles and political risks. He was certainly nothing like as evangelical as the only other adviser who rivalled him for Cameron's ear, Steve Hilton, who quickly established himself in Downing Street as a one-man policy and implementation unit. (Cameron, fatefully, decided to denude No. 10 of politically loyal, ideologically committed policy advisers.) 'Look Steve, you've never been to a parish council meeting,' Osborne would chide, when Hilton extolled localism. The only adviser who matched him for radical zeal was Rohan Silva, whose polymathic interests had taken him away from the Treasury brief over the years. The pair were the first to encounter something Osborne had always feared: the cloying inertia of a civil service that looks askance at plans for decentralisation. When Silva immediately found himself bogged down in a fight with bureaucrats, including O'Donnell, over the government's attempt to publish vast quantities of public data online, it was only a preview of bigger struggles to come.

In the bureaucratic civil war between reforming ministers and resistant mandarins, Michael Gove was the first to the frontline. Many believe that the Department for Education, which reverted to *dirigisme* after Blair's departure, undermined its own Secretary of State in the summer of 2010. A sympathetic Cabinet minister remembers, 'He had malicious leaks, he had a Permanent Secretary who was out of step, he had a private office that Ed Balls created.' Only tardily did Downing Street bolster Gove but help, when it came, was substantial and directed by Osborne, who allowed the Education Secretary to employ more of his own staff and provided extra money for free schools. He now regards Gove's policies as by far the most successful of all the government's public sector reforms.

The Chancellor regrets that his own career never took him anywhere near the education portfolio. For all that he tilts and triangulates on other issues, he feels real fervour for this one. He disdains left-wing educational fads and often interrogates Gove to test that his reforms are meaningful rather than symbolic. This is despite the fact that general elections are never won or lost on education. 'One of the things you learn as you work with George is that, over and above the political calculation, there is a set of things he really is bothered about and where he can be quite ideological,' confirms a senior figure in No. 10. 'He has never made any bones about the fact that he is giving his children the same private education as himself, almost exactly. He's not going to discuss that or feel difficult about it or go through all of the usual things that politicians do.' If there is such a thing as Osbornism, schools reform, along with fiscal conservatism, cultural liberalism and an interventionist foreign policy, is one of its four pillars.

Having set the 'envelope' of public expenditure with the emergency Budget, Osborne had to decide how to allocate it among

Whitehall's competing claims in the autumn spending review. He deputed Alexander to lead negotiations with departments, keeping himself in reserve to resolve impasses, which tended to occur with other Conservative Cabinet members. Osborne grumbled that right-wingers espouse austerity in principle but fight it whenever it imperilled things they liked (a cognitive dissonance that the columnist Matthew D'Ancona describes deliciously as 'fiscal nimbyism'). Liam Fox, the Defence Secretary who did not disguise his alarm at the government's Strategic Defence Review, was a case in point, but much the hardest Cabinet member to reach agreement with was Iain Duncan Smith, whose vision of welfare reform aimed to improve incentives to work rather than save money. 'IDS has no interest in spending less on welfare – he'd rather spend much more if it gets people into work,' says a Downing Street insider.

Osborne built an alliance in favour of his view by telling Cabinet colleagues they would face less swingeing cuts than the mooted 25 per cent if greater savings could be made in welfare. The Treasury also rowed with Duncan Smith over the very achievability of his welfare reforms, especially the consolidation of myriad benefits into a Universal Credit. Osborne questioned the analytical rigour of the Christian conservatives who hovered behind the project. 'He thinks the people pushing this are such total advocates and evangelicals that they blind themselves to any downside,' says a colleague. Many in the Treasury still regard welfare reform as the 'unexploded bomb' underneath the government. As Osborne hopes to make further cuts in welfare, his quarrels with Duncan Smith are not over.

Most of the other spending settlements were free of animosity, and the 'star chamber' of senior ministers that Osborne established to handle disputes had little work to do. Of all the Cabinet members haggling with the Treasury as summer turned to autumn, Jeremy Hunt was perhaps the shrewdest. He fought to limit cuts to Culture, Media and Sport to 24 per cent, and secured reductions in arts council budgets of no more than 15 per cent (the amount they told him they could live with) in return for promising to scythe the department itself, which is more or less halving in size. The Treasury credit this bargain with averting protests against austerity from the culturally influential arts lobby in recent years. Osborne has admired Hunt since he entered Parliament in 2005, once predicting to a colleague that he would become Foreign Secretary one day.

Other ministers were, in retrospect, perhaps too good at negotiating with the Treasury. Ken Clarke, whose liberal instincts on crime always made him a strange pick as Justice Secretary, accepted deep cuts that ruled out an expansion of prisons. 'He did it on purpose to trap us,' alleges a Downing Street adviser, who says Osborne remains 'incredibly skittish' about the coalition's vulnerability on law and order.

Before Osborne delivered the spending review, he learned who would be leading the opposition to his policies in the coming years. On 25 September, at Labour's annual conference in Manchester, Ed Miliband defeated his older brother David by an excruciatingly tight margin to claim the party's crown. The conventional view held the younger, leftier sibling as an unlikely winner who grew in stature and fluency throughout the campaign. Senior Tories, including Osborne, had almost the opposite opinion. Having initially feared the electoral potential of this clever and personable man, who despite his youth had more ministerial experience than almost any of them, they were reassured by a campaign they found 'waffly' and 'pandering' to left-wing activists. When he won with the help of increasingly militant trade unions, Osborne's team concluded that the result 'literally could not be better'.

For the Chancellor, Miliband evoked nobody so much as William Hague, another leader whose youth lulled his party into a sensation of change but who never really challenged their ideological certainties. At the Tory conference a week later, Osborne announced what remains perhaps his most popular policy: a cap on benefits that would prevent any household claiming more than £26,000 per year. He expected Labour to oppose it, compounding their image as custodians of dependency culture. (This was quite literally an 'image', as Andrew Cooper's research found that the picture voters typically drew to represent Miliband's party was a smoking and drinking welfare addict lounging on a sofa.) They obliged, furnishing Osborne with a 'strivers against the skivers' trope that he would deploy mercilessly until the next election.

However, at the same conference, Osborne was reminded of the right's own tin-eared solipsism. In an announcement that met several objectives at once, the Chancellor pledged to withdraw child benefit from higher-rate taxpayers. This would save money while leaving the vast majority of voters untouched, show that Conservatives were willing to impose austerity on their own natural supporters, buy Osborne the political licence to cut welfare to less well-off claimants, and, most profoundly, chip away at electoral support for the big state in the long run. Successive Labour governments had cannily given middle-to-high earners a stake in welfare through universal child benefit and tax credits. The Chancellor wanted to undo some of that, re-landscape the electoral terrain to make it more hospitable for the centre-right in the long run.

If Osborne is a political chess player, a metaphor offered by critics and admirers alike, then he uses one of those three-tiered chessboards. The lower tier is for tactics, the thrusts and parries that make up day-to-day politics; the middle tier hosts strategy, where moves are made with the next general election in mind; the upper tier is the venue for grand strategy, the calculated use of policy to gradually expand the share of the electorate with a rational interest in voting for his party. Diminishing tax credits for the well-off, scything the public sector payroll, capping child benefit – Osborne does not adopt these policies simply because they might boost the slice of the electorate that has a rational interest in voting Tory over time, but that potential outcome very much occurs to him.

More to the point, the child benefit cap was objectively, measurably, overwhelmingly popular.[119] To anyone even loosely conversant with Britain's income distribution, this is only natural. Most voters earn less than the £37,000 annual income at which the higher rate kicks in. However, most national political journalists are not among this majority, and their immediate reaction to Osborne's speech was broadly hostile. In the press pit of the Birmingham conference centre, Harrison stood besieged by reasonable enough quibbles about the anomaly that would see a single-earner household with an income of £38,000 lose their benefit while a home with two parents making £36,000 each kept theirs. But it was the very principle of what Osborne was doing that drew the real ire in the ensuing days, especially from the right-wing press.[120] It had always been fair to accuse the Tory modernisers of neglecting the striving classes, but some on the right now appeared to define these plucky, put-upon strivers as people in the top 15 per cent of the income scale, on the basis that they did not 'feel' rich. Call it post-modern economics.

Osborne was minded to resist pressure for even a minor revision of the policy but, by the Budget of 2012, skittishness on the part of No. 10 was enough to force some tweaks. The whole episode captured three themes of recent years: Osborne, with his brain for retail, authors the government's most punchy and popular (if not particularly 'modernising') policies; Cameron is usually more prone to trimming and tilting in response to clamour (as he had done in Davos); and, most worryingly for the Chancellor, many on the right only support austerity insofar as it affects other people. The fiscal nimbys would hound him just as much as the left.

The spending review, when it arrived on 21 October, was less vicious than Osborne had hinted in his emergency Budget. Extra savings in welfare allowed him limit departmental budget cuts to an average of 19 per cent over four years rather than 25 per cent. Schools and the NHS were spared, and Osborne honoured his (by now very odd-looking) pledge to increase foreign aid dramatically. But police funding was trimmed and half a million public sector jobs were scheduled to disappear, including many in the armed forces. Some of the deepest cuts were felt by Cable's department, whose efficiency measures included a big increase in university tuition fees to a maximum of £9,000 per year.

This policy was of Conservative origin; indeed, the Lib Dems had, incredibly, campaigned on a promise to abolish fees altogether. It was also a largely sensible continuation of the move away from exclusively state-funded universities that began under Blair. Still, it provoked a backlash against Clegg and his party that neither has overcome. As student protestors laid waste to Parliament Square, Osborne showed little patience with tremulous colleagues. 'This is what austerity looks like,' he said, with flat realism. 'What did you think was going to happen?' The political cynic in him also wondered why Clegg had not withheld his support for the legislation, as he was allowed to under the coalition agreement. 'George's view is that it was nuts for the Lib Dems to sign up to the tuition fees policy,' says an aide.

By now, Osborne was perhaps the most talked-about finance minister in the West. The IMF and the OECD joined the Bank of England in furnishing his approach with their *ex cathedra* endorsement. With the most aggressive austerity programme of any G7 country, even critics of the government acknowledged its daring. His ultimate virtue, however, was quiet, methodical delivery. The in-year cuts, the OBR, the overall fiscal strategy, the specific spending allocations – all of this was promised before the election, and all of it was in place by the end of the year. It is easy to underestimate the importance of this to the coalition's (and Britain's) international credibility. Osborne's first priority was to palliate doubts about the government's basic ability to act. He had succeeded, and the rewards flowed to households and the Exchequer itself in the form of lower borrowing costs – at a time when countries such as Spain and Portugal were seeing theirs go up.

His failing was complacency about the prospects for growth. The OBR's fanciful predictions chimed with his private assumptions. When, on 25 January, official figures showed that the economy had contracted by 0.5 per cent in the final quarter of 2010, a thrown Chancellor resorted to blaming an unusually snowy winter. He now regrets making too much of early signs of hope in the export sector and not heeding Clarke's advice, delivered in Cabinet during the first few months of the coalition, to warn voters of trying years to come. Days before the grim GDP numbers were published, Ed Balls became shadow Chancellor in place of Alan Johnson, who had resigned for personal reasons.

Osborne now faced perhaps the most pugilistic politician in Westminster, and the press had a rivalry they longed to write about. Balls had made his name as a fiscal hawk. He was Brown's *eminence grise* when the 'Iron Chancellor' followed two years of spending restraint with the decision to devote the bounty of a mobile phone spectrum auction to paying down public debt. More recently, though, he had emerged as Britain's foremost

Keynesian – a man who was known to worry that even the Darling plan would stifle the economic recovery. This was less a conversion than a reversion: as far back as 1992, during his time as a *Financial Times* journalist, Balls had authored a Fabian Society pamphlet warning that the 'Euro-monetarism' of the single currency would constrain the freedom of governments to 'use fiscal policy to stabilise incomes by borrowing when times are bad'.[121] He and Osborne, who wonders what kind of Keynesian would run deficits during a boom, avowed antithetical views on economics but shared a taste for the martial aspect of politics. Their struggle would be the political story of this parliament.

Balls's ascension to his coveted Treasury portfolio was not the only change of personnel that unsettled Osborne in January. On the 21st, Andy Coulson quit as the government's director of communications, explaining that 'continued coverage of events connected to my old job at the *News of the World* has made it difficult for me to give the 110 per cent needed in this role'. Cameron and Osborne fought to keep him, and not only because his departure might bring the resurgent hacking scandal closer to them. Coulson was extremely able and personally popular, at times serving as a spinner, a chief of staff and a political strategist simultaneously. Some insiders regard him as the only 'truly A1' back-room adviser to have ever worked in Cameron's immediate orbit. 'He immensely improved our operation,' says an ally of Osborne's, 'and we all counted him as a friend.' The decision to employ him, and then to take him into Downing Street, nevertheless remains perhaps the most controversial taken by the party during Cameron's leadership.

The Chancellor, in his role as the Conservatives' interface with high media, identified Craig Oliver, a BBC journalist who had edited the *Ten O'Clock News*, as Coulson's replacement. Cameron went along with his judgement. Oliver's arrival confirmed two truths usually lost in the sensational coverage of the Tories' relations with News International: senior Conservatives cared more about broadcast media than newspapers (as does, ironically, James Murdoch, the then executive chairman of NI), and if they had a strategy to woo a specific news outlet, it was the BBC. Oliver, for his part, is less of a political voice and managerial force than Coulson was, but he is masterful at influencing 'the six' and 'the ten'. 'If he does nothing else, that still justifies his salary,' says one insider.

Osborne's part in hiring Oliver showed something else. As well as striving to stoke a dampening economy and keep a new shadow Chancellor at bay, he took upon himself the general political management of the government. He spent stretches of his working day in Downing Street rather than the Treasury, often chairing the 8.30 a.m. and 4 p.m. political meetings in Cameron's absence. He shone in these settings, expounding on threats and opportunities that escaped the antennae of less worldly colleagues. When the government faced financial penalties from the European Court of Human Rights for denying the vote to prisoners, Osborne suggested defying the Court, charging inmates for the cost of their accommodation and using the money to pay the fines. As trade unions prepared to strike, he proposed raids on their financial resources. 'He thinks in 3D, 360 degree politics, 24 hours a day,' marvels one of the regular attendees of these meetings. 'He must be the first Chancellor who spends as much time in No. 10 as the Treasury. From a Conservative point of view, he is the Deputy PM. He is across everything.' One of Osborne's Cabinet colleagues agrees: 'He is as political as any Chancellor we've had since the war.'

But anyone who seizes such sweeping political influence had better be good at wielding it. One threat that eluded his radar was the government's own Health and Social Care Bill. In opposition, the Tories had renounced any 'top-down' reorganisation of the NHS – to the extent of resisting reasonable Labour reforms. Now, from Andrew Lansley's impenetrably technocratic cerebrum emerged proposals for a market-based overhaul of the system. Almost all commissioning of healthcare, which amounted to 80 per cent of the NHS budget, was to be done by GPs on behalf of their patients. A wider range of providers would vie for their custom. The hope was to improve quality and save money through choice and competition, reasonable enough at a time when rich nations contended with ballooning healthcare costs. But the prospect of disruption and private provision proved incendiary to nurses, doctors and other professional bodies. This was hardly proof by itself that the Bill was wrong, but the sheer weight of pressure forced Cameron to announce an ignominious 'pause' to the legislation by the spring of 2011. It was more of a ceasefire.

Osborne blames himself for not spotting the coming danger of the NHS Bill, and so do others. The wisdom of his double life as finance minister and political strategist began to be questioned more searchingly. The Bill appeared out of Lansley's department as the Chancellor occupied himself with the Vickers Commission, the spending review and his first Mansion House speech. He assumed that Lansley, who evinced no radical proclivities in opposition, had produced an appropriately soporific piece of work. He was further reassured when neither Clegg nor Alexander objected to it in meetings of the 'quad' – an embryonic Cabinet within a Cabinet, comprising the two most senior Tories and Lib Dems. When Osborne finally studied the contents of the Bill at the end of 2010, it was the first (and so far only) time he has lost his temper as Chancellor. In confirmed what colleagues call his 'Nixon in China' theory of healthcare reform: only Labour, the founders of the NHS, would ever be trusted to make it something resembling a market. Amid the chaos, it has been forgotten that many on the right deplored the Tories' timid NHS policy during their time in opposition, including some who now mock the attempted reforms as the most obvious political folly.

The NHS shambles revived doubts about the effectiveness of the political operation in Downing Street. Having disbanded the policy unit upon entering power, Cameron, confronted with his lack of grip on the rest of government, wisely ordered its revival. But he delegated this project not to Steve Hilton or any other Conservative, but to Heywood, the mandarin who replaced O'Donnell as the most powerful in the land in 2012. The result was a policy team staffed overwhelmingly by civil servants who, by definition, showed no fealty to either of the governing parties and who, by instinct, baulked at the Prime Minister's centrifugal vision of the state. Whereas Blair always searched for the most radical policy people he could find, Cameron was mired with a largely technocratic bunch who sometimes acted as a constraint on his own will to shake up government. They could, and did, and still do, hold meetings that include no political staff at all.

Even ministers without a reforming bone in their body complain of Downing Street's opacity and directionlessness. Some claim to have no point of contact in No. 10 at all during moments of trouble: the civil servants refuse to provide any help that might even loosely be described as 'political', while the few nominally Conservative staff are stretched supporting the Prime Minister. Osborne's view on all this is said to be ambivalent. He takes professionalism, political loyalty and organisational clarity more seriously than most, and runs one of Westminster's tighter operations. He has played a part in persuading Cameron to effectively give up his self-defeating cap on the number of special advisers in government. But he has not used his preponderant influence to overhaul the very centre of government.

Cameron is not, despite suspicions to the contrary, a natural friend of the mandarins who secretly cheers on the creeping Whitehall ascendency. He has views of his own, most of which are the very opposite of bowler-hatted *dirigisme*. But he does not trouble himself with the mechanics and plumbing of Downing Street. This is understandable of a head of government with global burdens, but it also creates a severance between his vision and his practical ability to execute it. Perhaps the ultimate tragedy of Tory modernisation was Rachel Whetstone's estrangement from the Camerons over her affair with Viscount Astor, the stepfather of the Prime Minister's wife Samantha, in 2005. Had it never happened, she would now almost certainly be Cameron's enforcer in Downing Street, perhaps offering order, coherence and no little ideological vigour.

Foreign distractions from these domestic travails emanated from the usual part of the world. Awkwardly for the government, insurrections against autocracies in the Middle East and North Africa began as Cameron visited the Gulf to drum up business for British exporters, including arms manufacturers whose clients included some of the region's least democratic regimes. This mercantilist take on foreign policy, which William Hague outlined in his early weeks as Foreign Secretary, was nothing like as tawdry as the government's critics pretended. Britain is often sloppy and squeamish in pressing its economic interests abroad compared to countries such as France and Germany; some in Downing Street regard UK Trade & Investment as the most useless branch of Whitehall. But the juxtaposition of a trade mission and a democratic uprising jarred nevertheless, and Cameron seemed to be failing his first foreign test. His subsequent support for military intervention on behalf of revolutionaries in Libya was at least partly driven by a desire to redeem himself politically.

Osborne argued in favour of the Libya mission, albeit less volubly than Gove, who irked Hague with his sonorous zeal. As a member of both the Cabinet and the new National Security Council, he also attended almost every important government meeting about the conflict – these numbered around sixty, another measure of the sprawling responsibilities he was choosing to add to his day job. Osborne's neo-conservatism is 'more teleological than ideological', according to a colleague. He believes that the tide of our times is towards greater freedom, democracy and prosperity, and that Britain may as well be on the right side of history. More crudely, perhaps, he also favours an active foreign policy for the same reason he pursues *grands projets* like high-speed rail: it is proof of power, the thing that he and his party have lacked for most of his career. If these seem like thin foundations for a worldview, then it explains why, according to some accounts, Osborne's enthusiasm for the Arab Spring as a whole was more tepid than he let on to journalists. As Egypt stirred, Osborne's most assertive interventions in meetings counselled the dangers of instability and of the government appearing naive abroad.

Cameron's leadership on Libya, which helped to prod an equivocal American President into the fray, enhanced his standing. Abroad, he was now a statesman with a tangible achievement to his name. At home, he radiated prime ministerialness. Downing Street already nursed few doubts about their man's personal superiority over Ed Miliband, regardless of the wider performance of the government. Focus groups and opinion polls yielded unforgiving appraisals of the Labour leader, who struck voters as light, odd and nebulous. An unwisely bombastic speech to an anti-austerity rally in London in March seemed to be purposely written to broadcast his flaws. Cameron, by contrast, looked, sounded and comported himself like a national leader. His team's confidence often verged on complacency, though. Cameron was a better politician than Gordon Brown, but failed to win an election against him. He was a natural communicator, but lost the television debates to Clegg. Only with a broad strategy could the Tories hope to be re-elected. At times, his inner circle appeared to believe that Cameron was their strategy.

Libya exhibited Cameron's leadership style in microcosm: he was poor at spotting emerging problems but adroit at dealing with them when they arrived. This combination of complacency and resourcefulness characterised his handling of the AV referendum campaign in the spring. The 'No to AV' group was paralysed by poverty, and polls suggested the Tories would end up on the losing side of the plebiscite. That result would boost Miliband and Clegg, both of whom campaigned for the change, and incur mortal wrath for Cameron from his own MPs, who suspected that the referendum was a needless compromise in the first place. Two events shocked Cameron out of his insouciance. First, Osborne told him that a putsch by angry backbenchers could not be ruled out if the referendum were lost. Soon after, Matthew Elliott, the head of the No campaign, gave a presentation setting out in stark terms his paucity of resources.

Cameron finally stirred, initiating a fundraising mission and instructing his team to schedule an anti-AV event for him at least once a week. These belated efforts helped to turn the campaign around but the decisive intervention was Osborne's. A month before the referendum, he told journalists that the Electoral Reform Society, which backed the pro-AV campaign, had a commercial wing (Electoral Reform Services Limited) which stood to profit from any change to the voting system. 'That stinks, frankly,' was the quote that carried.[122] The No campaign was everything the previous year's Conservative election campaign was not: immaculately clear, rigorously tested via polls and focus groups, and executed with discipline.

Victory came on 5 May by a crushing, two-to-one margin – but at the cost of coalition bonhomie. The No campaign exploited Clegg's unpopularity, insinuating in posters and leaflets that AV's triumph would thrill the man who betrayed his promise on tuition fees. The Tories struggled to deny their culpability: the No campaign was based across the river from Millbank, and dozens of Tory staffers would go back and forth across Lambeth Bridge every day. Clegg was understandably furious and his partnership with Cameron has never quite recovered its early sheen. Ever since their humiliation over AV, the Lib Dems have sought to 'differentiate' themselves from the Tories. Osborne regards that strategy as perfectly futile; the Lib Dems' immovably dismal poll ratings appear to make him right.

Osborne's roving political endeavours had always achieved mixed results. The success of AV was quickly followed by an unwelcome reminder of one of his less shrewd judgements: the decision to hire Andy Coulson in 2007. On 4 July, *The Guardian* revived the phone-hacking scandal by reporting allegations that his old employer, the *News of the World*, had intercepted voicemails left for a missing schoolgirl, Milly Dowler, in 2002. Three days later, the bestselling tabloid was shut down by its parent company News International. Although it was edited by Rebekah Brooks, not Coulson, at the time of the Dowler incident, Coulson himself was arrested the following day over allegations of both hacking and illegal payments to Metropolitan Police officers during his time in charge.

By the end of the month, Brooks had resigned as chief executive of News International, Rupert Murdoch's News

Corporation had withdrawn its contentious bid to take full ownership of BSkyB, and the Met had lost its Commissioner Sir Paul Stephenson and its Assistant Commissioner John Yates. In Parliament, it was Ed Miliband who led the admonitions of the Murdoch press. Cameron said that he regretted hiring Coulson, and set up a broad inquiry into hacking and the over-intimate relations between politics, media and the police under Lord Justice Leveson. Just two months after his prime ministerial pomp in the aftermath of Libya and the AV referendum, Cameron was asked by a journalist whether he would consider resigning.

The creation of the Leveson inquiry made more sense tactically than strategically. It relieved the immediate pressure on the Conservatives, allowing Cameron to impose some semblance of control on a gushing torrent of events. But such an expansive inquiry, which had the scope to recommend the statutory regulation of Britain's proudly free-wheeling press, antagonised newspapers without doing much to please the public, whose interest in the hacking saga remains, at best, fitful. Leveson alone has not turned the likes of the *Daily Mail* and the *Daily Telegraph* against Cameron, and neither of these newspapers were much taken with the Tory leader to begin with, but it has served an aggravating function.

Despite his preponderant role in hiring Coulson, Osborne managed to evade the blame and scrutiny to which Cameron was subjected by simply staying out of public sight. For critics, his ability to exert profound influence across government while disappearing at times of trouble evoked nobody so much as Gordon Brown during his own time as Chancellor. Downing Street sources claim that Osborne was asked to 'bat for Cameron' during the worst of the Murdoch scandal that summer, but declined, insisting that his intervention would only draw more fire towards the government. Similarly, when official figures revealed that the economy had grown by just 0.2 per cent in the second quarter of 2011, he turned down invitations from No. 10 to deliver a major speech on the economy.

In a profile for the *Financial Times Weekend* magazine that spring, George Parker wrote of Osborne's burgeoning reputation as the 'submarine' of the coalition, a silent colossus who surfaces only for set-piece events such as the annual Budget and the occasional, punctiliously rehearsed interview.[123] The motivation behind Osborne's elusiveness is as much self-awareness as self-interest, though. He knows his limitations as a public personality; the average voter's affection for the government hardly soars when this baronet's son turns up on television with his brittle voice and icy mien. He is neither troubled by this – 'I know I will never be a man of the people,' he once told a colleague, as breezily as if he were giving the time of day – nor inclined to do very much about it. One friend suspects that he takes a perverse, Mandelsonian delight in playing the pantomime villain. Certainly, unlike Brown, he will never embarrass himself with desperate pretences at ordinariness. There have been no compromises in his family life, with its upmarket holidays and expensive schools.

His only answer to his own unpopularity is strategic inconspicuousness. This makes immaculate sense for a Chancellor but it is unthinkable for a Prime Minister, and Osborne is thought to have designs on the ultimate office. In August, when urban riots ravaged parts of London and spread to other cities, Cameron was forced back from holiday to reassure an anxious nation from a lectern outside No. 10 and then at the despatch box. If Osborne is serious about replacing him one day, he will have to hand in his cloak of invisibility and accept an unrelentingly searching public gaze. Even some of those who are best-disposed towards him doubt both his ability and appetite to make the transition.

Even in the short term, a deteriorating economy made it ever harder for Osborne to hover above the fray. His speech to the Tory conference in October was as thorough a case against fiscal loosening as he had ever made. He portrayed Labour's 'Plan B' as the very definition of a low risk, high reward strategy: releasing a 'few billion' pounds into the economy would give a nugatory boost to demand, he said, while jeopardising Britain's hard-won credibility abroad. His immediate audience in the hall, many of whom craved tax cuts, were as disappointed as any Keynesians outside it. Osborne was stuck. He had to encourage growth without borrowing money. He planned to use his conference speech to announce his support for the labour market reforms proposed by Adrian Beecroft, a businessman commissioned by the government to look into burdensome employment laws, but the Lib Dems remonstrated furiously.

A month later, Osborne reported some of the bleakest economic news the country had heard since the Second World War. His autumn statement revised the growth forecast for 2011 from the 2.3 per cent predicted in the emergency Budget to just 0.9 per cent, and the projected peak in unemployment from 8.3 per cent to 8.7 per cent. Far from eliminating the bulk of the structural deficit by 2014/15, cuts would still be needed in the next parliament. 'There is light at the end of the tunnel but the tunnel is getting longer and the light is getting dimmer,' Osborne told colleagues.

Balls claimed vindication but Osborne pointed to upheaval in the eurozone, which was beginning to ensnare economies as large as Italy and Spain. Indeed, the debate over the deficit was beginning to transmogrify into an argument about foreign affairs. Osborne, backed by third-parties such as the IMF and OECD, insisted that it was fanciful to expect an open, medium-sized economy such as Britain to grow at a healthy clip while the continent on its doorstep was undergoing such convulsions. Balls, quoting sectoral statistics, countered that exports were actually holding up – it was constriction in the public sector that was suffocating demand and confidence. Europe was simultaneously Osborne's curse and *deus ex machina*: it made growth in Britain difficult to achieve but furnished him with a plausible excuse.

The electoral implications of the souring economy were even knottier. Osborne had always planned to go into the 2015 election with healthy public finances, a buoyant economy and a tax-cutting Budget that rewarded voters for their stoic endurance of austerity. That hope was now gone but he was far from dejected at the new terms on which he would have to fight the election. Instead of asking the country to retrospectively reward him for dealing with the deficit – always an optimistic plan – he could now set out more cuts and challenge Labour to match them. If they did not, he would accuse them of planning to raise taxes. His baseline theory of elections was back.

For all its noise and light, 2011 had been an eerily stable year politically. Taken together, Coulson's departure, the AV referendum, the re-ignition of the hacking scandal, the riots and the lugubrious economy failed to shift the underlying equilibrium of the opinion polls, which showed the Conservatives only narrowly trailing Labour, Cameron vastly preferred over Miliband, and the Lib Dems mired in existential unpopularity. The closest thing to a transforming event came at the end of the year when Cameron refused to sign up to an EU-wide treaty to palliate the euro crisis. His objections were not to the austere fundamentals of the text but to the lack of reassurances for Britain's huge financial services sector, which was and remains hounded by European regulation. The arrangement went ahead as an 'accord' without Britain, prompting some to question what Cameron had achieved, but voters applauded his defiance, sending him soaring in the polls.

Osborne was intimately involved in the veto from conception to execution. Britain's diplomatic demands were largely crafted by the Treasury, and the Chancellor was kept informed of the negotiations as they deteriorated during the early hours of 9 December. He held out hope that Nicolas Sarkozy would give ground to Britain's (rather modest) requests but the French President was immovable. Never, though, did Osborne – or Hague, or Cameron – doubt that they would exercise the veto if its demands were not met. 'We were surprised that everybody else was surprised,' says a member of Osborne's team about the media din that greeted the veto. Clegg, a former MEP who struggled to disguise his anguish in the following days, evidently never believed that his government was actually going to follow through on its threat – an assumption that says more about his own immersion in the cant and misdirection of Brussels diplomacy than anything else.

Nothing has surprised Osborne about the job of Chancellor as much as its international, and specifically European, dimension. From his first Ecofin meeting of finance ministers, which discussed a directive aimed at hedge funds, he has grappled with countries such as France and Germany that simultaneously deplore the unruly profiteering of the City and yearn to see more of it done in Paris and Frankfurt. 'There is endless regulation from Europe,' says a senior Treasury mandarin. 'When it comes out of the Commission, it always looks terrible. Then it progressively gets made acceptable. But it takes a lot of the Chancellor's time and energy.' One of Osborne's own advisers admits that 'we are always on the defensive'. One of Brown's worst follies was his handling of European Commission appointments in 2009, when Britain accepted the foreign affairs role (which went to the obscure Baroness Catherine Ashton) instead of insisting on a major economic portfolio. 'Michel Barnier is a big problem,' says an Osborne ally of the Frenchman now in charge of the internal market. 'Not only is Cathy Ashton crap but she's out of the country all the time so she can't represent British interests.'

While he fought financial regulations in Brussels, Osborne imposed them at home. His first two years as Chancellor yielded the Financial Services Bill, the Vickers Commission, minimum lending targets, onerous capital requirements and the empower-ment of a Bank of England that neither understood nor cared much for the City. Among his objections to the EU fiscal treaty was that it did not go *far enough* in constraining banks' ability to leverage. The Chancellor had to avert another bailout, of course, and some re-regulation of the City was inevitable. But his regulations shackle Britain's outstanding economic sector at a time of pitiful growth. Nor are they even offset by a resurgence of tangible industry. The 'rebalancing' that Osborne heralded with mystifying confidence in 2010 was both faulty in principle (financial services accounted for roughly the same share of the economy as manufacturing) and fiendishly difficult to deliver. A nation cannot switch its economic specialism by wishing hard.

The City, which never took to Osborne in opposition, regard him as schizophrenic on financial regulation, and commenta-tors such as Simon Nixon of the *Wall Street Journal* attribute the economy's sloth, in part, to the Bank's 'regulatory jihad'.[124] There are, though, signs of a revised approach from the Chancellor. A Treasury minister admits to a recent 're-calibration of our view of the role the City plays in the economy ... you need a banking sector that is in a good position to lend'. Osborne's fateful cut in the top rate of income tax in 2012 was partly aimed at gloss-ing the City's global appeal as a money-making crucible. But his great onslaught of regulation has already happened, and it will not be undone. Several years will pass before its impact on one of Britain's few truly world-leading sectors can be known.

Having feared a Labour lead of up to 20 percentage points within a year of taking office, astonished Conservatives found their party ahead in some polls at the turn of 2012. Osborne was the opposite of complacent, however. A cutting critique of the Chancellor was forming among the right, no less than the left, as an unimaginative Scrooge with no vision for economic growth. After GDP was shown to have shrunk again on 25 January, his sense of vulnerability found expression in private, *obiter dicta* musings about his own political mortality. 'If I'm still doing this job next year...' he said twice to one lunch companion, wholly unprompted. 'I don't know how many more Budgets I will give,' he told his team by way of justification for some daring tax changes he had in mind.

The dramatic Budget of 2012 grew from this period of angst. Osborne and Cameron respect and respond to one thing above all else: political pressure. If the clamour for a certain course of action threatens their electoral standing, they will concede enough to at least temporarily relieve the danger. Both men, and especially Osborne, are capable of strategy – their dogged fealty to his fiscal plan proves as much – but tactical concessions to pressure come to them more naturally. As his thoughts turned to the Budget, the pressure Osborne felt most intensely was from the pro-business right. Friendly newspapers cursed his supposed indifference to supply-side reform while chief executives deplored his capricious treatment of both Stephen Hester, the RBS boss who was hounded into returning his bonus in January, and his predecessor Fred Goodwin, who was relieved of his knighthood by the government soon after.

Besieged by his right flank, Osborne concluded that his unimpeachable reputation for fiscal discipline was not enough. He had to show that he was striving for growth too. As is his way, he reasoned backwards from that goal and calculated that he could only achieve it by announcing a pro-business policy that was vivid and divisive – or, as he put it, by 'picking a fight'. An accelerated cut in corporation tax was not controversial enough to suffice, though it would feature in the Budget. Hilton lobbied for the radical deregulation advocated by Adrian Beecroft but the constraints of coalition put paid to that. Osborne was already hastening infrastructure projects and the Bank of England's monetary policy – which included quantitative easing (the printing of money to buy government bonds) as well as near-zero interest rates – could hardly be looser.

So, the Chancellor alighted upon the idea of cutting the 50p rate of income tax levied on those earning more than £150,000. Since its introduction in Labour's penultimate Budget, it had served as both totem and trap. If the Tories cut it, they were the party of the rich. If they did not, a country that competed on its favourable tax and regulatory environment would be stuck with a punitive levy on globally mobile talent. In the months leading up to the Budget, Osborne could hardly attend a City event without fielding grievances about 50p. The Treasury itself doubted that the tax band was raising enough money to offset its repellent message to high-flyers.

For all this lobbying, Osborne, whose own liberal instincts were offended by the apparently confiscatory tax rate, had actually decided to do something about 50p more than a year earlier. His sleepy 2011 Budget was going to include a cut in the top rate, paid for by a tax on property. He secured agreement in principle from both Clegg and Alexander but Cameron, ever-skittish about anything that might compound his party's image as custodians of the wealthy, rejected the idea before it could be developed. Instead, Osborne prepared to revisit the issue a year later by announcing a review by Her Majesty's Revenue and Customs (HMRC) into how much money 50p was actually raising.

When he read the findings in the run-up to the 2012 Budget, his determination to cut the rate hardened. According to the report, the rise from 40p to 50p had raised a mere £1 billion as high-earners shifted their income across tax years; reducing the rate to 45p might cost as little as £100 million. Impressed by the rigour of HMRC's work, the OBR pronounced this figure a 'reasonable and central estimate'. (Osborne knew that the OBR's director Robert Chote had published research questioning 50p's revenue-raising potential during his time at the IFS.)

Brandishing this evidence, Osborne was able to once more secure the Lib Dems' assent to a reduction in the top rate. Clegg and Alexander were classical liberals who did not come into politics to take the majority of a person's income, and even their social democratic colleagues, including Vince Cable, were open to Osborne's case. Indeed, they were prepared to contemplate a cut all the way back to 40p as long as long as they made tangible gains for their own causes. Clegg yearned to hasten the increase of the income tax threshold to £10,000 by 2015, and expand the taxation of property. Osborne, who wanted the Budget to impose a net tax rise on the rich, was happy to oblige. He was increasingly taken by the theory advanced by some on the centre-right – including the influential blogger Tim Montgomerie – that the Tories could only shed their association with privilege by shifting taxation from earned income to property and assets.

Cameron, too, had grown less hostile to Osborne's plan to cut 50p – but he remained the quad's most anxious member. Property taxes also alarmed his political radar while offending his Shire Tory reverence for hearth and home. Partly to assuage his fears, Osborne settled for a cut to 45p and abandoned the mansion tax and council tax reform in favour of an increase in stamp duty. 'Forty-five pence is a reasonable resting place for now,' says a member of Osborne's team. 'It's less than France, Germany,

Italy, Australia, and only 1 per cent more than New York once you count local taxes.'

Although Hilton appreciated the political hazards (and economic benefits) of the tax cut, he had given up fighting. His frustration with the civil service, which now ran Downing Street's policy unit, and his personal connection to California, where his wife's career with Google was partly based, lured him away from Westminster and towards a sabbatical in the sun. For many, the announcement of his departure doubled up as the official end of the government's radical phase. Certainly, some of his disappointment was with his friend, the Prime Minister. Cameron had the power to impose order and direction on the government, to overrule cautious ministers and recalcitrant mandarins, to actually back Hilton's vision instead of merely indulging it.

Hilton also faced obstacles from the Treasury, though his personal relations with Osborne himself were better than outsiders assumed. It was the absence of intimacy, enforced by the protocols and sheer unwieldiness of government, that left him forlorn. In opposition, Hilton could advance his causes in personal, almost social conversations with Cameron and Osborne. In government, the two ministers were less accessible, and a wider chorus of voices drowned out their old friend, whose only other reliable ally behind the scenes was Rohan Silva. When Hilton did see Osborne one-to-one, he found him constructive. At his prodding in late 2011, the Chancellor was gradually brought round to the case for an expansion of airport capacity in London and its environs.

Hilton's exit is ultimately a story of class. If Cameron, Osborne and some of those around them lack a furious hunger to change things, it is because the world has always worked so well for them. It was Margaret Thatcher, the provincial arriviste, who spurned patrician exhortations to let her country slump into a kind of

graceful coma. It was John Major, anguished by his own experience of state education, who began to demand more from the
public services. In the current government, it is Michael Gove,
whose remarkable gifts might have come to little had he not
been adopted as an infant, who spends himself in the struggle to
improve education. Hilton's own story is one of long odds, near
misses and immigrant ambition; had he not won a scholarship
to a good school, he might have gone the way of many of his
childhood peers. 'There was always a subtle divide in the band
of "modernisers" who sought to make the Conservatives electable again,' this author wrote in *The Economist* in 2011. 'The posh
ones, namely Mr Cameron and Mr Osborne, are in one sense
the most old-fashioned kind of Tories: men interested above all
in power, and aware that ideology can be an encumbrance in its
pursuit. Modernisers from humbler roots, such as Mr Gove and
Mr Hilton, are fervent believers in things.'[125]

Believing in things is less noble than actually doing things,
Osborne might counter, and his worldly balance of ideals
and interests is generating more tangible change than any
Conservative politician has managed since the Thatcher years.
Austerity is the obvious example, but there is also the extra money
for free schools, the incineration of planning laws, his plan to end
national pay standards in the public sector and, the boldest of
the bunch, the demise of 50p. Indeed, the 2012 Budget could be
seen as the culmination of a journey Osborne had begun in the
wake of the crash, from political calculating machine to an agent
of change whose real flaw was, if anything, *too much* radicalism.

For their part, the Lib Dems were confident that judicious leak-
ing of the Budget in advance of its delivery would enable them
to claim credit for lifting the tax threshold while portraying the
cut in the top rate as a Tory whim. After the autumn statement,
much of whose contents had been surreptitiously revealed in

advance, Osborne warned his coalition partners of the risks
in this way of doing politics. The more that a Budget is adumbrated, he told them, the more the media dwells on its remaining
surprises. Indeed, in quad meetings to agree the 2012 Budget,
he insisted on limiting the number of extra attendees to one
(a Treasury civil servant) and sometimes none. 'It didn't make
a difference to the leaks,' says a source close to Osborne. 'We
told the Lib Dems it was counter-productive but they carried on
doing it.'

This incontinence brought serious trouble a week before the
Budget. Osborne returned early from Cameron's official visit to
America (where the presence of the Chancellor, so soon before
a Budget, seemed unwise) to find *The Guardian* reporting his plan
to cut the top rate. The story suggested the Lib Dems would
get 'a large increase in the personal allowance' in exchange, as
well as some kind of wealth tax. Almost every major aspect of
the Budget was now public knowledge. The fiddly tax tweaks
required to pay for these goodies – including a freeze in age-
related allowances – were likely to dominate media coverage of
the event. During a conference call between the quad the following day, Osborne, according to someone privy to the discussion,
'basically lost it, saying that it was totally unprofessional and no
way to run a government'.

The Chancellor was now resigned to a hostile response to
the Budget – indeed, he was counting on a skirmish over 50p
to distinguish him as a champion of enterprise. But he was not
braced for the scorn and mockery that commenced almost as
soon as he stood down from the despatch box on 22 March.
While Ed Miliband excoriated the 'millionaire's Budget', journalists, for whom Osborne's major announcements were not
news at all, dwelt on the revenue-raising minutiae. The freeze in
older people's allowances was deplored as a 'granny tax' while

the imposition of VAT on hot snacks became the 'pasty tax'. A cap on tax relief for charitable donations was condemned as a menace to the Big Society that ministers claimed to envision.

In retrospect, Osborne assured himself two kinds of trouble as soon as he took the decision to cut 50p. Tax cuts for the rich are unpopular. The top rate had not been lowered since the radical Budget of 1988, when Lawson, flush from the boom, was also able to offer ordinary voters a reduction in the standard rate. True, Osborne understood very well the contentiousness of cutting 50p and was deliberately picking a fight ('We didn't need to see polling evidence to know it would be extremely unpopular,' says an aide). But he underestimated exactly how ugly a fight it would be.

Compounding this was the fact that he could only cut 50p by giving the Lib Dems a costly rise in the income tax threshold in return. Osborne was ultimately undone by the challenge of paying for this. 'We got pulled out of shape by the need to deliver such a big increase in the personal allowance, which is so expensive,' confesses a member of his team. 'We ended up doing things to raise money that you would ordinarily never do. Age-related allowances had come up before and we always said "no fucking way" but this time we had to do it.' The same was true of the raids on pasties and charities.

All these policies were eminently defensible. There is no good reason for the bias towards older people in the tax system, or the anomalies in taxing food, or the prerogative of the wealthy to decide whether their social contribution should be rendered in taxation or donations to arbitrarily selected charities. Osborne could have advanced impeccably Lawsonian arguments for simplicity and equal treatment in the tax system. He is usually meticulous in preparing the political ground for any controversial policy by commissioning third-party research, making the case via newspaper columns and organising supportive letters from business figures. He neglected to do the work on this occasion because he assumed that such footling tax changes would be ignored in favour of the Budget's bigger announcements. The leaks did for that assumption, but the Osborne of 2010 would have left nothing to chance. 'We had become over-confident about our ability to sell tough decisions,' admits a member of the Chancellor's team.

Osborne was paying the price with his own reputation. After two years of global acclaim as a finance minister willing to make and defend tough decisions in the open, he was suddenly likened to Gordon Brown for his covert levies, misdirection and general shiftiness. Commentators – and, privately, some of his own MPs – disparaged him as a kind of Machiavelli manqué whose ardour for the game of politics exceeded his actual talent for it. He had not even secured his modest political objective of placating ideological free-market conservatives. Instead, the Tory right did what it always does with a generous gesture in its direction: it pocketed it, forgot about it, and demanded more. By April, a Chancellor who was enforcing spending cuts on a scale Thatcher never even vaguely entertained, and who had just endured a political disembowelling to give high-earners a tax cut, was, stupefyingly, still accused of managerialist wishy-washiness by the ideological heirs of John Major's tormentors.

Osborne was outwardly philosophical about his sudden fall, reminding friends that his soaring career trajectory had always been interrupted by brief, discombobulating nosedives, including Yachtgate and his unconvincing response to Northern Rock's collapse. Privately, however, Osborne was hurt. At Hilton's leaving party in April, the departing visionary strategically seated the Chancellor among guests who were unlikely to discuss politics (a kind gesture nevertheless thwarted when Chris Lockwood of *The Economist*, a friend to both Hilton and Osborne, seized a neighbouring chair and teased him about his unravelling Budget). Some of Osborne's colleagues suspect that the Budget has quelled the radical spirit that swelled inside him during his first two years in power, when he advocated planning reform, welfare cuts and the end of 50p itself. They fret about the original Osborne – cautious to a fault, fixated on power but bereft of vision – staging an unwelcome comeback.

The Conservatives suffered no less from the Budget than its author. The party had defied its own expectations by more or less matching Labour in the polls after almost two years of austerity. By the end of March, it trailed by more than 10 percentage points. A month later, official figures declared Britain's return to recession. The 0.2 per cent contraction in the last quarter of 2011 had been followed by another one (later revised further downwards) in the first quarter of 2012. The 'double dip' forecast by Keynesian critics of austerity had transpired. The government's previously strapping lead over Labour on perceived economic competence began to narrow. The eurozone's deepening woes remained a plausible excuse for Britain's sloth but Labour invoked the election of the Socialist Francois Hollande, who deposed Nicolas Sarkozy as President of France in May, as proof of a tectonic turn against failed austerity.

Osborne is a student of his own and others' mistakes; the lessons he derives from the 2012 Budget will inform the rest of his chancellorship. The avoidance of leaks is an obvious procedural priority, albeit a hard one to achieve. Exactly who was responsible for the ruinous disclosures remains opaque. Alexander seemed to share Osborne's exasperation at the incessant seepage of sensitive information, so suspicions fell on Clegg. But the Chancellor's team prefer to blame to 'the DPM's office' rather than the Deputy Prime Minister himself. Another theory holds that, whereas Tory MPs are happy for Cameron and Osborne to craft a Budget privately, a Lib Dem leader is forced by his party's internal culture to consult his colleagues. As a result, an unruly oligopoly of Lib Dems – including Vince Cable, Tim Farron, Simon Hughes and David Laws – were kept informed of the Budget negotiations as they happened. The leaks might have flowed from some or all of them.

But these indiscretions, whatever their source, were only tactical nuisances. The contents of the Budget were themselves politically misjudged. In drawing them up, Osborne neglected the two great themes of his career: fiscal austerity and the modernisation of the Conservative Party.

It was folly to move away from the core goal of deficit-reduction. Until the Budget, Osborne was weaving a story that was simple and resonant among voters: Labour had ruined the public finances, and fixing them was a matter of Britain's survival as a nation of the first rank. There is no shame in standing for just one big thing, not least because it is one more than most politicians will ever manage. As a political message, austerity had the extra advantage of not pretending that growth is something politicians can summon at will. Osborne was quietly cutting corporation tax, bringing forward infrastructure projects and nodding along to the Bank's monetary loosening – but he never raised expectations that all this would electrify an economy beleaguered by a heavy hangover of debt and a currency crisis convulsing off its shore.

2010 was Osborne's grand strategic Budget – every one thereafter could have been limited to modest and risk-free amendments, just as 2011's was. Instead, out of a curious mix of vulnerability and overconfidence in his own political prowess, Osborne sought to rebrand himself as the enterprising Chancellor, the restless agent of growth. 'The judgement was that a do-nothing Budget had more political risk than a maximalist Budget,' according to one of those who know his mind. Neither this aim nor the policies devised to achieve it were ignoble, and Britain will be benefiting from the lower top rate long after the Budget has been forgotten. In its unabashed support for enterprise, the policy was an example of what the West, faced with incalculably more competitive emerging economies, will have to do more of in future. But Osborne's over-arching message was muddied, leaving voters wondering whether their government really was grappling with an existential national crisis or not, as his team now recognise.

'Putting a tax up to pay down the deficit is not the same thing as putting a tax up to put another tax down – the politics are totally different,' says one aide. In other words, voters might have tolerated the granny tax and the pasty tax if the proceeds were being used to ease the country's fiscal plight. But spending the money on tax cuts elsewhere, such as 50p and the threshold, struck them as needless tinkering. The government's *raison d'etre*, which was to chip away at the deficit, was no longer so clear to the electorate.

Osborne also erred by forgetting how much the Conservatives were still seen as keepers of the rich. Since Michael Portillo's failed leadership campaign of 2001, modernisation's design fault had been a misdiagnosis of the Tories' electoral pathology. Ordinary voters in swing seats such as Bolton West and Birmingham Edgbaston were not shunning the party for its cultural narrowness, or supposed authoritarianism, or indifference to greenery. They simply did not believe that the Tories were on the side of ordinary working people. In Andrew Cooper's focus groups, participants were asked to conjure an image they associated with the Conservatives. The commonest picture was of a rich family posing outside a capacious detached home.

Of all the major modernising themes espoused by Osborne and Cameron – liberalism, environmentalism, fiscal responsibility, the NHS – only the last was ever designed to dislodge this image. This was compounded by the crash, which forced every mainstream party to accept austerity. Nor were the Tories helped by their own privilege; whether or not they were a party *for* the rich, they were undeniably, at least as far as their leadership went, a party *of* the rich. By 2012, seven years after they had taken charge of the party, it remained inescapably true that only a Labour Chancellor could cut the top rate of income tax without his motives being damned. Fifty pence was a cynical trap laid by a failing government, but Osborne walked into it.

Still, with a few paces backwards for a sense of perspective, he could discern myriad consolations. The government was only as reviled as Osborne had expected it would be within a few months of taking office; unpopularity had actually been surprisingly and gratifyingly slow to arrive. Mid-term, moreover, often brings a kind of political unreality in which incumbents suffer while their opponents swarm unfettered. Scrutiny, from both the public and the media, would turn to Labour in time for the next election. Away from the ire and the commotion, tangible, meaningful gains were clocking up. A quarter of Osborne's deficit-reduction programme was finished, including almost all of its tax rises. With 45p, Britain was better able to compete and to grow. Meanwhile, the country's international credibility, fought for tooth and nail by its Chancellor, was measurable by some of the lowest public borrowing costs for three centuries. As the continent writhed in paroxysms provoked by a monstrously conceived currency, the former sick man of Europe stood, along with Germany, as its safe haven.

More than all this, Osborne had the consolation of experience. He had tasted political adversity before. Indeed, he knew it better than triumph. Onlookers beheld his weightless voice and vaporous bearing, and assumed a fortunate, frictionless rise to eminence. The truth was an undulating story of loss and achievement. If he could toil through his party's decade-long dalliance with extinction, he would not be broken by a single scorned Budget. As he played the event over and over in his mind, the picture of himself at the despatch box might have evoked an older memory: a precociously political teenager holding forth in a private school debating chamber, covetous for the glory of power, only faintly comprehending of its burdens and agonies.

Epilogue

George Osborne never speaks of any ambition to hold the only higher office than his own, even in the company of friends and trusted colleagues. But it seems to seep out in the occasional oblique utterance. 'The person who becomes Prime Minister is the one with the fewest enemies,' he mused to one associate, ostensibly talking generally rather than personally. Anyone who has hankered after political power so fervently and for so long must, surely, define No. 10 as his ultimate destination. How else to explain his assiduous cultivation of MPs, journalists, businessmen and international potentates? For what else but a race for the Conservative leadership – ideally after the departure of Prime Minister Cameron in an opportune mid-term moment circa 2017, and perhaps against Boris Johnson – is this political empire being amassed?

Consider, though, a conflicting testimony. 'He doesn't have the slightest interest in being Prime Minister,' postulates a minister and friend, long before the 2012 Budget diminished those prospects anyway. 'David enjoys the exercise of symbolic power more than real power, whereas George is the opposite. Chancellor is the perfect job for him. He is a back-room boy who has managed to become front line while maintaining the back-room air of wheeling and dealing. He could never do that as PM.' If this seems too categorical, as it probably is, then at least it offers an account for some of Osborne's behaviour. For someone supposedly mono-maniacal in his pursuit of the premiership, he is stunningly insouciant about holidaying lavishly, basking in social exclusiveness and generally shunning even token gestures at populism.

Seen from a certain angle, all his empire-building might actually be defensive in design. Osborne rose to power with the patronage of a few leaders – Hague, Howard, Cameron himself – but he knows that he can only survive there with a deeper, wider base of support. His wounding year between the autumn of 2007, when he flailed after Northern Rock's demise, and the autumn of 2008, when scandal almost claimed his career, taught him the hazards of aloofness. He has painstakingly nurtured relationships ever since. 'Dance with the ones who brung you,' he advised a young aide at his fortieth birthday party, gesturing at the secretaries, researchers, advisers, dogsbodies, editors, grandees, Cabinet members, tycoons, intimate friends and half-forgotten acquaintances revelling in the grounds of his grace-and-favour residence Dorneywood, all of whom had played some part in his ascent, all of whom he was anxious to thank.

New Labour looms so large over modern politics that Cameron and Osborne are sometimes assumed to be ciphers for Blair and Brown. But just as Cameron nurses none of Blair's missionary commitment to causes, neither is Osborne anything like as gnarled with aggrieved ambition as Brown. His hunger for power is trammelled by realism – about his own limited public appeal, about the government's prospects – and by an ability to walk away from Westminster, if not from politics. As shadow Chancellor, he told one colleague that he could imagine himself in Washington, working as a high-powered political consultant while teaching at Georgetown University. In short, Osborne would probably rather become Prime Minister than not. But his hunger for the job is nothing like as ravenous as many imagine. He has been a Pauline, a Bullingdon boy and a Bilderberg panjandrum, but he now belongs to the most truly privileged elite in the world: those who are happy in their work.

Afterword

Anatomy of a Recovery

George Osborne sunk to a nadir as his hometown reached a glorious high. In the summer of 2012, London hosted the Olympic Games with a verve and slickness that made it hard to recall the years of cynicism preceding the event without a tinge of shame. This was the summer of purple-shirted volunteers, of Tube conversations between strangers, and hauls of British medals under beatific sunshine. It made flag-waving enthusiasts of bean-counting churls, and roused a country that was trying and failing to escape its worst recession of the postwar period.

Bread and circuses, maybe. But what bread. And what circuses. Osborne might have enjoyed it all from a distance had an invitation not arrived from an old friend that summer. Seb Coe, with whom he had worked for William Hague more than a decade earlier, had fronted seven years of preparation for London 2012. He asked the Chancellor to present medals at the Paralympic Games on 3 September. Under no illusions about his unpopularity with the public, Osborne queried whether this was really such a good idea but ultimately went along in the hope that some brief pleasantries at the podium could not go very wrong.

When he arrived at the Olympic Stadium on the night, he knew that hope was fanciful. Obscure dignitaries were already drawing scornful murmurs from the crowd during the medal ceremonies, so a hated politician in charge of a failing economy stood no chance. The official programme had him down to do the honours for the Men's T38 400m race. Pulling out would itself cause a scene.

The ceremony comes around, Osborne is introduced by the public address system and the boos commence. He laughs hesitantly but the din does not go away. By the time he is slinging circles of gold, silver and bronze around athletes' necks, the better part of 60,000 people are jeering him. He has faced a wall of noise at the despatch box, but he has never been exposed like this. The scene is beamed to millions and threatens to become a cultural reference point, like Michael Portillo's humiliation at the hands of Enfield's voters on election night in 1997.

Osborne felt two emotions as he left the stadium that night, and neither was personal hurt. He was angry with himself for going ahead with an idea that he knew could end ignominiously, and anxious about his family, who were watching from the sidelines. He is personally indifferent to unpopularity – to an extent that is foolhardy in a frontline politician, as he would soon accept – and sometimes wears it as an Olympic medal of his own, a proof of the largeness and contentiousness of the decisions he makes as Chancellor.

The trouble was that those decisions were coming to nought. The economy was, at best, stagnant, as was his central project of fiscal consolidation. When official GDP data showed a contraction of 0.7 per cent in the second quarter of 2012, the Treasury suspected the number overstated the crisis, but not by very much. 'The nominal [tax] receipts we were seeing were pretty bad too', says one of Osborne's team, 'and they don't lie.' The radioactive half-life of the Chancellor's shambolic Budget, which had included a provocative cut to the top rate of income tax, was also burning through to the end of the year.

His alibi for Britain's economic torpor was the crisis of the European single currency, a saga entering its third year and exacting a heinous cost in growth and jobs across the Continent's Mediterranean underbelly. He also intimated that Britain's financial sector was in worse repair than he had appreciated in 2010, clogging up the usual transmission of loose monetary policy into actual bank lending. The OBR took a similar view but, as long as growth was absent and his spending cuts were in effect, a plausible causal link could be drawn between government policy and economic failure.

Ed Balls drew it with metronomic regularity. Understandably incensed by what looked like an attempt by Osborne that summer to implicate him in the rigging of Libor – the interest rate at which banks lend to each other – Balls hounded his opposite number on the airwaves and in the House, goading him with economic data that refused to get better. Many Conservatives wanted 'Chancellor Zero' shuffled to the Foreign Office, denuded of his roving political role or sacked outright.

Osborne did not know it at the time but his recovery was already in train, thanks to an Italian technocrat running a German-based central bank on behalf of a seventeen-nation currency of which Britain was not even a member. Such is globalisation.

As the euro thrashed around in spasms of agony, Osborne became irked at what he saw as the tentativeness of the European Central Bank. Instead of pulling out all monetary stops to shore up the currency, the ECB's institutional culture continued to reflect old German dreads about indiscipline and cheap money. Some members of its governing council, and many politicians in Berlin, believed the burden was on indebted eurozone countries such as Greece to fix their public finances and restructure their uncompetitive economies. Too much monetary help would only encourage them to ease up on these 'internal devaluations'.

Osborne admired the Germans' insistence on fiscal rigour, which some portrayed as a sadistic Berlin imperium, but he had less sympathy for their monetary hang-ups. In truth, he had none. With some impatience, he pressed the case for a more active approach to the crisis in discussions with the ECB and the German government. 'Our analysis was always that the euro was the main cause of our problems', says a Treasury insider, 'and that the solution had to come from the ECB. Those meetings were a mixture of trying to influence them and gleaning intelligence on what they were doing.' What struck Osborne's team about the Germans was their legalistic take on economics. Because there are so many trained lawyers in the Berlin elite, they tend to assume that codified policies are what drive reality. The role of sentiment and irrationality, of sheer human impulse, was less appreciated. As a consequence, they were slow to see the ECB's potential to raise confidence with a dramatic gesture or two.

The Treasury's urgency sprang from all-too-detailed knowledge of the potential consequences to Britain of eurozone breakup. Under the strictest secrecy, Osborne was making contingency plans for that eventuality. Since the previous summer, he had held near-weekly meetings of a committee that included Mervyn King, Adair Turner (the chairman of the Financial Services Authority), a few relevant Cabinet members and representatives of the security services. This was war-gaming to chill the soul. They agreed that a disorderly exit of Greece from the currency union could, on its own, cause British banks to seize up, leave holiday-makers stranded there without access to cash and plunge businesses in the middle of sterling–euro transactions into an unprecedented legal limbo. Making provisions for all this was like looking into the abyss.

But whatever his eagerness to see the euro crisis curbed,

Osborne's influence over the management of a currency to which his country did not belong was nugatory. Any conversion to monetary activism would only happen if Angela Merkel decided it would, and that summer she did.

Accounts of how and exactly when the German Chancellor's epiphany took place differ, but they all converge on three essentials. She concluded that letting Greece fall out of the euro would be an event of comparable magnitude to the American failure to save Lehman Brothers four years earlier. She thought the contagion of panic could, in a realistic worst-case scenario, do for the EU itself. And she decided that conflicting messages emanating from her government had to be stamped out: any signs that Berlin regarded 'Grexit' as a containable event – a view associated with her finance minister Wolfgang Schäuble – were only inflaming the markets.

Ms Merkel's certainty gave the ECB's doves – including its president, Mario Draghi – encouragement to act. Osborne had already picked up hints that something big was about to happen when, in July, Draghi made an elliptical promise at a London conference to do 'whatever it takes to preserve the euro'.[126] A week later the ECB explained that it was prepared to buy the sovereign debt of troubled governments in bond markets. The purpose of these Outright Monetary Transactions (OMT) was to reduce borrowing costs for countries such as Spain and Italy, which had risen as investors began losing confidence in their ability to honour debts and in the euro's ability to survive in its present incarnation. If such large economies ended up requiring direct bailouts of the kind received by Ireland and Greece, the cost would be crushing. The ECB was willing to commit its theoretically unlimited firepower to stop this happening.

On 6 September, Draghi explained the terms of the arrangement. To deal with German qualms – including those of the

Bundesbank president, Jens Weidmann, who accused the ECB of testing the outer limits of its mandate – he said OMT would only go to countries who committed to budget-tightening and economic reforms. Even before any application for OMT could be lodged, the bond markets calmed. Spain's implied borrowing costs fell on the day. Two months later, its two-year bond yields had fallen from a high of 7 per cent to under 3 per cent. The equivalent bonds for Italy had fallen from over 5 per cent to just over 2 per cent.

The acute phase of the euro crisis seemed to be over, or at least suspended. The world exalted 'Super Mario', who became the *FT*'s Person of the Year. Osborne did not expect OMT to work so well and with such alacrity. It is said that Draghi did not either. To this day, no country has actually applied for the scheme. It does not exist in any practical form. And yet its impact is all around us in the form of relative calm. As a lesson in the primacy of animal spirits over material reality, it is exquisite. 'Draghi's statement worked not because of what it said but because of what it represented,' according to one of those closest to Osborne. 'It was a symbol of the fact that the political will existed to keep Greece in at all costs.'

Draghi's miracle was also a test for Osborne: if British stagnation really was down to the euro crisis, then he no longer had that excuse. The economy had better start moving. As his team convened in September after the parliamentary recess, the mood was 'phlegmatic', according to one. Short of a discretionary loosening of fiscal policy – the one thing they forswore – they believed everything that could be done was being done. OMT was already in effect, as was Funding for Lending, a policy that allowed banks to borrow cheaply from the Bank of England in order to make loans to businesses. Yet the economy lay dormant.

Osborne had one more opportunity to impose himself on

events. Appointing a new Governor of the Bank of England was, he knew, one of the two or three most important decisions he would make as Chancellor. The Bank's powers had expanded beyond interest rate-setting to include the oversight of the financial system. The candidate had to be an exceptional technical economist, an assured manager of an organisation and conversant with the City, a theoretically reconcilable set of traits but one that is hard to find in actual humans. Osborne also wanted someone who would counter the Bank's innate caution and devote the institution to the pursuit of growth. He was taken by the aggression and resourcefulness of the Federal Reserve, whose dual mandate required it to achieve maximum employment as well as stable prices. 'Whether it's Janet Yellen or Ben Bernanke, you always get the sense they're on the case,' marvels a Treasury adviser, reflecting the Chancellor's view.

By early 2012, Osborne had concluded that the obvious candidates for the job were able but somehow safe. There was Paul Tucker, the Deputy Governor of the Bank; Lord Turner, the head of the FSA; his predecessor, Sir Howard Davies; Lord Burns, the chairman of Santander; and Sir John Vickers, who chaired the Independent Commission on Banking. All were eminent and plausible, even if Tucker was rated more as an economist than as a manager. But none was likely to shake up the Bank or to signal to the world that Britain was doing 'whatever it takes' to recover. 'We really wanted to use this as a moment,' says one of Osborne's team.

The Chancellor's dissatisfaction with his options pushed him to consider a foreign candidate. He entertained the idea of Stanley Fischer, the avuncular Governor of the Bank of Israel, but his real object of desire was Mark Carney, who had distinguished himself in his time in charge of the Bank of Canada. The two first met while Osborne was in opposition, and got to know each other on the global carousel of conferences. A former Goldman Sachs man, Carney possessed an intimacy with real-world banking that was hard to find in the scholarly chambers of Threadneedle Street. His country and its well-capitalised banks had avoided the worst of the crash. He was known to be creative in using monetary signals to raise economic confidence. And his sheen of superstardom would electrify observers across the world – including, crucially, potential investors – in a way the conventional candidates would not.

When Osborne identifies an important person to cultivate, he puts in the work and lays on the attentive charm. This is how he inveigled his way into Hague's office as a twenty-something and built a strategic conviviality with Christine Lagarde, the head of the IMF, as Chancellor. In February 2012, at the G20 summit in Mexico, he approached Carney about the job. As they talked in a Japanese restaurant, the Canadian expressed his interest but winced at the burden of moving abroad. Osborne told him not to rush his decision, as he had most of the year to make the appointment. He knew that other avenues were open to Carney, including frontline Canadian politics and a lucrative return to investment banking.

By early summer, it was evident that Carney's preference was to accept Osborne's offer – but also that the upheaval of moving his family to another continent for eight years was too much to contemplate. He appeared to rule himself out of contention in remarks to the Canadian press in August, at which point the Chancellor lost some – but not all – hope of ensnaring him. Sir John and Sir Howard seemed the most convincing alternatives. One of them would probably now be Governor had things gone differently.

But Osborne still had time. In September, he telephoned Carney, ostensibly to get his thoughts on the shortlisted candidates.

After Carney offered them, Osborne reminded him that he was still the ideal choice and asked whether there was anything he could do to lure him. The call was not so innocent after all. Encouragingly for Osborne, it ended with Carney seemingly loosening his position from outright refusal to severe doubt. ·

Only seven people in the British government were aware of this prolonged campaign to hire the Canadian: Osborne, Cameron, Rupert Harrison, Ed Llewellyn, Kate Fall, the Treasury's Permanent Secretary Nick Macpherson and the Chancellor's private secretary Beth Russell. Even Jeremy Heywood, the mightiest of all civil servants, did not know, and neither did Danny Alexander, the Chief Secretary. A leak could nix the whole thing. Carney could not be seen to be toying with a foreign post while serving out his term in Canada, and Osborne did not want to upset the other candidates in case his first choice fell through. Indeed, as he quizzed the five shortlisted candidates with other members of the interview panel that autumn, he was preparing for Carney to ultimately say no.

The final act of this great chase took place in Osborne's hotel room in Tokyo, where the IMF was convening that October. During one last blitzkrieg of persuasion from the Chancellor, who was perched on his bed for want of a chair, Carney said no, and no, and no again, until finally relenting. The truncation of the Governor's term from eight years to five had made the prospect of relocation a bit less daunting. Osborne had pursued Carney across the world over the best part of a year and, like the Canadian Mounted Police, he got his man. But the deal was not yet official. Carney still had to go through a formal interview. He flew secretly to London, where he was met by Poppy Mitchell-Rose and Osborne's driver at Heathrow. To preserve discretion, the interview was to take place in a flat in Notting Hill belonging to Sir David Lees, chairman of the Bank. Carney arrived early, so he whiled away some time in Starbucks, where nobody recognised the soon-to-be third most powerful person in the land.

Once the formalities were over, Osborne's remaining duty was to keep the news quiet until the official declaration in Parliament. He and Cameron informed the Canadian government of Carney's imminent move and requested secrecy at their end. They were duly watertight, later remarking to Cameron that anyone who leaked information in their government was immediately fired. When Cameron recounted that conversation to some of his own government's advisers, there was some ironic coughing and shuffling of feet.

On 26 November, Osborne announced the improbable news. The Bank would have a foreign Governor. Any trepidation the Chancellor felt about the reaction to an outsider subsided when Balls cheerily endorsed the appointment at the despatch box, though there was a final flash of panic when Osborne arrived back in his office to see Carney on television giving a press conference in Canada. His new hire was, of all things, speaking in French.

'There is no protectionist argument in British politics on the left or the right,' Osborne would tell an American audience a few weeks later. 'We are a truly open country.'[127] This is not quite correct. Britons are relaxed about foreign ownership of their large companies and strategic infrastructure, but they desire – and are given by Osborne's government – a protectionist immigration policy. Still, his inclination to boast about openness confirms that he is, to his bones, at ease with the economic phenomenon of his lifetime: globalisation. The great planetary swirl of people, products, ideas and capital that got going when Deng Xiaoping opened up China in 1978 unsettles many of Osborne's countrymen and drives reactionary movements such as UKIP. But the Chancellor generally finds himself pushing it further, whether by turning the City into an offshore trading hub for the renminbi or by getting a Canadian to look after the Old Lady.

Osborne sought to accelerate any momentum eked out of the Carney coup by shaking up his team of advisers. Neil O'Brien arrived from Policy Exchange to offer roving policy counsel and a steering hand on the election manifesto. Mitchell-Rose made way for Thea Rogers of the BBC, who set about sprucing up Osborne's image with a new half-mod, half-Caesar haircut. This involved some subterfuge: the Chancellor had no idea how much hair was being lopped off his head as he sat for the stylist, with whom Rogers had secretly conferred earlier.

She also advised Osborne to be seen outside of Westminster more often, an idea that would transform his diary. He had always taken the Millwall line on his image: no one likes me, I don't care. He could now see that, for an elected politician, this was a dereliction of duty. His curiosity was also piqued by a conversation with an old hand from the Reagan White House, who said that mastery of visual communication lay in choosing an image to convey and sticking to it. Reagan's asset was his toughness on defence and his liability was his age, so his team arranged photo opportunities with uniformed generals or with beaming youngsters. Most other requests were given short shrift. Working on this logic, Osborne started scheduling visits to businesses and construction sites, and almost nowhere else. The image to promote was one of dogged purpose. When he started being teased for the hard hats and the fluorescent coats and the pointing at things, his team knew it was, in Westminster's parallel language, 'cutting through'. He now goes on these excursions twice a week, sometimes more.

Osborne's most expensive hire that autumn was on behalf of the Tory Party as a whole. He brought in Lynton Crosby, initially on a part-time basis, to run election strategy. Osborne knew this would be written up as a mortifying loss of face; strategy, after all, was supposed to be his game. But he shuddered when he recalled the shapeless farce of the 2010 campaign, with its bickering principals and garbled messages, and knew that Crosby could avert a repeat. Older and gruffer than either Osborne or Cameron, he is not easily contradicted. On matters of political communication, his brief was to establish a chain of command ending with one person. 'He is the only one who can tell George and the PM, "No, that's wrong, that's not consistent with our strategy,"' says one regular attendee of their meetings.

'It's not what he does, it's what he stops from happening,' is how another Tory describes Crosby's contribution. From his base in CCHQ, the Australian hones the party's basic pitch to the electorate – which majors on the economy and minors on Cameron's leadership – and watches vigilantly for any utterance by any significant Tory that contradicts it or even veers from it too far. Adam Atashzai, a young adviser of almost canine tenacity who does Osborne's old job as head of the political section, is authorised to tell ministers on behalf of Crosby that this speech or that press release is not in line with the party's central strategy. 'Sometimes Labour will announce something and we'll want to attack it,' says a Tory in the Treasury, 'but Lynton will stop us because it's not relevant to our core message.'

He also advised Osborne to condense his economic argument to a five-point plan that could fit on leaflets. 'He said he didn't care what the points were,' according to an Osborne adviser, 'but he said we had to be happy with them and keep talking about them.'

Like Atashzai, Crosby flits in and out of Downing Street. He rarely attends the 8.30 a.m. and 4 p.m. conferences that deal with the day's political business, usually chaired by Osborne if the Prime Minister is elsewhere. Yet one long-time fixture of the

No. 10 operation says Crosby has assumed some of the 'chief of staff work' that Osborne used to perform. 'George does less politics these days,' he says. 'Nobody calls him the part-time Chancellor any more.'

Osborne's reputation was no longer sinking by the week – one ally remembers late 2012 as his 'stabilisation phase' – but this was only because he was eliminating unforced errors. It was not down to any encouraging economic news. Indeed, the autumn statement brought Osborne the embarrassment of having to confess that he would not meet his target to have debt falling by 2015/16. Economic stagnation was one thing but, if he was not even 'dealing with our debts', what was he for? It could have been even worse: the original target was going to be 2014/15 but Harrison, in one of his earliest exertions of influence at the Treasury, insisted on the extra year of wiggle room.

Osborne's only distraction during this dismal end to the year was his role in the Tories' historic commitment to a renegotiation of Britain's EU membership, followed by a referendum. The policy was to be announced in a speech the following month by the Prime Minister. Osborne and Hague were consulted but it was largely drafted (and redrafted, and redrafted again) by Llewellyn in No. 10. Osborne observed that the only thing everyone in the Tory Party agreed on when it came to Europe was the principled case for a referendum. He also believed that the party's perceived betrayal of its promise to hold a plebiscite on the Lisbon Treaty had made them look tricksy. On top of all this, the backbench pressure for a referendum on membership was too vociferous to face down and something needed to be done about UKIP in time for the general election. Osborne put his team to work on reassuring business groups that the speech was not the beginning of the end of their access to a 500 million-strong single market.

Underlying all these political calculations was a subtle but unmistakable hardening of Osborne's own attitude to Europe. He remained a supporter of British membership and shook his head at the casualness with which some colleagues talked of exit. But he had arrived at two conclusions. The first was that exit was no longer unthinkable: a sequence of events leading to that end could now be imagined, and it was not just the crazies and the bores who were enthused by this. The second conclusion was that a large EU country outside of the eurozone was in an increasingly invidious position. The currency bloc was becoming the real decision-making crucible and voting weights were shifting in its favour on matters of vital British interest such as banking. Britain was one of the largest financial contributors to an organisation whose inner circle was doing its own thing. His mood on the subject varied but, at his bleakest, he wondered whether such an arrangement could last.

In January, while darting between bilateral meetings in Davos, Osborne received advance news of another quarterly contraction in the economy. When he was photographed later that night tucking into a pizza with Cameron and Boris Johnson, the image revived old accusations of insouciance. Being booed at the Paralympics was tough, but it lasted a minute or two. This ordeal stretched across weeks and months: Britain's credit-rating was downgraded, the IMF's Olivier Blanchard openly criticised the Chancellor's fiscal management and even *The Economist*, which has never seen a spending cut it did not like, advised him to borrow for the sake of more capital expenditure. This U-turn aggrieved Osborne, who prizes the support of elite opinion-formers. '*The Economist* were the only people we lost [on austerity],' an aide says now. 'We kept the other papers we had, the CBI, the chambers of commerce, the OECD.'

On 4 February, the first day back in the office after Davos,

Osborne convened a meeting with Cameron and their most important advisers. The atmosphere was as bleak as the data. One more quarter of negative growth and Britain would be mired in an unprecedented 'triple dip'. Only Harrison offered a beam of light. He insisted that the government just needed to tough out the next few months because, by the summer, the economy would be 'going gangbusters'. Everyone laughed at what they assumed was irony. The Tory Party, through sheer practice over two arduous decades, does a nice line in gallows humour. But Harrison said he was serious. The certainty of the prediction and the Wodehousian turn of phrase provoked Llewellyn into making a note of it, which he asked Harrison to sign. It is still pinned on the latter's office wall.

Why was Harrison so confident? Remember that he always attributed much of Britain's economic stagnation to the nervousness engendered by the euro crisis, which stopped banks from lending to households and businesses. Draghi's intervention had calmed that crisis, which went a long way towards settling those nerves. Funding for Lending was kicking in simultaneously. Sure enough, all the metrics that matter in Harrison's view of the economy – mortgage rates, the borrowing costs for banks themselves – were improving. Markets, clearly convinced that the worst of the tail-risks had passed, were relaxing. His hunch was confirmed when he saw the cannier hedge funds buying up eurozone periphery debt and British equities in late 2012 and early 2013. Martin Hughes, the founder of Toscafund, said with some clairvoyance that 'no one ever gets how good it's going to be until [the stock market] moves'.[128]

Osborne gave the 2013 Budget not knowing whether the imminent GDP data for the first quarter would indicate recovery or confirm Britain's third recession in four years. The pressure intensified as dissent against austerity crept into the coalition itself, albeit fleetingly. Vince Cable wrote a *New Statesman* piece entertaining the idea of a slowdown in deficit reduction.[129] Harrison had haggled with the Business Secretary's special adviser, Giles Wilkes, over the wording of the article, to little avail. Cable was the most persistent nuisance to the Treasury's side. Clegg himself mooted the idea of more capital spending but did not force the issue. Osborne's team suspect Chris Huhne might have caused them serious trouble had he not just been forced out of Parliament by scandal.

The theme of the Budget was, again, monetary. Help to Buy, a hugely contentious innovation that many economists said would inflate another property bubble, was brought in to assist aspiring homeowners. The remit of the Bank of England was broadened to take more heed of growth, though Britain's historic neuroses about inflation meant a Fed-style dual mandate was never on the cards. These were the intellectual fruits of a trip Harrison had made that winter along the east coast of America to hoover up the newest ideas in monetary thinking from academics and policy-makers. Osborne himself admires American economists for their ability to think big, and finds the British profession technically proficient but occasionally unimaginative. (Mervyn King is among those he regards as an exception.)

For years, the volcanic debate about austerity – conducted not only over the despatch box, but in the comment pages of the *Financial Times* and the *New York Times* – crowded out discussion of the other half of Osborne's macroeconomic policy: monetary activism. He has espoused it since opposition, citing Nigel Lawson's 1984 Mais Lecture as an influence. Not only has his preference for monetary policy as the instrument of short-term economic management remained consistent, it has actually intensified and accelerated during his time as Chancellor. Hence Funding for Lending, the 2013 Budget, the incessant badgering of the ECB and the German elite. His least effective wheezes in recent years, such as his shares-for-rights scheme for employees, have been fiddly deviations from his monetary focus.

At the worldlier end of politics, Osborne used a visit to a supermarket distribution depot in early April to announce further incursions into welfare. He then cited Mick Philpott, a father of seventeen children, recently convicted of an arson attack that killed six of them, as the creation of a squalid dependency culture that had festered under the previous government. The left accused him of bad taste but Labour took weeks to summon a convincing line on welfare. After months of sullen reticence in his Treasury bunker, Osborne was rediscovering his taste for the sting of battle.

The first sign that Harrison's bullishness about the economy was well-founded came with the quarterly GDP number in April, which was marginally positive and averted the ignominy of a third recession. The fact that 0.3 per cent of growth was a mercy to be cherished is a commentary on how bad things had become. A negative number would have been survivable but only because Labour had done so little to fix its own economic reputation. Osborne was living on his opponents' lack of credibility. In June, Ed Miliband tried to address this by promising to match the government's plans for current expenditure in the first year of the next parliament. Many commentators saw it as an intellectual capitulation to the Chancellor. 'Why bother voting Labour?' wondered an aggrieved left. The right crowed, and crowed even louder when the double dip of the previous year was revised out of existence by the ONS.

Osborne himself was less ebullient. Labour were still leaving the way open for more capital spending. That was a political vulnerability for him to exploit but it also meant that his fiscal policy was not yet the only game in town. Headwinds were also blowing in from across the world: America's quantitative easing was about to taper off and the Chinese were trying to perform the high-wire act of deflating their own bubbles. At least one more quarter of growth was necessary before he could claim any kind of success.

He got his wish. In July, the ONS reported a second-quarter expansion of 0.6 per cent. This opened the window to a summer of radiant economic data: the Purchasing Managers Index rose, unemployment continued to fall and, as the hedgies had predicted, the FTSE was rampant. The economy was, to an extent, going gangbusters. Any earlier reticence Osborne had felt about claiming vindication gave way to a certainty that this was, as he likes to say, 'a moment'. The danger of making a public declaration of victory was that he would 'own' the economy in a way he never had before. The economy was hitherto seen as a mangled creation of Labour and the bankers that he was trying to put right. Now he was inviting the country to see it – and its every quarterly movement – as a product of his own steward-ship. Any return to recession would be his fault.

Despite this risk, Osborne decided it would be quixotic to wait so long for a turnaround and then go all shy about cashing in on it politically. Osborne is many things: squeamish about exploit-ing partisan advantage is not one of them. So, in September, he made a speech at a construction site in the Aldgate area of east London. 'We held our nerve', said the Chancellor, in a brutalist setting of drills and cranes, 'when many told us to abandon our plan.' Britain was 'turning a corner' as a result, and a Labour government would be 'disastrous'.[130] It was, like all of Osborne's speeches at critical moments, unsubtle. He does not do ruminative lectures, with thoughts floating vaporously across an archipelago of disconnected subjects. His intent is to communi-cate an unambiguous message on a single issue, with a mental picture of the kind of newspaper headlines he wants to see the following day.

'We put a lot of effort into that speech,' says an adviser who drafted it. 'We wanted to kill Labour on the economy, kill the Plan B thing, and then totally stamp on it.'

That narrow purpose was achieved. Labour has not admonished the fiscal consolidation as 'too far, too fast' for some time. Plan B is now just a rapper from Newham. But macroeconomic management is one thing. Household incomes are another. Under pressure, and with the resourcefulness of an assassin down to his last bullet, Miliband ushered the economic debate from the broad to the specifically human. What good was a recovery, he asked, if wages were failing to keep up with prices? It was a promising theme backed up with a potent policy. At the Labour conference in Brighton, Miliband said he would freeze energy bills for homes and businesses for a twenty-month period if elected. It was an idea pregnant with technical faults and perverse consequences but it was also rapturously popular.

The Tories' response oscillated hopelessly from derision to half-baked emulation. A flustered Cameron was announcing new policies during PMQs – to the frustration of Crosby and the Liberal Democrats – and the energy companies made Miliband's point for him by raising prices as winter loomed. As a political phase, Labour won the last quarter of 2013. Its leader was showing guile. More troubling for the government was the gradual mutation of what voters regarded as 'the economy'. Was it the overall picture of output and employment? If so, the Tories were well placed for electoral victory. Or was it the lived experience of ordinary Britons, household by household? Under that definition, the economy was not doing well enough to save the government.

In the short term, Osborne could console himself with the

best press he had ever had. His parliamentary confrontation with Balls over the autumn statement in December was a rout, and written up as such. His performance rating in opinion polls was going up and there was excitable talk of his restoration as a plausible successor to Cameron as Tory leader. When he began 2014 by trying to cool economic expectations – it was to be a year of 'hard truths', and his work was 'not even half done' – it was the scripted vigilance of a man who knew that he could afford to sound magnanimous.

Even his nemesis, the IMF's Olivier Blanchard, recanted his earlier view that Osborne was 'playing with fire' by tightening fiscal policy so aggressively. It was in the IMF's backyard, Washington, where Osborne gave what his team regards as the 'international version' of the speech he made in Aldgate: an explicit claim of vindication, hedged with warnings of hazards to come. Two years earlier, when he had visited Washington days before his explosively ill-designed Budget, it was proof of a dilettante with his mind on everything but the day job. Now, an American outing ahead of a Budget suggested a Chancellor so on top of things as to have time to spare.

For Osborne, a government's electioneering Budget is not the one that happens just before the country goes to the polls, but the one held a year before. It takes that long for an announcement to become a technical change in the tax system. As early as 2011, he had decided that 2014 would be the saver's Budget. Low interest rates were punishing the frugal, including the heaving multitudes of older Britons who can be counted on to vote. 'It was a group we needed to win back,' says a prominent Conservative. Osborne had already begun the year by talking down any prospect of pensioner benefits being cut. While he was at it, he told the nation that housing benefit for under-25s might be a fruitful place to look for savings. In some eyes, the youngest

Chancellor for a century was turning out to be a generational traitor.

In December 2013, Harrison set to work on ideas to reward savers. One of the more promising options, suggested by Treasury civil servants, was to relax the rules that forced people approaching retirement to spend their pension pot on an annuity. These annuities provided pensioners with an income for the rest of their lives. But there was resentment of their cost, the income they yield, and the compulsory nature of the purchase. If the government was considering some loosening of the annuity rules, Osborne asked, why not just get rid of them altogether? Giving people full access to their pensions was inherently Tory in its respect for personal choice. It also had the advantage of clarity. Osborne doubts the potential of any policy to electrify voters, or even arouse their interest, if it is nuanced and technical. This is why in 2007 he had insisted, against the advice of colleagues, that the inheritance tax threshold be raised all the way up to the voluptuous figure of £1 million.

Treasury officials were skittish about going so far on annuities. It might damage the market for bonds and gilts, and encourage old folk to go on madcap spending binges that left them with nothing for their later years. Osborne and Harrison asked Nigel Lawson, David Willetts and Oliver Letwin for advice, all of whom egged them on. Cameron was notified and gave his approval. Osborne's mind was almost made up but he could not dismiss the concerns of his officials. 'The Treasury was extremely cautious,' says a member of his team, 'and right up to the last minute we had a Plan B, which was a consultation. There were even parallel Budget documents prepared.' Emboldened by an economic revival that was now a year old, Osborne went ahead with what might turn out to be the last big idea of the parliament.

In the days after, Osborne was variously cheered, admonished or – given the unfathomable complexity of pensions policy – asked to elaborate. The only point of universal agreement was that, having been the subject of events for so long, limply tossed around by a recessionary quarter here and a missed target there, he was now shaping them. The spring of 2014 was the completion of a personal convalescence that had more or less tracked the economic recovery. Osborne was being likened to Colbert, the *ancien régime*'s frugal finance minister, by a commentator as grand as *The Guardian*'s Simon Jenkins.[131] He had the IMF all but apologising to him. Then, the moment that his chancellorship had been building up to for too long. On 25 June 2014, the British economy was officially, finally, bigger than it had been on the eve of the crash in 2008. The recovery was tardy and uneven, and per capita GDP was still below the crest it reached in the boom years. Neither was the deficit gone, nor the debt falling. Still, it took some obtuseness to not see a Chancellor in the ascendant.

Seven convulsive years in Britain's economic history, inaugurated by those apprehensive queues outside Northern Rock, had at last reached a coda of sorts. Osborne's own story was still open, though. Two debates swirl around him nowadays. There is the economic question: was he right all along? And the political speculation: where does he go from here?

Some quantum physicists believe there are parallel universes in which alternative histories play themselves out. Without a peek at these, we will never know the fate of Britain under a different Chancellor pursuing a different fiscal plan since 2010. Keynesians recall a promising recovery snuffed out by hasty cuts that summer, followed by two years of avoidable stagnation. Their opponents remember the external shock of a sovereign debt crisis, one that menaced Britain in 2010 and poisoned its economic sentiment thereafter.

These arguments were finely balanced until 2013 but events since then have allowed Osborne to ask a question that has no obvious rebuttal. If tight fiscal policy caused the economy's inertia from 2010 to 2012, why did it not prevent the subsequent bounce-back? All that had changed were the external conditions. Namely, the eurozone calmed down. If we brandish Occam's Razor and cut through to the simplest explanation, we might conclude that Osborne was the principal author of neither the stagnation nor the recovery. Both emanated from Europe. Despite the grandly baroque job title, the Chancellor of the Exchequer is just the finance minister of a medium-sized and vulnerably open economy on the edge of a continent-sized currency union that spent two years toying with oblivion. Whoever manned the Treasury during this period was going to be the vassal of European events. The decisive moment of this parliament took place in London, yes, but it was not the emergency Budget. It was Draghi's three words. 'Whatever it takes' to save the euro was also enough to turn Britain around.

Osborne's contribution to the recovery was to give it endless monetary nudges and to fight for some semblance of macro-economic stability in an unquiet world. This meant cutting expenditure and raising taxes to keep the sovereign debt crisis from ensnaring Britain. Those who object that this was never really going to happen are rather asking us to take their word for it. In the spring of 2010, Britain's Budget deficit was 11 per cent of GDP. The Bank of England and the Treasury were sufficiently worried to steer the new government towards in-year cuts. A meltdown of British sovereign debt did not have to be probable, only seriously plausible, to justify some immediate fiscal retrenchment. For governments faced with threats of low incidence but high impact, plausibility must be the condition for action. This is why we retain a nuclear deterrent and gird ourselves for catastrophic climate change, both at great upfront economic cost.

The hardest thing a politician will ever have to do is persuade voters – and, ultimately, history – that a painful course of action helped to avert something much worse. Without access to those parallel universes, Osborne can never prove the negative. But when Lagarde says that she 'shivers' to think of what might have happened to Britain without some fiscal tightening in 2010, she should not be alone.[132] Judging by the public's preference for the government over the opposition as managers of the economy, she might not be. Osborne has erred in many and varied ways during four years as Chancellor. He counted on a resurgence of exports that was always fanciful. He talked up the ferocity of his cuts, which might have dampened market sentiment more than the cuts themselves. He envisioned a new kind of economy with industry instead of services as its piston, as though a nation's economic specialism were a matter of ministerial whim instead of ingrained history and culture. But it is becoming harder and harder to stand up the proposition that his mistakes included premature and excessive austerity.

Osborne's personal recovery makes his future less, not more, certain. A floundering Chancellor has few options, and is lucky to keep what he has. But what does a flourishing Chancellor do? Among most journalists and many politicians, there is a settled view on this question: Osborne hungers for the premiership, or at least the Tory leadership, and commits all his dark ingenuity to achieving these goals. This has become Westminster's *idée fixe*, and it is fleshed out with new details by the month: Osborne is fighting a triangular war with Theresa May and Boris Johnson, his likely rivals, and using Michael Gove as a licensed agent, and using ministerial reshuffles to populate government with his placemen.

The first edition of this book concluded that Osborne's ambition to become Prime Minister is much more hedged and nuanced and downright diffident than the hype allows for. That remains the verdict of this updated version. Osborne's present role and even his 11 Downing Street address give him near-perfect exposure to the office of Prime Minister. After observing it for four years, he is intensely aware, in a way he believes Gordon Brown never was, of how great a step up from the chancellorship it really is. The range of burdens is daunting, and he wonders whether he could bear them as Cameron does. This might be why, as one No. 10 insider claims, his deference to the Prime Minister has subtly increased. 'To take one example, he calls him David to his face but always Cameron when he is talking to other people, even his own staff. "That was Cameron on the phone." It always used to be David.'

Ultimately, the exact dimensions of Osborne's ambition cannot be established without a glimpse into his soul. Easier to dismiss is the notion that he is building a loyal party within a party in advance of a future leadership election, with reshuffles as his principal means of recruitment. The popularity of this theory testifies to the residual influence of the Blair–Brown years on the way journalists see politics. But Osborne is not Brown. He is not dissatisfied with being Chancellor. His political influence over the government comes with the Prime Minister's active assent. He helps to reshuffle personnel because he finds such things stimulating and Cameron finds them a tedious ritual. Sometimes Osborne's suggestions are accepted, sometimes they are not. Mark Hoban, a minister he admired, lost his job in 2013, and Gove was deprived of the education portfolio a year later against Osborne's preferences. He is Cameron's executive officer, not his equal.

And while there were many Brownites, there is no such thing

as an 'Osbornite', despite the bizarre ubiquity of the term. Almost every MP described as such is, as one of them points out, a party loyalist who happens to have passed through Osborne's office in opposition or in government. They are no more loyal to him than to Cameron. They do not confer or socialise as a set. There is no ideology that connects them. With the exceptions of Matthew Hancock and Greg Hands, most have only shallow and recent associations with the Chancellor. Some are consistently surprised to read that they are 'close' to him, and wish it were true. Some would support him in a leadership election, others would not. Some are less admiring of him than other MPs who have no relationship with him.

More than anything, they are promoted because they are highly rated, which is why Osborne brought them into his team in the first place. He has always been a more coldly meritocratic employer than Cameron, who tends to favour the familiar. Sometimes, as in the case of the prematurely promoted Chloe Smith, Osborne's scouting eye fails him. And the one 'Osbornite' in whom he invests almost infinite confidence, Sajid Javid, would have prospered under any conceivable Conservative dispensation. Osborne's grip on the parliamentary party is nothing like as vice-like as imagined. When Andy Coulson was convicted and jailed for his role in phone-hacking in July, it was not hard to find MPs, even ministers, who dredged up Osborne's decision to hire him back in 2007. The Chancellor has also put little work into winning over the Tory grassroots, who ultimately choose the leader and currently favour May and Johnson.

None of this is to pretend that Osborne has no desire to become Prime Minister, only that his desire informs exceedingly little of what he does now. Reading a narrative of self-serving guile into decisions that are actually disconnected and rather banal has come to pass for analytic sophistication in politics. Television dramas such as *House of Cards* and *Borgen*, in which every other character is a budding Machiavel, do not help. If Osborne were to die tomorrow, many in Westminster would wonder what he meant by that. But this credits Osborne with too much cunning, and politics with too much logic. It is a messy and often nonsensical trade. Sometimes a cigar is just a cigar, and sometimes a reshuffle is just a reshuffle. Osborne knows that the identity of the next Tory leader will hinge on the vagaries of timing and circumstance as much as anything in his control. His 'strategy', a word increasingly denuded of all meaning through overuse, is to keep his options open and see what happens.

One reason why Osborne spends so little time thinking about the leadership election is that he spends so much time thinking about the general election. Gove's move to the very centre of government has given him another whirring political mind to trade ideas with. As Education Secretary, Gove used to visit Downing Street only for PMQs rehearsals once a week. He is now there with Osborne in most 8.30 a.m. and 4 p.m. meetings. They and Cameron hope to form something of a hive mind in advance of the election campaign, so as to avoid the dissonance that marred the last one. And if the result of the election is indeterminate, and Cameron needs to persuade his party to go into another coalition, or finds himself having to govern without a majority, the office of Chief Whip will be crucial. Osborne knows that Gove's ultimate political achievement may take place in the weeks immediately after the next election.

This biography concludes with a tentative prediction. Chancellor of the Exchequer will probably turn out to be the first, last and only ministerial office Osborne will ever hold. If the Conservatives are evicted from power in May, the party would have to succumb to a mood of uncharacteristic magnanimity to reward him with the leadership. Assuming it does not, then hanging around as a shadow Cabinet member would be a dreary life for this Bilderberg regular, who will not want for other opportunities in business, academia or global technocracy.

If the Tories remain in government, there is speculation of a transfer to the Foreign Office.[133] The chance to front Britain's mission to loosen its membership of the EU would supposedly arouse Osborne's sense of history. This overstates the centrality of the Foreign Office to that project, which is too critical to be run out of anywhere but No. 10. Cameron will be his own Foreign Secretary, with Osborne sharing the burden as Chancellor. It also understates Osborne's love for the job he is doing. The Treasury gives him more power than every other department put together ever could, a cold reality of which he is extremely conscious. Its proximity to the very centre also allows him to chair Downing Street's twice-daily meetings in Cameron's absence. As Foreign Secretary, he would be out of sight and out of touch. Osborne knew William Hague wished to quit that job a year before he actually did. Had he wanted to replace him, he could have asked Hague to see out the parliament and then taken over at the start of a new term. Instead, Philip Hammond was appointed.

Then there is the matter of the economy. It is a rare and self-denying Chancellor who toils through years of blackness only to hand over to someone else for the radiant spell. When Osborne was being booed in his own city, he had to fight to preserve some faith. He has no wish to walk away from a recovery that he hopes history will remember as his own.

Notes

It's a London Thing

1 'Partygoers who had designs on the Chelsea set', *The Times*, 28 January 1995
2 'Blow the budget', *The Observer*, 12 July 2009
3 'Partygoers who had designs on the Chelsea set', *The Times*, 28 January 1995
4 'Profile: George Osborne', *Financial Times*, 6 September 2008
5 Interview, Ben Slotover
6 Interview, Mungo Soggot
7 Interview, Ben Slotover
8 'The irresistible rise of Boy George', *Evening Standard*, 12 May 2005

History Boy

9   Interview, Ed Vaizey
10 Interview, George Osborne
11 Interview, George Osborne
12 *The Andrew Marr Show*, BBC 1, 8 May 2011
13 Interview, Andrew Edgecliffe-Johnson
14 Interview, George Osborne
15 Interview, Andrew Edgecliffe-Johnson
16 'George Osborne: from the Bullingdon club to the heart of government', *The Observer*, 1 October 2011
17 'George Osborne: from the Bullingdon club to the heart of government', *The Observer*, 1 October 2011
18 'The George Osborne Supremacy', *Daily Mail*, 21 September 2008
19 Interview, Simon Heuberger

Desert Brats

20 'Heaven on earth', *The Sunday Telegraph*, 1 October 2006
21 'Culture Clinic', *Telegraph* online, 12 January 2008
22 Interview, Simon Heuberger
23 Interview, Simon Heuberger

Gorgeous George

24 Interview, Prof. Laurence Brockliss
25 Interview, Prof. Laurence Brockliss
26 Interview, Prof. Laurence Brockliss
27 'George Osborne: from the Bullingdon club to the heart of government', *The Observer*, 1 October 2011
28 Interview, George Osborne
29 Interview, Professor Laurence Brockliss
30 Interview, Mark Reckless
31 'The real George Osborne', *The Guardian*, 28 November 2011
32 'George Osborne: from the Bullingdon club to the heart of government', *The Observer*, 1 October 2011
33 Interview, George Osborne
34 Interview, Prof. Laurence Brockliss

Joining the Guild

35 'The George Osborne Supremacy', *Daily Mail*, 21 September 2008
36 Interview, Daniel Finkelstein
37 Interview, Malcolm Gooderham
38 'The waiting game', *The Times*, 23 July 2005

Belly of the Beast

39 Hywel Williams, *Guilty Men*, 1st edn (London: Aurum Press, 1998), p.251
40 Interview, George Osborne
41 'New friends', *The Times*, 1 April 1996
42 'Party strife', *The Times*, 13 September 1996
43 Interview, Richard Packer
44 Interview, Stephen Dorrell
45 Interview, Charles Lewington
46 Interview, Charles Lewington

Hague's Apprentice

47 Interview, Gideon Rachman
48 'Memories of Britain's new chancellor', *Financial Times* online, 12 May 2010
49 Interview, William Hague
50 Interview, William Hague
51 Interview, George Osborne
52 Interview, Keith Simpson
53 Interview, William Hague
54 Interview, Seb Coe
55 Interview, Seb Coe
56 Interview, Rick Nye
57 Interview, David Gold
58 Interview, William Hague

59 Tim Bale, *The Conservative Party: From Thatcher to Cameron*, 2nd edn, (Cambridge: Polity, 2011), p.132
60 Private interview
61 Interview, Daniel Finkelstein
62 Interview, Nick Wood
63 Interview, Daniel Finkelstein
64 Interview, Nick Wood
65 Interview, Daniel Finkelstein
66 Interview, Robert Meakin
67 Interview, Martin Bell
68 Interview, William Hague

Through the Portcullis
69 Interview, Mark MacGregor
70 Interview, Francis Maude
71 Private interview
72 Hansard, HC Deb, 3 July 2001, vol. 371, cols 143–234
73 Interview, Mark MacGregor
74 Interview, George Osborne
75 Interview, George Osborne
76 Hansard, HC Deb, 14 September 2001, vol. 372, cols 617–70
77 'Why I am so embarrassed to be an MP', *Daily Mail*, 19 July 2002
78 Interview, Mark MacGregor
79 Hansard, HC Deb, 26 February 2003, vol. 400, cols 256–60
80 Hansard, HC Deb, 18 March 2003, vol. 401, cols 760–858
81 Hansard, HC Deb, 20 March 2003, vol. 401, cols 1087–100
82 Hansard, HC Deb, 11 March 2003, vol. 401, cols 173–261
83 Interview, Andrew Mitchell
84 'Bush is giving the Tories a masterclass in how to win', *The Times*, 31 August 2004
85 'Osborne gets job on frontline', *Knutsford Guardian*, 15 September 2004
86 Interview, Michael Howard
87 Interview, George Bridges
88 Interview, George Bridges

Brown's Nemesis
89 Interview, Michael Howard
90 Interview, Ed Staite
91 'Osborne rules himself out of race to be Tory leader', *The Daily Telegraph*, 20 May 2005
92 Interview, Michael Spencer
93 Interview, Ian Birrell
94 Interview, Greg Barker
95 'Top Tory, coke and the hooker', *News of the World*, 16 October 2005

96 'Parties with a coke-snorting dominatrix', *News of the World*, 16 October 2005

97 'We want a Tory, not a new Tony', *Daily Mail*, 22 October 2005

98 'Why won't you behave like proper Tories?', *The Independent*, 2 October 2006

99 Interview, David Laws

100 Interview, Michael Gove

101 'Man and Time', *The Times*, 11 May 2007

102 'Now we have got something to say', *The Spectator*, 26 September 2007

The Big Bang

103 Interview, Matthew Hancock

104 Private interview

105 Interview, Oliver Letwin

106 'Voters don't get it, but they still have to pay it', *The Times*, 22 September 2010

107 *Great Lives*, BBC Radio 4, 5 September 2008

108 'The court of King Mervyn', *Financial Times Weekend*, 5/6 May 2012

109 Interview, Claire Perry

110 Interview, Ken Clarke

111 Interview, Rick Nye

112 Interview, Seth Cumming

113 Interview, Matthew Hancock

114 'It's ridiculous to pretend there won't be cuts', *The Times*, 15 June 2009

None of the Above

115 Michael A. Ashcroft, *Minority Verdict*, 1st edn (London: Biteback, 2010), p.105

116 Michael A. Ashcroft, *Minority Verdict*, 1st edn (London: Biteback, 2010), p.105

117 Interview, David Laws

Paying for the Past

118 'A question for chancellor Osborne', *Financial Times* online, 10 June 2010

119 'Big backing for change', *The Sun*, 6 October 2010

120 'There's plenty of welfare on offer to the Poles', *The Daily Telegraph*, 5 October 2010

121 Edward Balls, *Euro-monetarism: why Britain was ensnared and how it should escape* (Fabian Society, 1992)

122 'Chancellor calls for investigation into backer's "serious" conflict of interest', *Daily Mail*, 13 April 2011

123 'Osborne's long game', *Financial Times Weekend*, 19/20 March 2011

124 'Wanted: BOE chief to tackle "jihadists"', *Wall Street Journal* online, 27 May 2012

125 'Urbane guerrilla', *The Economist*, 6 August 2011

Afterword

126 Speech, Mario Draghi, Global Investment Conference, London, 26 July 2012

127 Speech, George Osborne, Manhattan Institute, 18 December 2012

128 Interview: 'Toscafund bullish on UK economy and stock market', Reuters, 17 May 2013

129 'When the facts change, should I change my mind?', *New Statesman*, 8–14 March 2013

130 Speech, George Osborne, London, 9 September 2013

131 'How Janus-faced George Osborne defied stereotype and triumphed', *The Guardian*, 16 April 2014

132 Media conference, Christine Lagarde, London, 22 May 2012

133 'Revealed: George Osborne's plan to become Foreign Secretary', *The Spectator*, 3 May 2014

Index

Also available from Biteback Publishing

Enoch at 100
A re-evaluation of the life, politics and philosophy of
Enoch Powell

Edited by Lord Howard of Rising

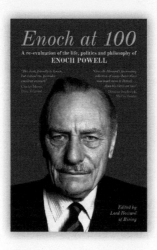

Enoch at 100 is a critical reassessment of the controversial
politician's legacy by some of the leading political figures and
writers of the current age. As well as a history of Powell and
his politics it features contributions, in the form of essays, by
figures as diverse as Iain Duncan Smith, Simon Heffer, Tom
Bower, Lord Salisbury, Lord True, Lord Lexden, Andrew
Roberts and Richard Ritchie.

'*This book, friendly to Enoch, but critical too, provides excellent answers.*'
Charles Moore, *Daily Telegraph*

352pp paperback, £12.99
Available now in all good bookshops or order from
www.bitebackpublishing.com

Also available from Biteback Publishing

The Margaret Thatcher Book of Quotations

Edited by Iain Dale and Grant Tucker

THE MARGARET THATCHER BOOK OF QUOTATIONS
Edited by Iain Dale and Grant Tucker

Margaret Thatcher enthralled whenever she spoke. Her political career spanned five decades and her influence on world politics is undeniable. From her followers she inspired devotion, from her detractors she induced unprecedented venom – but they listened all the same.

Margaret Thatcher is the most quoted British political leader since Winston Churchill and in this unique collection of quotations are the most memorable.

352pp paperback, £12.99
Available now in all good bookshops or order from
www.bitebackpublishing.com

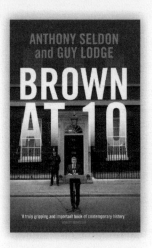